In Praise of When Your Perfect Partner Goes Perfectly Wrong

"This book should be a mandatory read for anyone in the world of dating, mating, and relating!" *Sheila Martin, founder Network Denver*

"So many people have been injured in relationships with people with Narcissistic Personality Disorder and they don't even know it. The victims just assume there is something wrong with them. This information and the descriptive personal stories can help them come out of the world of guilt, depression, and confusion."
Barbara L. Riste, MA, NCC, Licensed Professional Counselor

"This book is a real support for anyone who has to deal with these tough issues. This is a fabulous, in-depth reference!" *Donald Bross, Director of Education, The University of Colorado School of Medicine.*

"This roadmap through the mind of a narcissist, combined with so many stories from survivors and victims, left me stunned."
John Haney, Denver Police Detective

"This book, by one who learned from painful experience, can help those who are struggling (with difficult relationships), and provide insight for those who look on, feeling helpless. At least now they can recommend an excellent book." *Foreword Magazine*

"Fay strikes a decent balance between informing readers of Red Flag behaviors and the steps involved in extricating oneself from an unhealthy relationship. For most self-help collections."
Library Journal Review

"If you want to know what it is really like being the victim of relentless abuse by narcissists, *buy this book!* It masterfully combines first hand accounts of survivors with deep knowledge of the disorder." *Sam Vaknin, author of* **Malignant Self Love: Narcissism Revisited.**

When Your Perfect Partner Goes Perfectly Wrong

When Your
"Perfect Partner"
goes
Perfectly Wrong

A Survivor's Guide to
Loving or Leaving the Narcissist in Your Life

Mary Jo Fay

Out of the Boxx, Inc.
Parker, Colorado

Second Edition
When Your Perfect Partner Goes Perfectly Wrong:
A Survivor's Guide to
Loving or Leaving the Narcissist in Your Life

For more information and bulk discount orders, please visit us at www.OutOfTheBoxx.com

Or write us at:
Out of the Boxx, Inc.
PO Box 803
Parker, CO 80134

Cover design by Janice Green, Parker, Colorado
Editing by Barbara Munson, Munson Communications, Golden, Colorado

Printed in Canada

ISBN 978-0-9743504-4-8

Library of Congress Control Number: 2007941831

OUT of the BOXX
Inc.

To Scott –

*Thanks for teaching me that
there is not a narcissist around every corner.*

Other Books by Mary Jo Fay:

The Seven Secrets of Love
Unlocking the Mysteries Behind Truly Great Relationships

Get Out of Your Boxx
and Live the Life You Really Want...
*(But First Don't Forget to Drive the Carpool, Call Your Client, and
Make Love to Your Spouse)*

Please Dear, Not Tonight
*The Truth About Women and Sex...
What They Want,
What They're Not Getting,
and Why*

Contents

Survivors Anonymous
What the Victims Say...

"My husband made me recite to him every day, 'I'm only worth 29 cents ... the price of a bullet.' "

"My wife used to say, 'My life is perfect except for you. You're my only problem. In fact, I like you better when you're depressed.'... I always wondered what was wrong with *me*!"

"I felt like I was living in a cult. I was told what time to be home, what to do every minute I was home, and I wasn't allowed to contact my parents or friends anymore. He said that *he* was the only person I needed in my life."

"I'm the president of my company – successful and respected at work – but the minute I step in my own front door I'm told I can't do anything right at home. How can that be?"

"When my boss says, 'Jump,' he expects me to say, 'How high?' I run in fear of him every day. Why do I keep putting up with this?"

"I keep trying harder and harder to make my mother happy, but no matter what I do, it's just never good enough. I'm 50 years old and I've spent my life in constant exhaustion endlessly trying to please her, choosing a career she pushed me into ... and for what? She never seems to notice how much I try."

"My boyfriend doesn't think any rules apply to him. He thinks he's better than anyone and calls everyone else a bunch of idiots, including me. He says he loves me, but if that's true, why does he treat me this way?"

"Why do I feel so stupid? I have a master's degree in finance, but my husband says I'm too dumb to even know how to balance our checkbook."

"I had to quit my job because the emotional stress my boss gave me every day was terrible for my health. It was a great job but it was killing me."

"If he hates me so much, why won't he let me go?"

Ask Yourself These Important Questions ...

❑ Are you in a relationship where you feel that your partner is more important than you?

❑ Do you continually try to make your partner happy, but no matter what you do, it is never good enough?

❑ Do you often feel like a failure in your relationship and blame yourself for things going badly?

❑ Do you tell yourself, "If I just try harder, things will be fine"?

❑ Do you wonder what happened to the great person you were first involved with, and why he or she is so different now?

❑ Do you feel numb and exhausted from the constant strain?

❑ Do you keep hoping that "someday" things will get better?

❑ Do you have an overwhelming sense of guilt much of the time?

❑ Are you always told you're responsible for things going wrong?

❑ Have you given up your time, ambition, interests, and life for someone else?

If so, there's a good chance you're involved with a narcissist.

The next question is,
Just how much longer do you want to live this way?

Part One
Gaining Knowledge

"I think the saddest part of my journey to figure out what was wrong with our relationship was the lack of understanding by professional therapists about narcissism. Even those supposedly educated about this personality disorder cannot imagine what it's like to live in pure hell."
... The voice of so many survivors

> *"Every obstacle provides an opportunity*
> *to improve our condition."*
> *... Author unknown*

Chapter 1
The Master (or Mistress) of The Universe

"Have you ever considered that you're in a relationship with a narcissist?" a friend asked me. I looked at her confused. Not only did I not know what the word meant, I had never heard it before. I went home and got on the Internet to try to figure out what she was suggesting.

In searching Google for the word "narcissism" I discovered several informative sites that held my interest for hours as I learned about this little-known psychological disorder. I was dumbfounded by what I read and was especially mesmerized by one particular website (http://samvak.tripod.com) where it seemed like I spent forever reading and absorbing information that gave me amazing new insight. The site belonged to Sam Vaknin, PhD, author of *Malignant Self Love: Narcissism Revisited.* Unlike most of the heavily psychology-based information sites, Sam's was different – he was actually a diagnosed narcissist who found himself caught in his own web of unhealthy, narcissistic behaviors and then wrote about the journey. Through his words I began to see through the eyes of a narcissist and to suddenly understand so many of the difficult people I had encountered throughout my life.

Yet most importantly, I learned that narcissists think they are the "Master (or Mistress) of the Universe," and I'm not talking about the superhero action figures that save the world. Rather, I'm describing the ultimate authority personality. These people see the rest of mankind as underlings. They see themselves as being far superior to anyone else. They believe what they think is what everyone should think. And they see others in their universe as mere pawns in the game. As a result, the effect they have on those around them can cause profound and lasting damage.

I studied every site I could find to learn all I could and I was appalled at the fact that most of what I read was heavily text-bookish. It was hard to wade through and really didn't tell me what to do about my situation. While I did discover that I was not alone in my feelings, nor was I going crazy, I still felt highly frustrated and lost.

On the hopeful side, I learned that the confusing feelings and convoluted beliefs I was experiencing about myself in my current relationship, as well as in several past relationships, were not entirely my fault. On the downside, however, I discovered that malignant narcissism is a psychological disorder that leaves family members, friends, employees, and colleagues of narcissists with feelings of low self-esteem, guilt, pain, suffering, anguish, inferiority, and constant self-doubt. In addition, they can feel confused and at a loss as to how they became this way. But most of all, they can spend a lot of time wondering how a relationship that seemingly started out with the "perfect partner," went so "perfectly wrong" somewhere along the way.

As I learned more about this poorly understood behavior, I began to understand more about myself. I realized that I had finally found the tools to best deal with the narcissists in my life.

> *I began to understand that things were not just my fault, but that I had unknowingly contributed to the situation with my own behaviors.*

Now, I hope I can share with you what I learned. In addition, since the first printing of this book in 2004, I have received so many new stories and have consulted with such a variety of clients that I felt obligated to write this second edition to include what I had gleaned since that first printing.

You should know, however, that I am not a psychiatrist, a psychologist, or a life coach. While I do have a master's degree in nursing and years in professional roles, none of that entitles me to write this book. So what does? Actually, the truth of the matter is that I'm a survivor of several narcissistic relationships throughout my lifetime. Some were personal friends, some coworkers, and some were romantic partners. Some were people in a position of trust when I was a child. I am a survivor of months and years of living in environments that chipped away at my innermost soul. That left me doubting myself. That left me blaming myself for all that was wrong in my relationships. That left me fighting depression and various physical ailments. And at my darkest hour, left me at the edge of taking my own life. And after navigating that minefield out of the darkness and into the light, I now help others in their own personal journey to healing as well.

While psychotherapy does wonders for many victims, there are so many therapists who still do not understand the crazy world inside the universe of narcissism. Unless they have walked the path themselves, they frequently misunderstand or misdiagnose this tricky pathology.

I can't tell you the number of clients who have come to me after spending years and thousands of dollars in traditional therapy, only to still feel totally lost about why they feel the way they do. Believe me – the pain is incredible. And the constant confusion is ultimately one more step in the destruction of a once perfectly healthy adult.

Armed with this knowledge I wrote this not as a typical textbook for students of psychology – at least not from the usual mode of diagnostics, medications, therapy sessions, counseling techniques, and technical jargon. Rather, it is written from the viewpoint of many who are still victims as well as those who are survivors. It contains personal stories of people who have lived with the Master or Mistress of the Universe; those who have endured, those who are still suffering, and a few who have thankfully managed to escape. It is my hope that psychologists and students alike can learn different lessons from this book by understanding the first-hand accounts from real cases. Perhaps then they can help other survivors and victims better see themselves through the eyes of those who have walked the path before them.

I first wrote about narcissism in my book, *Get Out of Your Boxx ... And Live the Life You Really Want!* That book examines a variety of what I describe as "Behavioral Boxxes" that hold many of us captive; Boxxes like Perfectionism, Workaholism, Fear, the Expectations of Others, Your Past, and many others, *including* Narcissism, which is really someone else's boxx that we take on as our own. (I intentionally spell boxx with two x's to distinguish it from a plain, ordinary storage container.) Little did I realize when I wrote the book that the chapter on narcissism would cause the response it did. It seemed to strike a chord with so many people that it motivated me to write an entire book about it. People would say to me, "Wow, now I understand my husband (boyfriend, mother, boss, friend). Thanks so much for helping me recognize this rarely talked about disorder." But at the same time they wanted more information. I had only shown them the tip of the iceberg. And while the information on the Internet proved to be a lifeline to many in understanding the specifics of the disorder itself, they also begged for suggestions on how to live through the pain. How to pick themselves up afterwards. How to move on. And how to avoid the pitfalls again.

So I decided to compile this book to include factual narcissism information, personal histories from many survivors, and tools to aid in the healing process. It isn't written in technical, psychological terms, but in everyday language that we can all understand. Some of the following accounts are my own, but many are from men and women throughout the country who responded to my request for interviews with people involved with narcissists. I have changed the names and simplified the stories to provide some protection from any potential retaliation from the narcissists in our lives.

Our journeys are varied and shocking. My own encounters seemed minimal compared to most. Discovering light at the end of the tunnel did not happen for all of them. Several remain in their unfulfilling relationships, although most can't explain why. Many have left (or were left by) their narcissist years ago, yet they still feel the fear, anger, sadness, and anguish of a relationship that revealed itself to be a Pandora's Box: a "boxx of horrors" that held them captive for years. Yet for some unexplained reason, a boxx that many of them still wish they could return to, if it were possible.

It is my hope that as you read these personal journeys, combined with facts and knowledge about narcissism (much of which, unless otherwise specified, are taken from Dr. Vaknin's website or book[1]), that you will avoid making many of the mistakes we made. You will be able to recognize the signs and symptoms earlier than we did. You will learn to fully understand what you're getting into and be prepared for the lifestyle you have chosen, or through this education, you will make well-informed choices about the role you choose to play in the life of a narcissist. And perhaps some of you will do what we didn't do early enough – you'll run away. You'll run very far away. Whichever way you choose, at least you will have the education that we did not have before you get in over your head. You will have unmasked your narcissist early enough to recognize him for what he really is, "a legend in his own mind." And you will have the foresight to avoid getting boxxed in with him for a lifetime – a lifetime that will prove to be "perfectly wrong," despite the ever-so-perfect picture he paints for you at the beginning.

According to the American Psychiatric Association, the majority of narcissists (50 – 75 percent) are men.[2] Because of that, and for the sake of convenience, I will most frequently refer to the narcissists throughout this book as "he." Be assured that, in most situations, "she" will apply equally well. And if you're a guy you'll find plenty of information here about dealing with narcissistic women as well.

As you begin to learn about narcissistic behaviors and causes, it may be helpful to understand that this condition wasn't even recognized in the *Diagnostic and Statistical Manual* (the psychological Bible of diagnoses) until 1980, although Freud originally identified many of the behaviors almost a century ago. And unfortunately, many psychological professionals still do not understand it very well.

More importantly, many narcissists are such good actors they can even fool the best of them. With all of that in mind, how is the non-professional community supposed to be warned of the perils of getting involved with one of these people? How is the "girl next door" supposed to know what she's really falling for?

These were my questions and I went on a quest to find the answers. As a result, I made it my mission to help others understand this complicated disorder. It is also my hope that this book will be a tool to help prevent more victims from falling prey to these people; or at least to learn to recognize the situation and better deal with its repercussions afterwards.

I will also give you some tools to evaluate your relationships and how they make *you* feel. You can learn to spot some "Red Flag" behaviors in others that can help you decide whether you choose to get involved with, or stay involved with them, or decide to leave the relationship entirely. In addition you can begin to recognize and understand your own behaviors that possibly contribute towards an unhealthy relationship. Recognition is the key, for until we can recognize our own role in the dance, we can do nothing to change it.

Now you can unmask the narcissists in your life. You can discover the underlying issues that make these people tick. You can make informed choices in your relationships. And you will never be fooled by the Masters of the Universe again.

The most important piece of information, however, is to understand that while it certainly takes two to tango, and while we each bring our own set of baggage to any relationship, the issues brought to the table by a narcissist can make you feel like everything wrong in the relationship is your fault.

This book will teach you why it is not …

Chapter 2
Narcissus –
The Myth and the Real Story

The term "narcissism" comes from the mythological story of a Greek youth named Narcissus, who rejected the romantic advances of a nymph named Echo. As punishment for his behavior she cursed him to fall in love with his own reflection in a pool of water. He became so infatuated with his own image that he was unable to leave it and eventually died on the spot, where he was mystically transformed into the flower still bearing his name today.

We are all narcissistic to some degree. If you watch any group of two year olds it is obvious that they think they are the Masters of their own Universe! They have no concept of the fact that there is a higher world around them. When they want something, they want it right now! They do not understand consequences, responsibilities, or what their demands and needs might mean to someone else. It is all about them. And they are miffed when the rest of the world doesn't bow to their demands. The tantrums begin! The expression, "the terrible twos," gives powerful meaning to envisioning the behaviors and antics of the youngest narcissists!

By the same token, many youngsters become more narcissistic as they evolve from childhood to adulthood. Their idiosyncratic view of the world oftentimes leads them to think that others should understand that *their* needs are the most important. Any family who has lived through the whining, complaining, and door-slamming behavior of a teenager who doesn't get his way, will understand this phenomenon as well.

Fortunately, most healthy two year olds and teenagers outgrow these behaviors with age and maturity. They begin to realize the importance of having other people in their lives. They start to form valuable skills of compromising and taking turns. They learn to develop feelings of empathy and compassion – crucial life skills that will enable them to have deep, meaningful relationships with other people throughout their lives.

These are necessary ingredients for caring deeply and loving someone. These emotions and abilities are also key in understanding that other people have feelings too – whether those people are close family and friends, or the check-out clerk at the grocery store. Most importantly, healthy humans develop recognition that they are *not* the only person in their universe and the world doesn't revolve around them ... even though we may wish it did sometimes!

> *We all need to have a certain degree of "healthy" narcissism in our lives to function optimally in society. It's what lets us successfully face the world each day.*

People with healthy narcissism have strong self-esteem, believe in themselves and their abilities, and are satisfied in their careers or else choose to change them. They have strong but balanced egos. They can compete successfully and feel good about their successes and also can handle their losses well. They do not see losing a competition as a crisis. They occasionally get cocky, angry, or disappointed, but even then they do not believe they are complete and total failures. They generally pick themselves up and move on. They learn from their mistakes, understand they are not perfect (and that it's OK not to be), and try to find joy in life. They enjoy being in relationships because they like sharing their lives with others, and they understand that give and take, compromise, and caring are the foundations of any healthy partnership.

"Malignant narcissists," on the other hand, have some vastly different beliefs about themselves and others ...

Adolf Hitler and Saddam Hussein come to mind as perhaps two of the best known and most extreme narcissists of our time. These men came to believe that their view of the world was the only one acceptable and the rest of the world should recognize that as well. As leaders, they both were charismatic, sometimes (in the early days of their rise to power) charming and dynamic. At the beginning of Hitler's rule he was seen by many as visionary. People rallied around him, wanted to be affiliated with him, and never saw the dark side of his personality beneath the façade until it was too late. That dark side would lead to the extermination of millions of innocent people, to overtaking other countries in an attempt to rule the entire world, and to history labeling him as one of the most evil leaders of all time. When he started out appearing as the "perfect partner" for his country, who could have imagined that he would become so "perfectly wrong" for the entire world?

Saddam Hussein was no less demonic, slaying thousands of his own people and thinking nothing of it. He ruled his country through force and fear. Encouraging his soldiers to rape, murder, maim, and destroy, he demonstrated God-like power to his people and the world. A leader of but one small country (in actuality, a somewhat "big fish in a small pond"), he none-the-less believed that he was the Master of the *entire* Universe. I suspect he never dreamed it possible for anyone to touch him or rein him in, much less take away his power.

Yet what a picture he was the day he was captured in 2003 — hidden away in a tiny spider cave in the desert, looking dirty, old, disheveled, and weak. This was certainly not the image of the proud dictator who had erected statues of himself throughout his country. This narcissist was definitely unmasked for who he really was; a pathetic substitute for a human being. Yet the most telling insight to his character was revealed after his capture. When questioned about his participation in the genocide he had ordered in his country, he not only showed no remorse, he still stood by his decision to do what he saw fit. He thought no more about the thousands of people he had put to death than if he'd killed a plague of locusts. He remained the true narcissist to the end, still believing in his well orchestrated omnipotence while also wondering what happened to his "universe" he'd called his own for so long.

Certainly many of our world leaders, military officers, and corporate presidents are narcissistic to some degree or they would not be able to make tough decisions in times of difficulties. They would not be able to bear the constant criticism of others and the daily onslaught of the media. They would not believe in themselves and go forward in times of adversity. They would not be risk takers when others around them cling to the old or safe ways of doing things. These leaders forge ahead and many times, save the day, as they believe in their way of doing things, and they frequently prove they are right. Their charisma and apparent self-confidence often make others follow them without being aware they are doing so. Many of these leaders are extremely bright, well-educated, highly respected individuals, revered by their colleagues and others as well.

Yet, sometimes these same wonderful leaders overstep the bounds of healthy self-esteem and let their narcissistic tendencies take over. They become blind to reality. They can't see things from another point of view. They forget that others are involved and may be affected by their self-centered decisions. And eventually some of them make mistakes – big mistakes. Huge corporations like Enron have lost everything at the hands of leaders whose malignant narcissism left them blinded to the differences between right and wrong and kept them from acknowledging the needs of others. The results were that a once-perfect company turned into one of greed and led to tragedy for many.

Bill Clinton could certainly be considered narcissistic in his behaviors – at least for the way he handled his role with Monica Lewinski. Despite being impeached and caught lying to the American public, he maintained his air of charisma and confidence. It almost appeared that he was miffed that anyone should bother him about such "details" that stirred up the press and kept him from running the country. "I didn't do anything wrong" was the message he conveyed, when most of the country saw him for what he really was – someone who thought his title gave him carte blanche to be "Master of the Universe." Narcissists do love to show us just how "above the rules" they are, whenever they can get away with it.

I can point to plenty of examples of malignant narcissists in other roles in our society. Professional athletes and those in the entertainment industry, who are constantly striking for more money, amaze me with their entitlement beliefs. While already earning millions of dollars, it is just never enough. More interesting still is when they get in trouble with the law. How many of these people do we see acting as if the laws shouldn't apply to them? Drugs, alcohol, or domestic abuse issues with some of these celebrities seem to be minor issues in their eyes, while, for the rest of us, they are life changing.

However, narcissists do not have to be world leaders, military officers, or corporate managers. Many other lesser-known narcissists in our society inflict their own level of damage upon those they live with, trapping their victims in boxxes of guilt, fear, shame, and self-doubt. They are doctors, teachers, construction workers, and secretaries. They are blue collar as well as white. They are rich or poor. They are the guy or gal next door. They are your mom, your spouse, your boyfriend, or your best friend.

Abusive husbands are probably the most easily recognized examples of narcissists. Whether physically, sexually, or emotionally abusive, they are the ones we see on television and in movies, wreaking havoc upon those around them. *Sleeping With the Enemy* and *Enough* are two movies portraying husbands with deep-seated narcissistic behaviors. Both men exhibit absolute power and control over every aspect of their wives' lives, while inflicting abuse as "punishment" for perceived poor performance of any kind. On film, it's easy to see that this type of relationship is dangerous. In reality, any and all abuse (whether physical, sexual, verbal and/or emotional), is unacceptable in any relationship! It should go without saying, taking care of *yourself* is crucial, especially in these situations, and even more so when your children are involved. Do *not* feel responsible for the abuse you receive. It is the abuser's boxx, not yours.

> *Equally destructive are the many narcissists who live quietly in all areas of society. I'll call them "Stealth Narcissists."*

They can be anyone and be in any role. Many are highly respected members of our communities. On the outside they may wear a mask of sincerity, kindness, and friendliness. They may belong to civic organizations and donate hours of volunteer time to help others. Their public demeanor demonstrates competence, compassion, understanding, and often a great sense of humor. They may give their time and resources in a manner that seems completely humanitarian. Yet, beneath this veneer lies a personality that can inflict incredible damage upon others. What goes on behind closed doors can be something completely different than their friends, extended family, or colleagues might ever imagine.

Most narcissists appear self-confident and sometimes egotistical, yet just the opposite is true. Their inner self is full of fear and a self-loathing, which most likely began in early childhood when certain needs of love and compassion were not provided by their primary caregivers. Out of this emotionally unhealthy upbringing, these children oftentimes developed defensive and/or maladaptive coping behaviors to keep themselves safe from additional injury at that time. While that may have worked in childhood and adolescence, most of those behaviors no longer work in the adult world. Unfortunately, the adults they become neither see nor understand this truth and their destructive behavior only continues; causing harm not only to themselves but to so many others in their paths as well.

The end result of a lifetime of being raised in an unhealthy environment, they are left unable to love themselves or anyone else. Yet, they believe the world should, and does, love them. By wearing the mask of Master of the Universe they hide their innermost fears. They reflect a false self to the world, hoping that no one will ever discover their true, contemptuous self, buried deeply inside. For if that were to ever occur, they fear they would surely be abandoned, alone, and unloved once again, just as they were in their family of origin.

Their constant need to affirm their false self is their daily chore. They look for others who will reflect this unrealistically perfect image back to them, every minute of their lives. And so it is they see others as their "drug," their "fix" to keep them going each day. Without this, they fear they do not exist.

Keep in mind that it doesn't really matter if your response to them is positive or negative – it's simply that *you do respond* to them that matters. For example, if you and I were sitting on a couch having this conversation right now and you brought your two year old along, odds are the child will want to be the center of attention sooner or later. (That's just how two year olds are.) And so as you and I get deep into our conversation, your little one would probably start out by trying to hug or kiss you, crawl up in your lap and get in your face, or whatever. He'll likely try the nice guy angle first.

Yet if you and I were intent on our conversation, you'd tell your child that he'd have to entertain himself until we were done talking. At that point, desperate to be recognized, your directive to him might lead him to pull out some not-so-nice behaviors *just to get your attention!* He might even work up to a temper tantrum, which he knows from past experience will definitely interrupt our focus and direct the attention towards him. And even if you end up punishing him somehow, it won't matter, for he was the one who truly won, because guess what? He got your attention! And that was his "fix."

While most narcissists prefer that we praise them constantly and remind them of how wonderful they are, they are also willing to get their fix through our negative responses as well, just as long as it's attention. If they get us to cry, feel bad, or get quiet due to their aggression towards us, that will do as well. They still get attention at the same time they exhibit their control over us. And as long as we're willing to keep playing their game, they're glad to keep pulling our marionette strings, as we think we have no say in the matter and continue to do their bidding.

To understand some of their behaviors on another level, it may also help to think in terms of an analogy of a force field. Imagine the Star Ship Enterprise from the old TV show *Star Trek*. Now consider just how vulnerable the ship was whenever its force field was down. Why, there was a whole crew of engineers assigned to keep it intact 24/7, for if the force field was broached, the odds of death for all were extremely high.

Now think of a narcissist as having a similar force field. It is his daily mission to keep it strong and impermeable, lest others break through and reveal his true self to the world. It is his constant mission to make sure you don't break through and upset his paradigm of what life is really like.

This is one of the biggest reasons these folks are always attacking everyone else, for if they can *keep you off balance,* the odds of you attacking them are between slim and none, and their force field stays firmly intact.

> *Thus, the frequent switch from Jekyll to Hyde sets the stage to keep you wondering if you're coming or going, and that's just how they like it.*

These people love to be admired and adored by others and will find a way to meet that need at all costs – even if they have to play a role they might disdain in order to achieve it. Their image of being perfect leads them to believe they excel at whatever they attempt. From there they begin to believe they are God-like and others are only on this earth to meet their needs. This façade allows them to be on the offensive rather than the defensive. It's always easier to be on the attack than to have to fend one off!

It is a convoluted dance they play with us.

Narcissists most generally fall into two main categories:

1) Somatic: those who demonstrate unusual physical prowess or accomplishments, such as body building, sexual claims, or pure physical attractiveness, and 2) Cerebral: those who exhibit their intellectual brilliance. A subcategory also exists, where the narcissist can be either of the first two, but with a shy, quiet personality. The ego is not so obvious. He is not particularly charismatic. Don't let this shy persona fool you – there is still a narcissist under the surface. No matter which type, when their needs are not met to the degree they deem appropriate, they feel justified in punishing those who are responsible.

The sad truth is that no one can *ever* make these people happy as they are not happy with themselves to begin with. Anyone attempting *to make them happy* is on an endless mission that will always fail. This vicious cycle is self-perpetuating. The results are as malignant as cancer. The more the victim tries to please the narcissist and fails, the stronger become the victim's feelings of low self-esteem. She then believes she is to blame for the problems and that the narcissist has every right to be disappointed or angry with her performance. In the end, the victim is held captive in one of many "behavioral boxxes" not of her own making, wondering how she got there in the first place. As her self-esteem continues to erode, she develops a stronger belief that her narcissistic partner is right and that she is incapable of living without his direction and supreme intellect. He is indeed the Master of her Universe. How could she possibly function without him?

Of course, as I mentioned earlier, some narcissists are women. Years ago in Colorado a high-ranking military officer attempted to kill his wife by injecting a toxic substance into her intravenous line when she was hospitalized for a minor illness. Caught in the act, the military wasted no time in court-martialing him for "conduct unbecoming an officer." The man claimed his wife had abused him for years, and his defense was that he had finally "snapped" under the pressure. Who can say? While she wanted the charges dropped (lots of military benefits were involved, of course) the military found him guilty of conduct unbecoming an officer and he spent 18 months behind bars, in addition to losing full military benefits.

Another woman I know named Jackie runs her household with an iron fist. Her husband and children are terrified of her and she makes no attempt to appear as the doting, selfless mother. She is the "Almighty" in her house and what she says is Gospel. Her children count the days until they are old enough to escape her domination. Her husband, however, has become a puppet, jumping and asking "how high" whenever she barks. This is *not* a healthy boxx, and those who continue to live in it develop lifelong scars as a result. Jackie's own children may become sarcastic, negative, abusive, withdrawn, frightened, shy, or rebellious. They may even build a similarly narcissistic environment for their own children, thus perpetuating the cycle.

It may help you to better understand narcissistic people if you realize that they don't sit up at night plotting to "get" their victims. They don't plan each and every move throughout their day to make their partners crazy. Quite often, they don't even understand they are doing anything "wrong." Or if they do understand their behaviors are bothering someone, they just really don't care. Most of all, they are in total astonishment when anyone questions their behavior. After all, does anyone question "God"?

> *Unfortunately, being narcissistic is not a choice.*
> *Narcissists can't just quit being narcissistic*
> *because someone tells them they should.*

It's much like someone with diabetes deciding not to be diabetic anymore. They might be able to change some behaviors which help the symptoms, yet they are still diabetic.

Perhaps an analogy that explains their behavior more clearly would be to compare them to a male lion. The king of the beasts doesn't sit up all night plotting which antelope he's going to kill for lunch the next day. He simply knows that he must eat and when he's hungry he will hunt. He might sit at the edge of a herd of antelope all afternoon, just assessing his best options. He has no feelings or emotions about which victim he chooses to dine on. He simply finds the one that will give him the least resistance. When he picks the best candidate, he attacks, makes his kill, and has his lunch. There's nothing more to it than that.

The lion isn't mean. He isn't spiteful or angry. Nor does he have any consciousness of the life he takes in order to eat. He knows he must eat to survive. He knows that antelope are prey. More importantly, his world is all about him. He's king of the beasts and, outside of man, he has no enemies. He is the Master of his Universe.

In my early journey to understand narcissism, I met three women who shared their stories with me. I suddenly began to see these controlling and confusing behaviors in others outside my own personal world. I came to realize just how powerful and detrimental these difficult folks can be to the loved ones in their lives.

I will be forever grateful that God let me connect with these women who first began to open my eyes to the overwhelming pain borne by the victims of malignant narcissism. These are their stories.

Irene...

I met Irene in Cancun, while we were both waiting at the airport. She was a 40-year-old black woman and vice president of a bank in a big city. She successfully managed 65 people and millions of dollars, was the president of several professional organizations, and a pillar of the community. In her career, she was very successful, having worked her way up the ranks one step at a time. She went to work excited to see what she could accomplish each day. Everyone thought her life was "perfect." Yet, there was another side to Irene's life. I could see the pain and confusion in her face as she told the personal side of her story.

She had been married for 20 years to a successful businessman who owned several shops throughout the community. They had two great teenage boys and the family had a substantial income. Yet, despite all these seemingly wonderful things, Irene was miserable. She told me that the minute she walked into her own house at the end of the day she felt two inches tall. Her extremely narcissistic husband reminded her on a regular basis just how incompetent she was. She didn't cook right. Didn't keep the house clean enough. Certainly didn't make love adequately or often enough. No matter what she did, it was never enough. She described one particular day when she was about to take the boys to soccer practice. At the last moment, she had to return unexpectedly to retrieve something from the bedroom she shared with her husband. There she found him vacuuming the tops of the curtains, furious with her that she had enough time to take the boys to soccer, but not to keep his house immaculate!

Although he never called her names or abused her physically, his constant criticism and controlling behaviors kept her locked in boxxes of self-doubt, fear, shame, sadness, depression, anger, resentment, and complete emptiness. Despite all her great career accomplishments, nothing she did mattered in her husband's eyes. He considered her no better than a servant, and a useless one at that when she didn't meet all his needs instantly and to his liking.

As she told me this story, tears of confusion and despair streamed down her face. How could she be so successful in her career and be such a failure as a person?

She didn't understand that no matter what she did, she would never be able to please her husband because he was unable to find satisfaction with himself. The result: her "Mr. Right" was tearing her apart in her efforts to win his approval, and was a definite "Mr. Wrong" for her long-term, emotional health.

Julia...

I met Julia when she and her boyfriend Fred were on vacation in Cozumel, Mexico where I was working at the time. They were both in their late 30s and had lived together for several years. Fred hoped Julia would marry him. She was a very short woman and he was well over six feet. Their dramatic difference in size was just as symbolic as their inequality in the relationship. While on vacation, they decided to take the Introduction to Scuba Diving class offered by the hotel's dive shop. I was free that afternoon and decided to join them on their dive and I arrived on the scene as their lesson in the pool was coming to a close. Four couples were in the pool with two dive instructors, and they were all practicing their underwater skills, getting comfortable with the equipment.

Suddenly, Julia and Fred surfaced while the others continued practicing. Julia was sputtering and panicking as she realized she was not the least bit comfortable with the situation. She pulled off her mask and began to babble to Fred about how she just "couldn't do it." As she sobbed, her words began to suggest more than a simple fear of diving. She gripped Fred's arm pathetically, begging him to continue the dive without her as she knew he would enjoy it. But the last thing she said was, "Please, Fred, *please* don't be mad at me."

The look of sheer disgust on his face told me that what she had feared the most – his disappointment with her – had already occurred. I saw her shrink emotionally before my eyes. Had she been in a relationship of unconditional love – a relationship where caring, compassion, empathy, and understanding were regularly practiced and demonstrated – this woman would never have had to fear her partner's reaction. Yet, why didn't she get compassion and understanding from him? Why didn't he support her in her decision not to go ahead with the dive? My guess is that his narcissistic tendencies had already taught her that it was *her* responsibility to meet his expectations and his needs, and when she didn't meet the mark, it was *her* fault.

When she saw me on the side of the pool she came up to me and started apologizing to me for her "incompetence" all over again. Recognizing her situation, I immediately reassured her that diving isn't a sport for everyone and that it was perfectly OK for her to back out of something she was uncomfortable with, especially since she was unhappy in only three feet of water. I knew that 40 feet was not going to be better! She hesitatingly asked, "Well, do you think it's OK if I come back and try again tomorrow?"

I supported her and told her that if she felt a continued interest she could surely try again the next day. However, I suggested that she not bring her boyfriend. She had been unable to see the pressure he had put upon her to perform to his standards. I hoped that without him she could relax enough to learn the scuba skills without his condescending attitude. She would be one-on-one with an instructor who had frequently helped people with similar fears. The end result was that she did come back for another lesson – without the critical boyfriend – and she mastered the skills, allowing them to dive together later in the day. The Boxx of Fear holding Julia captive was due to Fred's controlling, narcissistic behavior stripping her of her ability to determine her own capabilities in the situation. Yet she did not readily recognize that his Boxx of Narcissism was not her own.

Is this Mr. Right or Mr. Wrong? It was becoming clear to me that physical or sexual abuse need not play a role in every harmful relationship, but the emotional abuse one carries from situations like this leaves scars just as deep.

Bobbie...

Bobbie was a critical-care nurse. She and her teenaged son were vacationing in Mexico over the holidays and when I asked her if her husband had stayed at the hotel instead of going on the day tour she and her son had taken, she told me he never vacationed with them. He couldn't be bothered to go places with them or do things they liked to do. He just lived in front of his computer all day, ruling his domain as he deemed fit.

Then she shared with me that she was just biding her time for one more year until her son graduated from high school, at which point she was planning to leave her husband. As she told me about some of his behaviors, I could understand why. In addition to his ongoing lack of involvement with his family, he insisted the house be spotless and nothing be out of place – *ever*.

She told me about one particular incident when she was preparing an educational demonstration for the new nurses who had just started working in the Intensive Care Unit where she was the educator. The day before her presentation she was at home practicing her speech and had laid out all the items she would need to teach the class, including syringes, tape, and other nursing equipment, on her kitchen counter. In the middle of her rehearsal, she stopped for a short bathroom break. To her surprise, when she returned, all of her items had disappeared! She discovered that her husband had wandered into the kitchen, and upon finding the display of "disallowed" items on "his" counter, had promptly thrown them all in the trash!

Although we were interrupted and I didn't hear the rest of the story, the one thing this woman demonstrated throughout was defiance. She was strong within herself and had already begun to make her plans for the future. How she maintained her confidence and drive was unclear to me, but she had decided not to let herself get walled up in his Boxx of Narcissism. She was gathering her ammunition to be ready when the time was right.

Did these women recognize Mr. Wrong from the beginning? Of course not.

> *One characteristic of narcissists is that they know how to play the role of the charming, caring, kind, compassionate partner during the courting phase of a relationship. They are great pretenders or chameleons while they search for a mate.*

Since they can oftentimes go unrecognized by professional therapists, the general public can easily be fooled as well. Thus begins the road down into the convoluted world of narcissism. Once caught up in the web of confusion, the victim doesn't even know what hit her and more problematically, doesn't know how to get out.

Chapter 3
Who Are They and
Why Do They Behave Like That?

The American Psychiatric Association publishes the *Diagnostic and Statistical Manual of Mental Disorders (DSM)*, its reference manual for diagnosing psychiatric illness. It defines Narcissistic Personality Disorder as "an all-pervasive pattern of grandiosity (in fantasy and behavior), need for admiration or adulation, and lack of empathy, usually beginning by early adulthood and present in various contexts."[3] It lists nine official behaviors that constitute Narcissistic Personality Disorder, with clients who meet at least five of those criteria falling into the disorder category.

Yet, there is a wide scale of narcissism, from people who exhibit some tendencies to those with the full-blown personality disorder. It is not my wish to teach you how to diagnose people as I am not qualified to do so myself. Whether or not these difficult people in you life are diagnosed with full-blown Narcissistic Personality Disorder (NPD) is left to the psychiatric community.

However, the key question I ask you to consider is not whether or not the difficult person in your life is a true narcissist or not but rather,

Are you healthy in this relationship?

While understanding narcissism is crucial to realizing why these people behave this way, understanding yourself and whether or not your emotional health is being compromised, is the most important question to study.

Nature or Nurture

Are narcissists born this way or did their environment make them this way? This is a question continually debated by the scientific community. Although there are some studies in progress attempting to define the possibility that there are specific genes involved, this has not yet been proven. What we do know is that there seems to be a great deal of environmental influence on the development of individuals who display narcissistic behaviors, frequently occurring in the very first years of development.

We all need loving, caring environments to develop trust, intimacy, and love. Even infants can quickly determine if their needs are met regularly, if they are provided comfort, and are nurtured and loved. Yet when a child's environment proves to be inconsistent, abusive (physically, sexually, verbally, or emotionally), neglectful, or one of abandonment, the child can develop patterns of unhealthy coping behavior. A parent who does not offer unconditional love leaves his or her child always guessing. If the parent ignores the child or abuses him, the child questions his value and learns to fear. He learns that the world is not a safe place and begins to believe that love does not exist. The child anticipates and expects inconsistency and an unstable environment. As a result, he continually strives to be perfect, to avoid the wrath of doing something wrong.

This child may escape into a pretend world where he is no longer the person he knows himself to be. In his own mind, he is the one who is loved and cared for. Yet he knows in his heart that this is not true, and while he may harbor anger for his abusive parents, he dares not show it for fear of more retaliation. This child is thus abandoned emotionally, while he may not be physically. He does whatever he can to form a safe environment within his own walls of defense. He learns to feel nothing.

Then there is the child whose parents expect constant perfection out of him and are always entering him in competitions or sports for the mere purpose of living vicariously through him so they, in fact, are the ones to receive accolades for the child's performance. Think of the five-year-old child beauty queens or black belt karate stars. Talk about pressure. Frequently it is this same extremely competitive parent who tells his child who won the second place ribbon that second place is really "the first loser," and directly teaches his child that the parent's love is conditional on his performance.

When there are conditions to being loved, it is a precarious love at best; one that leaves children fearful of their value within their family and to the world in general.

Since no one is perfect, this expectation is a huge burden for any child to bear. In fact, the child may fear punishment if his perfection is not maintained 100 percent of the time. Unfortunately, as he grows up and believes that perfectionism is the norm, he will expect that from everyone around him as well, much to the chagrin of those in his intimate circle.

On the opposite extreme, children who are idolized by their parents, who are placed on a pedestal and can never do anything wrong, may also fall prey to this disorder. Loving someone too much is actually another form of abuse, for it is like treating someone as an extension of oneself. For these children who have never been taught that they are not perfect (and that no one is), the real world is a constant reminder of their imperfect selves – for they are never quite accepted by the rest of the world as they were by their grandiose parents. No one else coddles them. No one else showers them with never-ending praise. In their ongoing search throughout life for this expected outcome, they are in a constant battle with themselves about their own validity and are confused why the rest of the world doesn't honor their supreme existence. With this in mind, they don't trust, are paranoid, and tend to be on the attack, lest anyone attack them first. In light of this, you can understand why idolization by a parent is actually abusive behavior, especially in situations where the parent may be trying to live vicariously through the child and doesn't allow the child to be an individual.

Don't get me wrong ... loving your child unconditionally is what we all strive for, but the child also needs to understand that he is not perfect and will make mistakes along the line. That he will certainly be held accountable for his actions and punished for wrongdoings, but fairly and reasonably punished. That his world will provide him clearly outlined expectations so that he knows how to function. And that when he does make mistakes, it is his behavior, and not himself, that is not approved of. And that whoever and whatever he is, he is loved for being his true self and doesn't have to change himself in order to be loved by his intimate family. When these elements are not in place, the pain begins. The end result?

Hurt people hurt people.

While all the above-mentioned examples seem to vary widely, the resulting behaviors of the unhealthy grown-up child towards those around them are essentially the same. Coworkers, neighbors, and family members stuck in any relationship with the narcissist created by this environment are constantly at a loss as to how to deal with them. They do not understand the quizzical behaviors, the anger that comes out of nowhere, and the ongoing moodiness. They are left doubting their own sanity and blaming themselves for the erratic behavior of the narcissist.

So what are narcissistic behaviors? What should you be on the lookout for? Instead of using the nine criteria put out by the American Psychiatric Association, I developed my own list of specific behaviors that I have found are common in a wide variety of people with unhealthy narcissism – from those with only tendencies, to those with full-blown Narcissistic Personality Disorder. The bottom line is that no matter what level of behavior they exhibit, these people can still be detrimental to your health and well being, both physically and emotionally.

The following is a list of Red Flag narcissistic behaviors. These may help you to gain a clearer understanding of how a narcissist acts. Somatic narcissists may have more behaviors related to their bodies, while the cerebral ones will be more intellectually oriented. Not all of these behaviors will necessarily show up in each person, and, in fact, many of us will likely have some of them ourselves. But if you have checked off a vast majority of the boxes on this list, the odds are in your favor that you are on treacherous ground.

Red Flag Narcissistic Behaviors

❑ Extreme infatuation with oneself, self-centered, expects to be recognized as superior
❑ Is preoccupied with fantasies of unlimited power, success, brilliance, beauty, or ideal love
❑ Sees himself as "special" and should only have to affiliate with others of a similar stature
❑ Takes advantage of others to achieve his needs
❑ Demonstrates a constant need for admiration or approval
❑ Exaggerates personal achievements while minimizing those of others
❑ Is convinced that he is unique
❑ Feels entitled to special treatment and that rules frequently don't apply to him
❑ May propose love and marriage within only a few weeks of starting a relationship
❑ Very charismatic or charming at first, but can quickly switch from Dr. Jekyll to Mr. Hyde without apparent cause
❑ May insist that he know your whereabouts at all times
❑ Demands compliance with his expectations
❑ Is unable to demonstrate or understand empathy or compassion
❑ Does not seem to feel real happiness or positive emotions
❑ Often criticizes and/or puts others down
❑ Assumes himself to be more knowledgeable than those around him
❑ Panics, cries, begs, and becomes emotional if he anticipates an end to a relationship
❑ May harass or stalk you if you do break up
❑ Quick to anger or feel insulted or slighted
❑ Rages with anger or inflicts the "silent treatment" when upset
❑ Denies he has issues to work on – sees himself as nearly perfect
❑ May often take unnecessary risks
❑ Frequently humiliates or abuses others, although he doesn't see it as abuse

- ❑ Sulks when he doesn't get his way
- ❑ Nothing is ever his fault
- ❑ Drives recklessly and/or way too fast
- ❑ Exaggerates the truth or blatantly lies
- ❑ Rarely treats anyone with respect or kindness
- ❑ Doesn't acknowledge or respect other's boundaries
- ❑ Always wants to be in control
- ❑ May drink and drive regularly
- ❑ His needs for attention, time, and space matter – yours do not
- ❑ Has difficulty putting himself in another's shoes
- ❑ Uses sex as a weapon – through withholding, controlling, or being overly demanding
- ❑ Rarely recognizes the accomplishments or abilities of others
- ❑ Doesn't appear to have a conscience
- ❑ Does not take criticism well and becomes defensive easily
- ❑ Rarely expresses appreciation of others
- ❑ Is easily hurt and insulted
- ❑ Considers most others in the world "idiots"
- ❑ Shows no feelings of remorse or guilt for his mistakes or the hurts he dishes out
- ❑ Wins most arguments through the use of rationalizing his behavior
- ❑ Blames others for all his problems
- ❑ Frequently complains that whatever you do, it isn't "good enough"
- ❑ Is often paranoid – thinks people are talking about him behind his back
- ❑ Has a hard time accepting the opinions or ideas of others
- ❑ May attempt to limit loved ones from spending time with others
- ❑ May want to have complete control of the family money
- ❑ Always has to win any argument
- ❑ Is often envious of others, or thinks others envy him
- ❑ May feel entitled to go through your purse, closet, or other personal belongings without your permission
- ❑ His attitude is generally haughty or arrogant
- ❑ Rarely can understand another's point of view

- ❏ Expects you to read his mind when he wants something
- ❏ Hates to stand in line – he shouldn't have to, as his time is more valuable than others
- ❏ Frequently "forgets" to give birthday and holiday cards and gifts to loved ones
- ❏ May ignore you or be indifferent to you for no reason
- ❏ Leaves others feeling as though they need to "walk on eggshells" around him
- ❏ Hates to be thought of as ordinary or average
- ❏ Is desperate to have the biggest house, car, bank account, or title
- ❏ Often leaves you feeling guilty, drained, fearful, exhausted, just plain stupid, and most of all, wondering how you got there

The Victim's Feelings and Actions

Now that you have begun to see some Red Flag behaviors that are common to narcissists, let's look at some feelings and behaviors frequently reported by the victims.

- ❏ Feeling guilty for "making" the narcissist feel the way he does
- ❏ Chronically confused about their partner's sudden changes in behavior
- ❏ Frequently exhausted from never knowing what might happen next
- ❏ Feeling like they have to "walk on eggshells" to avoid "rocking the boat"
- ❏ Coming home to find Dr. Jekyll and suddenly discovering Mr. Hyde, and never knowing what caused the change
- ❏ Always apologizing for "never doing things right"
- ❏ Trying to keep a low profile to avoid being noticed
- ❏ Making up stories to their friends and family about how they got the latest bruises
- ❏ Blaming themselves for never doing things well enough
- ❏ Always feeling anxious when they walk in their own home (or workplace if the narcissist is at their place of work)
- ❏ Never completely trusting their partner

- ❏ Never feeling respected or equal in the relationship
- ❏ Always worrying about their performance in any role, including in the bedroom
- ❏ Often wondering if it's OK if they phone or meet with friends or family
- ❏ Having to ask permission to do anything
- ❏ Not being allowed free access to their financial accounts
- ❏ Not being able to give their opinion for fear of being chastised
- ❏ Never being able to win any argument
- ❏ Always wondering what they did "wrong"
- ❏ Avoiding arguments at all costs
- ❏ Always attempting to "try harder" to make things better
- ❏ Chronically feeling empty
- ❏ May periodically have suicidal thoughts
- ❏ Wishing for "someday" when things will change, but someday never comes
- ❏ After breaking up with their narcissistic partner, all they want to do is run back to them
- ❏ Repeatedly making excuses for and forgiving their partner's unacceptable behaviors, which continue to happen
- ❏ Often wondering how they got into this situation to begin with
- ❏ Always being told everything is their fault
- ❏ Oftentimes feel humiliated by their partner
- ❏ Constantly fearing abandonment by the partner, so "doing whatever it takes" to keep him
- ❏ Doing things they are uncomfortable with because they feel pressured to do so
- ❏ Compromising their values, needs, and beliefs because their partner wants them to
- ❏ Discovering that the narcissist has frequently lied or misled them
- ❏ Feeling like no one else could possibly love them
- ❏ Believing they are not as important as their partner
- ❏ Taking their partner's advice, although their gut tells them not to
- ❏ Feeling like they're living a lie – that the outside world sees them one way, while the inner reality is definitely something entirely different

❏ Feeling subservient or less-than their partner
❏ Rarely feeling like their needs are being met or even acknowledged
❏ Never doing anything unless their partner says it's OK
❏ Their friends tell them they are being abused, but they just can't see it
❏ Feeling like they are being parented – that they're too immature or childish to be able to think on their own
❏ Often wishing they would have never gotten into this mess to begin with and now don't know how to get out
❏ Frequently feeling numb or depressed
❏ They no longer know who they really are
❏ May end up looking like the "crazy one" in the relationship

These are just some of the behaviors and feelings of narcissists and victims. If you find yourself recognizing many of these feelings, perhaps you are realizing you are in your own narcissistic relationship. Extricating yourself from the grips of a narcissist who wants to keep you entrapped in many of his boxxes is complicated at best. You may or may not want to leave this relationship, but at least, by acknowledging and understanding it, you can make better decisions and educated choices about your future.

Just remember one thing … It *is* all about choices. Unless they literally have a gun to your head, nobody can *make* you do anything you don't want to do. No one can determine your attitude unless you let them. Deciding to move on or to remain a victim of a narcissist depends upon your own circumstances.

Yet, when children are involved it certainly complicates things. For many individuals, the implied security of having a partner may feel safer than being alone in the big, wide world. As a result, you may feel like you are stuck in your situation. However, as you learn the devastating effects a narcissist can have on those around him, it is important to weigh the effect he can also have upon your children. Do you want them to learn that these destructive and abusive behaviors as normal, and fulfill a never-ending legacy of narcissism in their own lives? Or would you do whatever is in your power to help them avoid growing up to become a narcissist, or perhaps even the victim of one themselves?

Have you thought outside your usual boxx to consider all possible options for your future? Or will you submit, give up, and continue to let your narcissist control your life?

There is yet much to learn. Read on…

"Knowledge is power.
Know everything you can about narcissism.
It did me a world of good to be armed with information and realize that this wasn't all just my fault."
Angela – survivor

Chapter 4
A Narcissist From the Inside

*M*ost narcissists are oblivious to their condition. In addition, they are generally unwilling to listen to psychologists or other professionals who might suggest to them they are anything less than perfect. They certainly won't listen to *you* telling them they have something to "work on." So for God's sake, don't give them this book to read, as they will either deny that it is about them, or they will fly into a rage at your suggestion that they may not be God after all.

Yet there are a few who have recognized that something isn't quite right with their lives, who perhaps have hit rock bottom and are now interested in finding out how they got there – even if it is only to avoid this pain again. One such person is Sam Vaknin, who I mentioned earlier. He is highly intelligent, highly functioning, and a classic example of a hard-core narcissist. (With an official diagnosis of NPD.) While he recognizes that he will never improve, he has learned to use his intelligence and his condition to actually make a living informing others about this convoluted disorder.

Ironically, even though Sam offered his story for this book as a means of helping others, it is also clear that he did so because he is a narcissist. For him, having his story published is one more layer of attention, one more avenue that makes him unique. (For how many other narcissists can even admit they are narcissistic, much less be an expert in the field at the same time they help others with their information?) Mind you, he does not do this altruistically – he readily admits that he does it to continue to receive his own narcissistic supply. As such, he has agreed to share his story with me here, so that you can better understand what makes these people tick … and to make his presence known to an even larger audience at the same time.

The long and the short of it is this: Born in Israel, he attained his PhD in Philosophy in the United States. In 1990 (thinking he was above the law) he participated in a business scenario that the Israeli government defined as "stock fraud and manipulation." This yielded him 11 frustrating months in an Israeli prison in 1995-1996. His world crumbling around him, his marriage in shambles, his financial world ruined, and finding himself in jail with crooks and other lowlifes, he spent countless hours attempting to figure out how he got there and just exactly what happened to upset his perfect world: The world he once ruled. The very same world where others acknowledged him as omnipotent, perfect, and God-like. How could such a terrible thing happen to *him*? It was beyond his comprehension.

He shares his story with us so that you can begin to appreciate the twisted thought processes created in the lives of a narcissist. You can recognize the plotting, the anger, the hate, and the self-loathing. And perhaps you can begin to understand that the feelings you may have as a result of living with one of these troubled people are not simply your fault.

Yet, for all his self-discovery, Sam readily writes on his website and in his own book, that he is no better off today for all his searching and work, than he was that day he hit rock bottom in prison. He admits that he has not changed, nor will he ever change. He will be a narcissist until the day he dies. He has neither the ability nor the intention to change. This is his story, adapted from his journal entries (http://samvak.tripod.com/narcissist).

Sam Vaknin...

I remember the day I almost died. I could think of nothing but my wife. She left me two months after my incarceration in an Israeli prison. She said that my brain did not excite her as it used to. This is why I had planned to grab the warden's gun and kill myself. Death has an asphyxiating, all-pervasive presence and I could hardly breathe. Then it passed and I knew that I had to find out real quick what was wrong with me – or else.

How I obtained access to psychology books and to the Internet from the inside of one of Israel's more notorious jails is a story unto itself. In this search of my dark self, I had very little to go on, no clues, and no Della Street by my side. I had to let go – yet I never did and did not know how. I forced myself to remember, threatened by the imminent presence of the Grim Reaper. I fluctuated between shattering flashbacks and despair. I remember holding myself, white knuckles clasping an aluminum sink, about to throw up, as I was flooded with images of violence between my parents; images that I repressed to oblivion. I cried a lot, uncontrollably, convulsively, gazing through tearful veils at times.

The exact moment I found a description of Narcissistic Personality Disorder is etched in my mind. I felt engulfed, encapsulated, and frozen. It was suddenly very quiet and very still. I met myself. I saw the enemy and it was I.

The article was long-winded and full of references to scholars I'd never heard of before, but it described me to the last details in uncanny accuracy: grandiose fantasies of brilliance and perfection, sense of entitlement without commensurate achievements, rage, exploitation of others, lack of empathy.

I had to learn more. I knew I had the answer. All I had to do was find the right questions.

That day was miraculous. Many strange and wonderful things happened. I saw people – I *saw* them. And I had a glimmer of understanding regarding myself; the disturbed, sad, neglected, insecure, and ludicrous thing that passed for me.

The first real important realization I had was that there were two of us. I was not alone inside my body.

One was extroverted, easy going, gregarious, attention-consuming, charming, ruthless – and at the other extreme, manic-depressive. He required admiration and frequent praise. Everyone loved him. The other was a schizoid, shy, dependent, phobic, suspicious, pessimistic, and helpless creature – a kid, really.

The first, I'll call Ninko. He would appear to interact with people. It didn't feel like I was putting on a mask or that I had another personality. It was just like I was *more* me. It was a caricature of the true me, of Sam. Yet Sam hated people. He felt inferior, physically repulsive, and socially incompetent. Ninko also hated people. He held them in contempt. They were inferior to his superior qualities and skills. He needed their admiration, but he resented this fact and he accepted their offerings condescendingly.

This is but a piece of my self-discovery. The layers of me were deep and confusing.

No woman has ever wanted to have a child with me. It is very telling. Women have children even with incarcerated murderers. I know because I have been to jail with these people. But no woman has ever felt the urge to perpetuate us – the "we-ness" of she and me.

I have been married twice, but women are very hesitant with me. Most definitely do not want anything binding. It is as though they want to maintain all routes of escape clear and available. It is a reversal of the prevailing myth about non-committal males and women huntresses.

But no one wants to hunt a predator.

It is an eroding task to live with me. I am infinitely pessimistic, bad-tempered, paranoid, and sadistic in an absent-minded and indifferent manner. My daily routine is a constant rigmarole of threats, complaints, hurts, eruptions, moodiness, and rage. I snarl against slights, true and imagined. I alienate people. I humiliate them because this is my only weapon against the humiliation of their indifference to me.

Gradually, wherever I am, my social circle dwindles and then vanishes. Narcissists don't necessarily hate people – they simply don't need them.

> *I am torn between my need to obtain attention and my overriding wish to be left alone. This wish, in my case, is peppered with contempt and feelings of superiority.*

Such an unpredictable but always sickening and festering atmosphere is hardly conducive to love or sex. Gradually, both become extinct. My relationships are hollowed out. Imperceptibly, I switch to a-sexual co-habitation.

I am heterosexual, so I am attracted to women, but I am simultaneously repelled, horrified, bewitched, and provoked by them. I seek to frustrate and humiliate them. The sexual and emotional lives of us narcissists are perturbed and chaotic. We are unable to love in any true sense of the word. Nor are we capable of developing any measure of intimacy. Lacking empathy, we are incapable of offering our partner emotional support of any kind.

I have been asked many times if I miss loving, whether I would have liked to love, and if I am angry with my parents for crippling me so. There is no way I can answer these questions. I never loved. I do not know what I am missing. I am not angry for being unable to love. I equate love with weakness. I hate being weak and I hate and despise weak people. I do not tolerate stupidity, disease, or dependence – and love seems to encompass all three. These are not sour grapes. I really feel this way.

I am an angry man, but not because I never experienced love and probably never will. No, I am angry because I am not as powerful, awe inspiring, and successful as I wish to be and as I deserve to be. Because my daydreams refuse so stubbornly to come true. Because I am my worst enemy. And because, in my constant state of paranoia, I see adversaries plotting everywhere and feel discriminated against and contemptuously ignored. I am angry because I know that I am sick and that my sickness prevents me from realizing even a small fraction of my potential.

My life is a mess as a direct result of my disorder. I am a vagabond, avoiding my creditors, besieged by hostile media in more than one country, hated by one and all. Granted, my disorder also allowed me to write my book, *Malignant Self Love*, the rage to write as I do (I am referring to my political essays), a fascinating life, and insights a healthy man is unlikely to attain. But I find myself questioning the trade-off ever more often.

But at other times, I imagine myself healthy and I shudder. I cannot conceive of a life in one place with one set of people, doing the same thing, in the same field, with one goal within a decades-old game plan. To me, this is death. I am most terrified of boredom, and whenever faced with its haunting prospect, I inject drama into my life, or even danger. This is the only way I feel alive.

I guess all the above portrays a lonely wolf. I am a shaky platform, indeed, on which to base a family or future plans. I know as much. So, I pour wine to both of us, sit back and watch with awe and with amazement the delicate contours of my female partner. I savor every minute. In my experience, it might well be the last.

Even in the darkness of my deepest valleys I was not afraid. I carried with me my metal constitution, my robot countenance, my superhuman knowledge, my inner timekeeper, my theory of morality and my very own divinity – myself.

When my first wife left me, I discovered the hollowness of it all. It was the first time that I experienced my true self consciously. It was a void; a gaping abyss, almost audible, a hellish iron fist gripping, tearing my chest apart. It was horror.

It was then that I came to realize that my childhood was difficult. At the time, it seemed to me to be as natural as sunrise and as inevitable as pain. But in hindsight, it was devoid of emotional expression and abusive to the extreme. I was not sexually abused – but I was physically, verbally, and psychologically tormented for 16 years without one minute of respite. Thus, I grew up to be a narcissist, a paranoid, and a schizoid. At least that's what I want to believe. Narcissists tend to blame others for their troubles. In this case, psychological theory itself was on my side. The message was clear: people who are abused in their formative years (birth to age six) tend to adapt by developing personality disorders, amongst them Narcissistic Personality Disorder. It was simply not my fault

Another area of dysfunction is my sexual life. To my parents, sex was ugly and dirty. My rebellion led me to experience orgies and group sex on the one hand, but other times practicing strict self-denial. While I have experienced bouts of promiscuity (after major life crises), I typically engage in sex very rarely (despite long-term relationships with women). My sexual non-availability is intended to frustrate women who are attracted to me. I frequently use the fact that I have a wife as an alibi to avoid contact with women.

I am pompous, grandiose, repulsive, and contradictory. There is a seriously huge mismatch between who I really am and what I really achieved, and how I feel myself to be. It is not that I think that I am far superior to other humans intellectually. Thought implies free will and willpower is not involved here. My superiority is ingrained in me; it is a part of my every mental cell, an all-pervasive sensation, an instinct, and a drive. I feel that I am entitled to special treatment and outstanding consideration because I am such a unique specimen. I know this to be true – the same way you know that you are surrounded by air. It is an integral part of my identity; more integral to me than my body.

This opens a gap – rather, an enormous abyss – between me and other humans. Because I consider myself so special, I have no way of knowing how it is to be them.

In other words, I cannot empathize. I am not a bad person. Actually, I am a good person. I have helped people – many people – all my life. So, I am not evil. What I am is indifferent. I couldn't care less. I help people because it is a way to secure attention, gratitude, and admiration. And because it is the fastest and surest way to get rid of them and their incessant nagging.

My narcissism has always done two things for me: It isolates me from the pain of facing reality at the same time that it allows me to inhabit the fantasyland of ideal perfection and brilliance. These once-vital functions are bundled in what is known to psychologists as my "False Self." What you see is not the real me. I wear a mask so that you will never see the real me, for I fear if you do, you will abandon me. You will hate me, the way I hate myself. And you will no longer need me. The result – I will lose you – my source of attention – my "Narcissistic Supply." My "fix," as if I were a drug addict. That is the worst fear I have. That you will no longer be here to validate me and praise me. To need me. To respond either positively or negatively to my behaviors – for either are equally strong sources of my necessary supply. I really don't care if I make you cry or cower or smile – just as long as you keep reflecting me back to me. It is when you leave me and my supply shrivels up and disappears that I disappear. This thought is worse than death.

I don't have an extended family of my own. I don't have children. While I have married again, families to me are hotbeds of misery, breeding grounds of pain, and scenes of violence and hate. I do not wish to create my own. I certainly did not find my own family of origin a safe and happy place.

Even as an adolescent I was looking for another family. Social workers offered to find foster families for me. It pained my parents and my mother expressed her agony the only way she knew how; by abusing me physically and psychologically. It was not a nice place, our family.

My father always said to me that their responsibilities ended when I turned 18, but they couldn't wait that long and sent me to the army a year early. I was 17 and terrified witless. After a while my father told me not to visit them again, so the army became my second, nay, my only home. When I was hospitalized for two weeks with kidney disease, my parents came to see me only once, bearing stale chocolates. A person never forgets such slights; they go to the very core of one's identity and self-worth.

I dream about them often, my family whom I haven't seen for five years now. My little brothers and one sister, all huddled around me listening intently to my stories of fantasy and black humor. I remember every detail in stark relief and I know how different it could all have been – how happy we all could have been. If only circumstances had been different. I dream about my mother and my father. A great cavern of sadness threatens to suck me in and I wake up suffocating.

I guess that, at the bottom of it all, I do not want to live. They took away from me the will to live. If I allow myself to feel – this is what I overwhelmingly experience – my own non-existence. It is an ominous, nightmarish sensation, which I am fighting to avoid even at the cost of foregoing my emotions. There is in me a deeply repressed seething ocean of melancholy, gloom, and self-worthlessness waiting to engulf me, to lull me into oblivion. My shield is my narcissism.

Whatever it is that I experience as emotions I experience in reaction to slights and injuries, real or imagined. My emotions are all reactive, not active. I feel insulted – I sulk. I feel devalued – I rage. I feel ignored – I pout. I feel humiliated – I lash out. I feel threatened – I fear. I feel adored – I bask in glory. I am virulently envious of one and all.

I can intelligently discuss other emotions, which I never experienced – such as empathy or love – because I make it a point to read a lot and to correspond with people who claim to experience them. Thus, I gradually have formed working beliefs as to what people feel. It is pointless to try to really understand, but at least I can better predict their behavior with this ammunition.

So, here I am: An emotional hunchback. A fossil observing my environment with cold, dead eyes. We shall never meet amicably because I am a predator and you are the prey. Because I do not know what it is like to be you and I do not particularly care to know. Because my disorder is as essential to me as your feelings are to you. My normal state is my very illness. I look like you, I walk the walk and talk the talk, and I – and so many others like me – deceive you magnificently. Not out of the cold viciousness of our hearts, but because that is the way we are.

We cannot delay gratification. We do not accept "no" for an answer. And we settle for nothing less than the ideal, the sublime, the perfect, the all-inclusive, the all-encompassing, the engulfing, the all-pervasive, the most beautiful, the cleverest, and/or the richest. We are shattered by discovering that a collection we possess might be incomplete, that our colleague's wife is more glamorous, that our son's grades aren't as good as the kid down the street, that our neighbor has a new, impressive car, that our roommate got promoted, that the "love of our life" signed a recording contract. It is not plain old jealousy. It is not even pathological envy (though it is definitely a part of the psychological make-up of the narcissist). It is the discovery that we are not perfect, or ideal, or complete. That is what does us in.

I feel entitled to more. I feel it is my right – due to my intellectual superiority – to lead a thrilling, rewarding, kaleidoscopic life. I feel entitled to force life itself, or at least people around me, to yield to my wishes and needs; supreme among them the need for stimulating variety.

My personality is inflexible. This rigidity means that I have pre-set, determined, invariable reactions to changing situations. Of course, very often my reactions are counter-productive. I am self-destructive and my behaviors are self-defeating. I hate myself so much that I am content only when I suffer and am on the verge of complete devastation. It is a common mistake to believe that understanding something is halfway to curing it. I understand pathological narcissism as very few people do. I correspond with psychologists and psychiatrists all over the world, giving them advice on this subject. Yet, even if I am fully aware that my actions will cause me great, irreversible harm, I cannot change my course. I cannot avoid committing these tragic errors. I want to be constantly punished.

I have emotions and they are buried in a pit down below. All of my emotions are enormously negative and all encompassing. I cannot feel anything, because if I open the floodgates of this cesspool of my psyche, I will drown.

And I will carry you with me.

At the same time the voices in my head constantly say: "You are a fraud." "You are a zero." "You deserve nothing." "If only they knew how worthless you are."

I know I am loved by many.

But –

I don't feel loveable at all. I attribute the fact that people love me to their stupidity, naiveté, gullibility, ignorance, or pathology. Had they known me, the *real* me – I assure myself – they would have never been able to love me. As it is, it is only a question of time before they get to know me better and turn to hatred and repulsion. So, I am on a constant state of alert, awaiting the inevitable rejection/abandonment and trying to maintain my image (false self) half-heartedly (this being a doomed effort).

And all the love in this world, and all the crusading women who think that they can "fix" me, by doling out their sickly sweet compassion, understanding, and support, cannot change me one iota in this maddening, self-imposed verdict meted out by the most insanely, obtusely, sadistically harsh judge:

By me.

The biggest difference between you and me is that you can leave this prison … I am here for all eternity.

"If you find yourself in a relationship with a narcissist, run away! Run very far away!
We do not change. We never change."
Sam Vaknin, narcissist

Chapter 5
The Perfect Partner

*I*n the many accounts I have received from respondents, one thing is clear: there is an incredibly similar pattern to each story. While the details, occupations, ages, parts of the country, and many other factors may vary substantially, the perverse dance of becoming enmeshed with a narcissist seems to be nearly the same. From the perfect beginning to the ugly and painful end, it is almost as if all narcissists and their victims read the same manual: the first group about how to hook themselves a victim, and the second group how to become one.

How do these narcissists do it? How do people with such absurd and damaging behaviors convince seemingly normal people to follow them? To fall in love with them? Or even more confusing, to continue to stay with them, despite ongoing heartache and, oftentimes abuse? What's more – what spell do they place upon their victims that leaves them still in love with their user, sometimes months and years after the relationship has ended? It's almost like the Pied Piper – they come swooping down with their magical music and mesmerize their victims into being blind, deaf, and dumb to the reality that is engulfing them.

In short, predators begin by building up the unsuspecting loved one's self-esteem to a point she had never experienced before, and then slowly, painfully, horribly tear her apart, leaving her shattered and wounded for a very long time.

And it's not as if this scenario only affects the less educated, or people from poor social classes or neighborhoods. Some victims have PhDs. Some are attorneys. Some are successful business people. Some are big, strong men. No socio-economic, racial, or educational group is exempt. Even psychiatrists have been fooled. Although women seem to make up the majority of the victims, anyone can fall prey to the magical spell of a narcissist.

The following story is a good summary of this phenomenon.

Sally and Tom...

Sally met Tom at a friend's barbeque. Out of the 30 or so people attending, Sally noticed Tom right away. He was tall and handsome with a great smile and loads of charisma. It was obvious that he worked out regularly and his muscular build had the eye of most of the women in the group. He was the life of the party, always telling jokes and getting people to laugh. It was readily obvious that everyone loved him.

When Sally realized that Tom was gazing at her periodically, she was flattered. She considered herself petite, plain, and quiet compared to the many gregarious, beautiful, single women who were flaunting themselves upon him. Yet, she was certain that he was intently looking her way quite often. As the evening progressed it became more obvious and eventually Tom extricated himself from the women with the dominant personalities in favor of Sally.

As he struck up a conversation with her, she instantly felt flattered and awestruck with his appearance and self-confidence. He told her that her quiet shyness combined with her simple yet raw beauty intrigued him. He was tired of "pushy, independent women." He really liked the more "down to earth" women who liked old-fashioned romance and chivalry. Sally was swept off her feet instantly and they ended the evening with him walking her to her car. He was ever so polite; opening the car door for her, thanking her for such a nice evening, and in a very gentlemanly way, asking her if he might call her sometime. Of course she was thrilled and gave him her phone number.

When he called her a few days later, he suggested they meet somewhere neutral so that she would feel safe. She was so impressed that he didn't press her to find out exactly where she lived. She had been with pushy men before, so his kindness and apparent empathy made her head swell. They met at a nice restaurant where they enjoyed an expensive meal, talked and laughed for hours, and discovered they had many things in common. At the end of the evening Tom picked up the tab (despite Sally insisting they go Dutch treat), and once again walked her to her car. This time he asked her permission to kiss her on the cheek. She was delighted! She seemingly had found a non-pushy man who treated her with respect and adoration. Who could ask for more?

When Tom sent a dozen roses to her office the next day, she was hooked. After that they began to see each other a couple of times a week. At first it was movies, walks in the parks, or trips to the zoo. They talked about their mutual love of children, the church, and volunteerism. Tom was always super polite, holding doors, paying for everything, and telling Sally how much he loved her little "quirks." Within a few weeks, they appeared to all their friends to be madly in love.

Sally's friends thought Tom was an angel. They had seen her be unappreciated by men before and were delighted that she had found someone who would take care of her. Not that she needed to be taken care of per se – after all, she was a successful accountant with a big firm and had a great income of her own. It's just that Sally felt more comfortable in the more behind the scenes situations than in the limelight and thus it was harder for her to find nice, eligible bachelors. As she wasn't much of a drinker and didn't smoke, the bar scene had not been comfortable for her either. Sally was pretty but was about 20 pounds overweight and didn't like to wear makeup or dress provocatively, so she felt she probably wasn't appealing to the average man. Yet, Tom told her that she looked "genuine" without all the makeup worn by most women.

She was in heaven.
She felt more beautiful than she'd ever felt in her life.

Tom was a contractor and managed several building operations around the city. He often talked about his job and the people he managed. Occasionally Sally sensed his frustration with the type of employees who worked in construction, as he routinely mentioned what idiots they were and how hard it was to find good workers, but not being familiar with his environment, she thought nothing of it. She was happy and that's all that mattered.

Eventually, the couple became intimate and Sally thought Tom was a wonderful lover, although she was a bit uncomfortable with him on top of her, simply due to their size differences. It seemed to be his preferred position and as she enjoyed making him happy, it was not something she mentioned to Tom. She just waited for her turn and anticipated that he'd do the same for her.

Tom began to speak of marriage when the two had only been dating for six weeks. While Sally was flattered, she did think it was a bit fast and shared her concerns with Tom. He laughed wholeheartedly with his big smile and said, "Oh, come on, don't we love each other? Isn't that what people in love do? They get married – right? What are you worried about? I'll take care of you and pretty soon we'll have a house full of little ones running around."

While she was a bit unsure about the time frame, she agreed that they should be engaged and the wedding date was set for three months down the road. Her friends were overjoyed with her news, as they continued to see Tom as the father figure she had always needed in her life. Whenever Tom visited Sally's office, everyone stopped to chat with him as he frequently brought them cookies or coffee or other such goodies.

The wedding was big, beautiful, and stunning. The only minor glitch in the entire evening was that Tom drank way too much and started getting loud, laughing more boisterously than usual. Some of his friends from work got drunk too and Sally just took it as a symptom of normal, healthy celebration. The fact that she didn't drink at all and still had her wits about her, she realized, meant that she was probably just a bit more inhibited than the rest of those celebrating. However, she did think it a bit unusual that Tom danced several dances with the secretary from his office – a woman Sally thought he might have once had a relationship with – yet, she still threw it off as everyone letting their hair down and having fun. After all, the rest of the day had been spectacular.

However, by the time she and Tom arrived at their honeymoon hotel room he was vomiting profusely – a direct result of the alcohol, and the fact that he had actually eaten a cigar someone gave him, as a joke. He passed out as soon as they walked in the door. By morning he was a bit grumpy – something she hadn't seen before, and he asked her to "give him some space" until he felt better. She was a bit sad that their wedding night was not quite as she had envisioned, but she had always known that Tom was a bigger partier than she was, so how could she blame him for his behavior? So, she looked on the bright side and towards their future together. The joy he had brought her during their time dating would surely return as they settled into their new life together. The wedding behind them, the newlyweds set up housekeeping.

It wasn't long after that when things began to change ...

Once married, Tom insisted that he and Sally have joint bank accounts. While Sally had lived on her own for years, at age 34 she had never thought about merging her money with a partner. Yet, she realized that marriage brought with it many changes and as she had been able to save a fair amount of money over the years, she wanted to feel like an equal to Tom, contributing her share to their mutual financial stability. So, she conceded and joint checking and savings accounts were established.

The next thing Sally noticed was that Tom's workload seemed to increase dramatically. He told her that he'd gotten two additional contracts and would need to be spending some late hours in order to meet all the needs required by the increased demand, in addition to helping pay for the new house they had bought. She was completely understanding of the situation and busied herself in the evenings and some weekends by setting up their new home in a manner she thought would please Tom.

For the next several months Sally kept the home fires burning and still maintained her job at the accounting firm. They spent some evenings together, but Tom's work schedule remained hectic and sometimes even took him out of town. He suggested that since he was "her provider" now, she really didn't need to work anymore. In addition, hadn't they agreed to start having children right away, since their biological clocks were ticking? After enough discussions on the subject, Sally agreed to become a full-time homemaker and sadly said goodbye to her co-workers.

Occasionally there were times when Tom reminded Sally that she shouldn't "need" her friends or relatives so much anymore, now that she had him "taking care of her." In fact, he frequently seemed hurt if she was on the phone with her mother or a girlfriend when he arrived home. If she didn't end the conversation right away he had a tendency to get angry with her and they would spend much of the night with an uncertain distance between them. As a result, she made a conscious effort to limit her outside family and friend time. Since she rarely knew which nights he would be home on time and which would be late, it became harder and harder to set up outings with others and, over time, many of her outside relationships began to disappear.

And so, Sally spent hours making meals, decorating their lovely home, hosting parties for Tom's friends from work, and trying to get pregnant. Yet Tom's frequent traveling and late nights at work seemed to leave him little energy for lovemaking. He would come home late, eat the dinner she had made, watch a little TV, and fall in a heap in bed. When they did make love, it had become quite clear that he was pretty insistent that he take the top position at all times. She had hoped there would come a time when he would ask her what she liked, but when she gently tried to show him her likes, he either didn't seem interested or told her he was too tired to take care of her too. Lovemaking seemed to slowly diminish and Sally started blaming herself for being too demanding in the bedroom. As a result, and thinking that Tom might like it, she made a trip to Victoria's Secret to buy some enticing bedroom outfits, but when Tom didn't even seem to notice, she started to believe that he no longer found her attractive.

With so much free time on her hands, she started to go to the gym to get her body in the best shape possible. She lost weight, toned up, got strong, and was the envy of most women in her circle. She was driven to look good for Tom – for how were they ever going to have children if they didn't make love? At 34, she knew her time was growing short.

Despite her efforts, Tom seemed to have less and less libido. One day out of sheer desperation, Sally asked him if he'd ever considered Viagra. The result of that question left her shocked and astounded. Tom flew into a rage the likes of which she had never seen in anyone before. He began to call her names, curse at her, and blame her for all their sexual incompatibilities. He grabbed the Victoria Secret clothing and ripped it to shreds. He called her a whore and a slut and told her that she was revolting and fat at 118 pounds, that she looked like a dyke, and that she didn't have a clue what a man wanted in lovemaking.

She was mortified.

He finally slammed the door and left the house. As he drove away in the dark, Sally looked around at her torn clothing and wondered what on earth had just happened. Tears rolled down her cheeks as she relived the horror, constantly questioning herself about exactly what she had done to ignite the situation in the first place. Of course – she had asked him about Viagra. As she thought about it, she decided that the fight had been her fault. It must be. Obviously Tom was sensitive about the issue and she had walked right over his feelings. Of course anyone would react that way. She felt terrible about her behavior and hoped that Tom would come back soon. She would do her best to make it up to him and she promised herself that she would never mention Viagra again.

Tom didn't return for a week and Sally was beside herself with worry. When she called his office, his secretary said that he was at work, and so she knew he was OK, but she was terribly sad that he wouldn't even call her and she wondered where he was staying. More than anything, she hoped that she hadn't strained their relationship enough that he would leave her permanently.

She dreamed of their first months together when life had been so perfect. Tom had always listened to her, asked her questions about her interests and ideas, was so polite, and wanted to spend hours together. Now he barely asked her about her day. Looking at the empty house, she suddenly realized that she was spending more time alone than when she was single. She kept wracking her brain about what to do to get him back. She would just have to try harder.

When Tom finally returned he acted cold and distant, barely speaking to her as he came in late and went straight to bed. In the morning she got up early and fixed him a big breakfast, hoping to get a few minutes with him before he had to head out the door. As she poured his coffee and served up his eggs the way he liked them, he barely spoke to her except to offer a curt "Thank you" or "No thank you." That was it.

She tried to apologize for starting the fight, but he shut her down with a short, "I don't have time to talk about it now." The only other comment he made was as he was walking out the door ..."By the way, 'Sweetheart,' (he said sarcastically) everyone knows that you're not supposed to make eggs that way – you're supposed to cook them in butter like my mother does. What's wrong with you, anyway?"

Sally was left in total confusion. She had been making his eggs that way for weeks. He had always told her specifically how he liked them and she had changed her original style of cooking eggs in butter to using olive oil at his suggestion. She kept going over and over this new information in her mind, trying to figure out how she could have gotten it so wrong. She distinctly remembered him telling her at the beginning of their marriage that he did not like the taste of butter on his eggs. So when had he changed his mind? And why did he wait until now? And why did he have to tell her this way?

For three days his conversation and behavior remained the same. Stilted. Cold. One- and two-word sentences. He didn't initiate any conversation. She felt as if she was being punished with his silence and it felt deafening.

When at last he spoke, he informed her that it was not a woman's place to ask a man about his sexual performance and that he would never tolerate it again. As she stared at the floor, avoiding his steely gaze, she just kept wondering what had happened to their previously perfect relationship. Everything seemed to have gone from perfect to perfectly wrong in a matter of a few weeks. She knew this wasn't how things were supposed to be, but she didn't know what to do about it.

The next day Tom pulled in the driveway with a new car. Sally was completely surprised. While Tom made a good salary, she really hadn't considered that they needed a new car and as he proudly showed her the fiery red Corvette he had bought for "them," she hesitatingly asked him when he had decided to make such a purchase. The accountant side of her personality was doing quick mental math regarding their monthly expenditures and she couldn't figure out where he had gotten the money. Tom brushed aside her worries and insisted that she go for a test drive with him and so with the top down and the sun shining, they drove for a couple of hours, with Tom lavishing her with laughter and his big smile. He was obviously happier than she had seen him in a long time. In her heart, she had hope that things were getting back on track, while at the same time she had that little nagging feeling in the pit of her stomach that something just wasn't right.

A few days later, when that feeling still hadn't gone away, Sally called their bank. To her amazement, tens of thousand of dollars that had been in their joint account was no longer there. She started to feel nauseous. What had Tom done with the money? Had he paid cash for the car or had he squandered it on something else? She had no idea, but suddenly she was feeling like she was in quicksand. If she dared say something to him and he flew into a rage again, things could become as horrible as the last time. Yet if she said nothing and the situation continued, it wouldn't take long before all their savings disappeared. She held her breath and asked Tom about the money when he got home.

His fury erupted instantly and he slapped her across the face. She crashed to the floor in utter amazement, her face burning with the pain. He began throwing things, yelling, and calling her vile names she'd never heard before. As she started to cry, he began to berate her further, telling her she was worthless. That she had no business sticking her nose into "his" financial business. That she was a useless, stupid, fat pig and that no one would ever want her for a wife besides him, so she'd just better get used to it. Then he picked her up by the neck and threw her out on the lawn and proceeded to lock the doors.

Lost, alone, dazed, in pain, and totally confused how she got there, she went to the neighbor's house to use the phone. She hoped like mad that her parents were home.

It wasn't long after that she returned to Tom and once again mended fences. She was sure that if she just worked harder, tried harder, that she could get things right again. She believed in her marriage vows and found the idea of divorce appalling. Over the next few months there were brief times when things would go well, like the afternoon they drove the new car all over town. Yet, Tom's growing pattern of hostility seemed to get stronger. His mood swings went from outrageously manic on days when things had gone wonderfully well, to total silence and withdrawal on days they had not. Some days he got irritated by the smallest thing – like when Sally's mom would stop over to bring them a dessert she'd made or if Sally wanted to go to a movie with her girlfriends. Tom didn't like sharing his "Sally time" with anyone. The end result was that she only isolated herself further.

There were other outbursts of anger, each one leaving Sally more confused than the first. One day he was furious that she hadn't remembered to pick up beer when she went grocery shopping. Since she didn't drink beer, she relied on him to tell her when he was getting low. Tom didn't feel it should be his place to do so – she should "just know" he was low.

Another incident that blew up over seemingly nothing was when he saw a cobweb on the top of the curtains. He flew into a rage that she didn't keep the house neat enough. When he noticed she'd taken it down a few days later, he questioned her as to *how* she took it down. When she explained that she'd taken it down with a piece of paper towel, he closed his eyes in disbelief and let out a huge sigh in disgust. While a pregnant pause filled the air, Sally wondered what could possibly be wrong, as Tom whispered in contempt, "You *can't* do it that way. Don't you know anything? You have to vacuum these things down or they just come back! How stupid are you?"

> *To make things worse, for the longest time*
> *her friends didn't believe her*
> *when Sally described the abuse.*

She certainly had no scars to show them. The Tom they knew – charming, friendly, and charismatic – was who they still saw. Just like always, he remained friendly to them. He continued to make everyone laugh. And then told them confidentially that Sally was close to having a nervous breakdown from spending so much time alone and discovering that she couldn't have children. They nodded their heads sadly, understanding how difficult it must be for him not to be able to help her. And not to have her be understanding with him for all the overtime he was working to provide them a good home.

Sally was left in a total state of confusion when even her friends didn't believe her. They seemed to be in Tom's corner and she couldn't understand why. At last, hoping to find someone who she could talk to, someone that she could trust, someone who might help her understand her feelings, she went to see a therapist (which, of course, Tom only used to validate her confused mental state to others). She tearfully described Tom's behaviors to the therapist and how so many things had seemed to change over time. She explained her feelings of confusion, sadness, guilt, depression and utter despair and at the same time described her love for her husband and her desire to make the marriage work.

While the therapist was sincerely concerned with Sally's health and emotional status, he got off the subject of Tom fairly quickly and assured Sally that she had to face her fears from some childhood trauma in order to help her surmount these issues which she had apparently "blown out of proportion" in her mind. He realized the stress she was under after leaving her job of the last 10 years and also knew her sadness at not having a child yet. He prescribed drugs for depression. And so Sally began a course of medications that would last for years and only confirmed for her that the problems were her own doing.

Over time, the Sally that everyone knew and liked when she was an accountant had slowly disappeared. She pulled into herself. She became jumpy, nervous, anxious, and fearful of everything and everyone. Her eyes looked empty. She had a hard time sleeping. And her physical health slowly eroded.

She longed for the wonderful, beautiful days when she and Tom first met. She prayed each day that he would change and the "old Tom" would come back to her. She was convinced that if she would only try harder to make him happy, that she could succeed … that they could be happy again.

The final straw came after three years of this roller coaster behavior. Thin, pale, withdrawn, depressed, and numb, Sally's friends barely recognized her. The long and the short of this journey is that Sally left Tom eventually, but not before he took almost every dime she had. But that wasn't the worst. Her self-esteem in ruins, her belief in her own abilities in shambles, her convictions that she was a valuable member of society with something to contribute totally dismissed – she was left a mere shell of herself.

After the divorce she found out that Tom had been sleeping with many other women during their marriage. This knowledge left her stunned, as the Tom she knew hadn't had much interest in sex, despite all her efforts to stay fit or dress seductively for him. It certainly explained why he didn't have anything left for her.

Despite this new information, she didn't care. She still loved him. She couldn't live without him. She just wanted her "perfect partner" back again. And try as she might, she simply couldn't understand what had gone so "perfectly wrong."

The Usual Story

Not all relationships with narcissists are this extreme. Some are much more subtle and are difficult to pinpoint, as the abuse is a series of ongoing little "digs" that erode the victim's self-esteem away in microscopic pieces over a course of years. "Death by a thousand cuts," so to speak. However, some relationships are much worse. They may involve years of beatings, sexual abuse, and in extreme cases, even death. Sally's story is a very typical dance played by those in the confusing maze of the narcissist. Life seems to start out perfect for those who eventually become victims. The charm. The charisma. The looks. Or, in the case of the cerebral narcissists, the incredible intellect. All are absolutely, perfectly wonderful. The unknowing victim gets swept off her feet. All the subtle signs and little gut feelings that something just isn't exactly right simply get swept under the rug, as these victims share ...

"My downfall started when I thought, 'How can anyone be so mean?' It must be me misinterpreting things. It snowballed from there."

"The first night I spent with him I was terrified. I knew something was wrong. Yet I stayed anyway."

The narcissist is like a chameleon – he changes colors with his environment, with his needs, when it suits him in hunting and surviving. Especially when he is looking for his next target.

The important thing is recognition. Once you understand that there is no such thing as a "perfect partner" to begin with, you're on the right track. We all have faults. We all have bad days. But we all also have those little gut feelings that tell us when things aren't quite right.

Learn to listen to your gut. And remember to take care of yourself. When someone doesn't respect you or your desires, fears, and needs, then you're probably not in the right relationship.

When he suggests marriage when you've barely known each other long, ask yourself why? Is he suggesting that you give up your job so he can "take care of you"? Does he want to know about your finances? Does he seem to want to be in control of everything?

Take lots and lots of time to get to know people you get into relationships with. It takes time to see if you like each other (despite your "quirks"), and to see if your commonalities outweigh your dissimilarities. Remember to set your behavioral expectations of your partner and stick with them. If you really don't like smoking or drinking, don't abandon that position just because some cute man makes you feel special. It is not likely that he will abandon that behavior for you once your relationship evolves. If you're not into drugs, closing your eyes to the fact that your boyfriend does drugs is not a healthy place to start a relationship. He's not likely to change either and the issues that you will face when one of you likes to get high and the other doesn't will be significant. If you are shy and quiet in the sexual department and prefer someone who is gentle and kind, do not give up your requirements for a different type of partner who is aggressive and demanding, just because he or she is the only person who pays you the attention you crave. These issues will become overwhelming over time and can lead to significant pain and suffering.

Above all, do not think that you are a lesser player in any relationship. While you do not have to dominate your mate either, a balance between you is ideal and *is* attainable in healthy relationships. Once you feel that you are subservient or less-than, things can only snowball in a bad way. Remember, there are many, many people out there. There is bound to be someone for you if you are patient, open, and yet particular about what you need.

Most of all, if you got caught in the maze of a narcissist and are still held captive or are striving to recover, it is incredibly important to strongly remind yourself that you are in love with what you *thought* was a perfect partner. It was really just an illusion. It was a mask that he was wearing. This is not the person you thought you knew and life can never go back to those perfect times. The sad truth is that they were never real to begin with.

You were in love with a lie.

> *"I was just an image on his arm –*
> *the perfect wife, mother, and socialite.*
> *It was a must that I was visible at all social events, although*
> *he rarely spent one second with me once we got there."*
> *Alexandra – survivor*

Chapter 6
Why Me?

Sally and so many other people like her have asked themselves a million times:

- ❑ "Why me?"
- ❑ "What did I do to deserve this?"
- ❑ "Why did he treat me this way?"
- ❑ "Why do I feel so guilty all the time?"
- ❑ "Why did he change?"
- ❑ "What did I do wrong?"
- ❑ "Why did he choose me to begin with?"
- ❑ "Why do I feel like this?"
- ❑ "Will I always feel this way?"
- ❑ "Why do I want him back when he treats me this way?"
- ❑ "Why do I still love him?"

Although many victims will have friends and family members who do not see the pain and suffering they endure (mostly due to the chameleon-like talents of the narcissist), others clearly see the truth. These supporters are often confused about their friend's behaviors and feelings. As a result, they frequently ask themselves...

- ❑ "Why don't they just leave their situation?"
- ❑ "Why do they keep taking that abuse?"
- ❑ "Why can't they see this isn't normal?"
- ❑ "Why don't they think they deserve better?"
- ❑ "Why can't they see the danger?"
- ❑ "Why do they think this is love?"

There are no pat answers to any of these questions. Each individual brings a lot of baggage to any relationship. While the narcissist is a specimen of a dysfunctional childhood, his victims have their own pasts that have led them to be who they are and to respond the way they do.

I hesitate to even use the term "dysfunctional family" as something unusual, because I don't think there are perfectly normal families to begin with. We all have things in our past that make us vulnerable. While not all families are abusive, neglectful, or underprivileged, I think that the stress we all deal with everyday can take its toll on members of every family and lead to the development of various coping behaviors and underlying beliefs about ourselves – despite the fact that many are actually inaccurate.

For example, being a child of a military family may mean that you move every couple of years. Having to establish new friendships and school relationships may lead some children to feel insecure or unhappy. A family where divorce or death of a parent occurred may produce a child with abandonment issues. A family with seven children may put undue pressure on the oldest children to end up being a "parent" for the younger children at a very early age – thus developing caretaker beliefs and roles early. A child with parents who are perfectionistic may become perfectionistic as well, as he fears he will not be loved if he is not. Certainly children who are abused, whether physically, sexually, or emotionally, may struggle with huge issues related to self-worth.

When people have healthy self-esteem they are better able to take care of themselves in a variety of situations. They have strong boundaries and do not compromise them easily. They do not require praise and recognition from others to determine their value.

They listen to their own instincts and recognize when things don't feel right. They are more able to objectively look at their own situations without getting blinded and engulfed by their feelings. They also know that they need to take care of themselves and not compromise their beliefs or values for someone else. And they know what healthy compromise with others looks like.

In Sally's case, many pieces of the puzzle may have led her down her path with a narcissist. Let's look at some specifics in her story that should help us understand her particular behaviors and choices.

Sally's Issues

In studying Sally's case, we don't have her childhood to examine, but we can learn much about her upbringing from some of her behaviors and beliefs. First of all, Sally was not like the aggressive, independent women who threw themselves at Tom at the barbeque. He accurately assessed her as one of the less powerful, more unsure-of-herself gals that readily fell victim to his charms. Sally didn't see herself as attractive to the average man and Tom could readily sense this, and as such, saw her as a likely target. She may have seemed a bit uncomfortable with the party environment, as she was really more of a behind the scenes person. When he told her that he was tired of "pushy, independent women" and that her "quiet shyness, combined with her raw beauty, intrigued him," she was pleased and flattered. Odds are, her self-esteem, as least as it pertained to her physical self and the dating world, was not one of her strengths. Tom kept stroking her needs by being chivalrous and polite: walking her to her car, opening the door for her, and then asking her for permission to call her sometime.

He had started to build her trust.

As Tom kept up his role of the perfect partner, Sally kept believing in this wonderful man she had found. He was careful to suggest they meet at a neutral place on their first date so that she'd feel safe. As she had been with more aggressive men before, this was a welcome behavior and led her to believe that Tom was only concerned for her comfort. She saw compassion and empathy in him, even though it was only his great acting ability on display.

Next, Tom worked his way into the world of Sally's friends and colleagues. He won them over with his cookies, gifts, and charm so that they too thought Sally was a very lucky girl. They saw her as getting a great father figure in addition to a boyfriend. (An intimate relationship should never be parental, so even her friends did her no favor here!) He left no stone unturned in setting up the environment he needed to lure Sally into his web of deceit, control, and manipulation.

Once he had her in the palm of his hand, he was able to slowly win her over to his way of thinking. The marriage proposal, although too early for Sally's comfort, didn't seem out of line as she had built such trust in him by that time that the feelings of uncertainty she had were swept under the rug. She may also have thought to herself, "What if I say no? What if he leaves me because of that? Where will I ever find someone so perfect again?" Her common sense and intuition were thus ignored. If she'd had stronger self-esteem in place, she might have looked at this situation with logic and listened to her own beliefs of what more healthy behavior is in dating, love, and marriage.

One of Sally's big mistakes from the beginning was not clearly establishing her boundaries with Tom. From lovemaking, where he insisted on a position that left her uncomfortable, to pushing for a marriage commitment before she was ready, Sally simply allowed Tom's needs to be more important than her own. She didn't feel that she was an equal, yet she was also unable to recognize this view as emotionally unhealthy. Unfortunately, she didn't realize that by not expressing her own needs early in the relationship, she would never learn how her partner's responses to compromise would be – responses that would prove crucial to their ongoing health as a couple.

In addition, Sally had a vague hope that eventually Tom would ask her what she wanted and needed. This type of thinking – "he'll change eventually" – is deadly! Liking someone for his *potential* and not for who he is can only lead to unhappy surprises! While some people can and do change their behaviors, most of us simply stay as we are. Ask anyone who has ever wanted to quit smoking or lose weight. Unless there is a major crisis or life-changing moment, it's easier for people to remain the same than it is to change ... and it's even more difficult if change is desired by someone else and not themselves. It is even harder to get someone to change if they do not recognize they have a problem to begin with. Tom saw no need to change anything he did because Sally never gave him reason to. As a narcissist, in his mind his view was always the right one. She kept hoping that Tom would read her mind and figure out what she wanted. Unfortunately, it just doesn't work that way.

Once the marriage took place and things began to change dramatically (even before the first blowup), Sally continued to let her boundaries erode, right along with ignoring those gut feelings that something just wasn't right. At first she merged her finances with his without any plan or conversation as to how they would handle money. She just gave him carte blanche to an open door. Next, when he pressured her to quit her job, she didn't stand up for herself — for what was important to her. She quit taking care of herself and meeting her own needs for growth and career, once again letting Tom's beliefs and needs take precedent over her own. Then when Tom fumed at her for needing to talk with friends or family on the phone, she gave up her ability to have needs outside of him. She didn't recognize throughout all these issues that what Tom was really doing was controlling more and more areas of her life.

Then, of course, he began to withhold sex from her. While it appeared to Sally that Tom was just overworked or overtired (which certainly occurs for many of us in this fast-paced culture we live in), Tom had simply found another way to manipulate Sally and keep her confused and off-base.

Sex can be either what I call a "Bed of Understanding" or a "Position of Power." When it's a Bed of Understanding a couple can share their bodies, their love, their fears, and their joys, while acquiring a deeper acceptance of each other. The intimacy of sex can provide a closeness and opportunity unavailable in any other dimension. However, when it's a Position of Power, the goal is to control, hurt, deny, or dominate through withholding, anger, abuse, intimidation, and/or humiliation. As it turned out later, we find out that Tom, in fact, was having affairs with other women at the same time that he was not allowing Sally to get her needs met.

When at last, the *real* Tom surfaced, Sally was so uncertain of the world around her that she didn't know what had hit her. By this time, her self-esteem had been chipped away to nothing. Her job, once a source of satisfaction, friendship, and value, was no longer available as a supportive environment. Her money had dramatically disappeared. Her friends had gradually backed away as she was brainwashed into believing she only needed him. His constant criticism and belittling had further eroded her beliefs in herself as worthy, loveable, and someone who anyone else could possibly want.

Then there was the issue of trust. She had trusted him implicitly and she had trusted her friends when they told her how great he was. She had trusted herself to do the best job of taking care of him by putting his needs first. She had also trusted that time would improve things.

And, most disturbing, she had trusted a well-meaning therapist to help her deal with the horrific issues that were strangling her. Unfortunately, the particular professional she chose to visit did not have detailed enough knowledge to adequately diagnose the situation as one engulfed with Narcissistic Personality Disorder.

Despite ongoing education regarding NPD,
it is still poorly understood by many professionals.
In addition, the narcissists themselves are such great actors
that they oftentimes fool therapists completely,
thus only damaging and discounting the victim even further.

In the end, Sally was a mess. And yet, with Tom's brainwashing she still thought that she loved him and needed him, and no one else would ever love her again. She longed for the once perfect relationship that had now become something unrecognizable. And unfortunately she got stuck in the Victim Boxx, mourning the past, desperately wishing for things to go back to the way they were, and all the while unable to see a future of happiness for herself.

If only she knew that she is very much not alone.

No Visible Scars

There are hundreds of thousands of Sallys — all victims of narcissists. Many are obvious. We see the bruises. We know the stories of abuse. We hear of murder in the news. One in three murdered women is killed by her spouse, current or former. (In the year 2000 alone, 1,247 women and 440 men were murdered by their one-time intimate partners.)[4] Yet this is only the tip of the iceberg.

There are so many stealth narcissists out there that no one sees or recognizes. They are not nearly as blatant as their more obvious counterparts. Some are so subtle in their behavior that an observer would literally have to live in the house with them for weeks to truly be able to detect the barely perceptible, but ongoing pattern of destruction that occurs behind closed doors.

In my opinion, the stealth narcissists are the worst because they are so careful in their emotional abuse that the victim may never begin to understand what's happening to her until it is too late.

With them, there is no physical abuse. Possibly no sexual abuse either. Yet the undermining is constantly there all the same. Little nagging comments about how the food's not hot enough, the house could be a little cleaner, the lawn mowed a little more often.

Or he might like to tell her how "everyone does it this way, dear — don't you know that?" — implying that she's too stupid to do something the way normal people do. Or maybe he just ignores her for days, giving her the silent treatment as a punishment for some perceived injustice towards him, which she probably doesn't even know she did. Unless of course he wants sex, and then she's expected to demonstrate her love for him, despite the lack of affection he gives her on a daily basis. When she doesn't desire him in the way he expects, she's chastised for that as well. And for each new attempt the victim makes to work harder to make her partner happy, there's always something that could "just be a little better." She's constantly chastising herself for just not being good enough – ever. She is on a never-ending attempt to make him happy, yet he will never be happy with himself – no matter what she does.

So, hour after hour, day after day, week after week, this continues, with the tension in the air so thick you can cut it with a knife. Everyone walks on eggshells around the narcissist to avoid rocking the boat. Yet what they don't realize is that no matter what they do, the boat is already rocking, and has been rocking for some time.

As you can clearly see there are no bruises. No broken bones. No screaming or hollering fights. Certainly no breaking of the law. It's all so insidious. All so taxing. All so blaming.

And all the while the victim doesn't recognize or understand that this is not normal.

And she absolutely doesn't understand or believe that this is indeed abuse.

Additionally, it's certainly not healthy for her or her children to live in this toxic environment, which no one understands and everyone keeps pretending is just fine. And worse yet, where the neighbors and relatives think all is absolutely wonderful, when in fact it's horribly destructive to all those within.

There is a name for this phenomenon. It is called Ambient Abuse.[5] Its goal is to leave the victim living in an atmosphere of fear. Fear of violence, of the unknown, of inconsistency. Fear of simply not knowing when the other shoe will fall or about what. Fear of unpredictability. Fear of ongoing criticism. Fear of rejection. Fear of abandonment after the abuser has done an excellent job of convincing the victim that she cannot live without him. That he is her caretaker. That she is truly incapable of existing without his knowledge, his skill, his talents, and/or his financial means. And that she's so unlovable that no one else would ever take her in, much less love her.

This behavior is very difficult to identify or quantify. It is a game of mental manipulation that leaves the victim questioning reality as well as her abilities. So what's the end result? Eventually the victim's self-esteem is literally worn away to nothing. She begins to appear to be the sick one ... the one who obviously needs therapy. How could anyone else want her then? And so she becomes caught in the web of her narcissistic mate, and without help, will rarely escape the emotional torture chamber she's trapped in ... unless, of course, he pulls the plug without warning when he's found a partner he wants more, as Connie experienced:

"The first I heard that my husband wanted a divorce was when I came home and found that our apartment had a 'for rent' sign on it. When I asked the landlady what was up, I found out my husband told her we were getting divorced and would be moving! I was in total shock."

Boundaries? What Boundaries?

Part of what defines us is our boundaries, yet many of us somehow missed the important lessons on how to set healthy boundaries for safety and love. I doubt most of us even heard the word in our early dating years, much less understood the meaning. Many are still in the dark even today. Psychiatrists weren't even trained about boundaries until the last couple of decades. And Sally also missed those important lessons. She wasn't exactly sure what her boundaries were and she absolutely didn't know how to protect herself by establishing them in the first place. And this is where so many make their first mistake in getting involved with a narcissist. With that in mind, I want to spend a few moments making sure you completely understand this concept.

Simply put, a boundary is a bit like a fence around someone's property; a line indicating where one thing stops and another thing begins. (Your property. My property.) It also keeps things in or out.

You also might define setting boundaries for yourself as a way to tell the world, "These are some of my beliefs and rules about how I expect you to treat me." Of course, it's also important that you recognize others are saying the same thing to you with their boundaries as well.

Your boundaries define you.
They convey your thoughts and needs about your body as well as your feelings, beliefs, behaviors, needs, and desires.

Your boundaries are more than likely quite different from mine or anyone else's, as they need to be. These are the unique facets of who we are that make us all such different people.

By not smoking, for example, you define your beliefs about smoking and your health. By choosing to date only partners who are athletic, you define yourself as someone passionate about being active and taking special care of your physical body. By choosing an outdoorsy partner, you are saying you embrace nature as a big part of where you spend your time. By living a Christian lifestyle (or other religion), you also take on a variety of beliefs and behaviors that define your faith through your actions. For example, you may not believe in premarital sex.

Telling others about your specific boundaries doesn't mean being aggressive, abusive, or angry. You can do it with a simple statement, a genuine smile and perhaps a touch, depending upon the circumstances. You are not being mean. You simply are defining what is important to you and who you are.

We don't always consciously share our boundaries with others. As a matter of fact, sometimes we don't even recognize that we have a boundary until someone breaks it. Of course, since we don't all run around screaming out our boundaries to others, there will be times when someone steps on them. That's why it's important that we let them know our boundaries upfront. The respectful and understanding person who treads on your boundary (usually quite accidentally) will generally acknowledge his or her infringement and will not need to be reminded again if you point it out in a kind but firm manner.

So let's examine a few general boundaries ...

I DO NOT ALLOW ANYONE TO:

❏ Touch my body unless I give them permission.
 (Including friends and family members.)

❏ Call me names.

❏ Smoke in my house.

❏ Make decisions for my safety or health.

❏ Perform something sexual with me I'm not comfortable with.

❏ Threaten me in any way.

❏ Maintain control of my money.

❏ Tell me how to think or feel.

❏ Force me to have sex with them.

❏ Mistreat my children and pets.

❏ Drive recklessly with me in the car.

These are just a few specific boundaries, but you get the idea. Keep in mind that people who do not respect your needs once you have informed them of your boundaries are those you need to watch a bit more closely. Oftentimes they will continue to ignore your boundaries and keep pushing harder for more than you are willing to give, or they will simply not understand your needs and issues to begin with.

Their message to you: They do not respect you.

And if they don't respect you and your feelings early on in the game, they certainly won't become more understanding over time, as was clearly the case with Tom.

So stand up for your boundaries. Be determined about them. But keep in mind that emotionally healthy people also know that their boundaries can be changeable and flexible throughout their lifetime, as circumstances and relationships change. For example, once you establish deep trust with someone, your boundaries with that individual will likely be much different than they were the day you originally met. Just remember that you are the only one who can decide when they need to be changed, and when it's smarter to change the relationship instead!

No Means No ... Sometimes

Many times victims of narcissists struggle not only with their boundaries but also with their definition of the word "no." Because, quite frankly, their no often means "maybe," and that's the first chink in their armor that lets the narcissist slide in, almost unnoticed, changing the rules and changing the direction of the relationship bit by bit.

Many of my clients are mystified as to how they got into an abusive or otherwise difficult relationship to begin with and I can just about guarantee you that their no never meant no. To more clearly demonstrate this interesting phenomenon, go rent the video *9½ Weeks*, starring Kim Basinger and Mickey Rourke. It's ages old (1986) but you can generally get it at most video stores.

This film depicts Elizabeth, an intelligent but insecure character, fresh out of divorce, who falls for a bad but wealthy guy, John, and the relationship is an emotional roller coaster from the get-go. The problems start at the first date when he takes her to a remote island house and immediately starts changing the sheets on the bed, to which she says, "I'm uncomfortable. Take me home." Other dates follow, which include all kinds of outrageous, demeaning, or otherwise inappropriate demands by John, all because Elizabeth's no never really means no. (Having a *second* date with him if she was uncomfortable with the first date is the first time she didn't really mean no.) One particular scene where Elizabeth's needs and wishes are not respected is when John puts her on a Ferris wheel (she's the only one on it) and has the operator take her to the top and leave her up there. Then John and the operator go off for coffee, leaving the screaming Elizabeth hysterically sobbing for God knows how long. And yet she goes back …

The long and the short of it is at the end of 9½ weeks she looks like she's been dragged through an emotional meat grinder and finally realizes that she's killing herself staying in a relationship where she is neither respected nor valued, much less loved. At least it only took her 9½ weeks to understand that things were absolutely unhealthy and to run, not walk, from the abusive, narcissistic creep.

Your weak "no" also can get you in trouble in your work environment. When a colleague or boss asks you to do something that you really don't want to do (work late when your child is playing in the school band that night) but they bully you into doing it anyway, you have taught them that your boundaries are meaningless here as well. And guess what? Doing it once simply teaches them that you're someone that they can probably win over by bullying again.

> *By not sticking up for your no meaning no the first time out, you set yourself up for more irritating behaviors down the road.*

What does your no mean? To your kids? Your partner? Your boss? And most importantly, to you? *It is consistency that counts,* because of course, it was the *original inconsistency* that got those around you to believe it didn't mean no to begin with.

We Teach Them How to Treat Us

I get so many letters from those who have found themselves victims of narcissists and one of the most common questions is, "Why does he (or she) treat me this way?" And the simple answer is – "Because you have taught him to."

Of course I don't tell people that right off the bat, for two reasons: 1.) they don't want to hear it, and 2.) they wouldn't believe it right away anyway.

> *Of course, if I did try to explain it right away*
> *I would probably hear something like,*
> *"I never taught him to hit me," or*
> *"I never taught her to call me names."*

But they would be so wrong. In actuality, we teach the narcissists in our lives exactly those things, but they are not obvious to us at the time. Here's how it starts ... the slow, unconscious teaching of someone exactly how to treat us badly ...

Let's look at Susan, age 35, with her long-term boyfriend Jim. She wonders why he regularly calls her names like "bitch, slut, and stupid," doesn't speak to her for days on end when he is mad, tells her that no one else could possibly love her because she's so incapable of taking care of herself, and reminds her how selfish she is whenever she wants to spend time with her parents. (Obviously time taken away from him!) He tells her what time she must be home, when and how to make love, and exactly how she must keep their house. She has no idea what their finances are and he doesn't even allow her access to the family checkbook. He gives her checks with only a certain amount of money to use when she goes to get groceries.

The look on her face is distant, distrustful, exhausted, and frightened. She tells me that she loves Jim but doesn't understand why he yells at her continuously, calls her names, and does all the other things described above. (Funny, this doesn't look like love!)

When I ask her if he has physically abused her she protests, "No, Jim would never hit me. He may have shoved me a couple of times, but he would never hit me."

So here's my guess as to how Susan has taught Jim to treat her this way ...

The first time Jim told her she was stupid, Susan probably bit her tongue and didn't establish her boundaries, didn't stand her ground and let him know in no uncertain terms that not only was she not stupid, but if he was interested in continuing their relationship, he would be wise to never call her that again.

There are many women like Susan (and their male codependent counterparts) who are so shocked the first time their partner calls them names, they don't even know how to respond. Or they may look at the situation and blame the bad behavior on their partner having a bad day, a little too much to drink, or some other stress in his life. In other words – they make excuses for him.

Then, instead of looking at Jim and analyzing *his* behavior, they look inward instead, asking themselves, "Might he be right? Might I be stupid? Was my behavior something I should rethink?"

Another possibility is that some victims like Susan were raised in abusive homes, so being called stupid and any other variety of not-so-nice names seems normal, since everyone in the family of origin called each other names all the time. While Susan may not have liked name-calling growing up anymore than she likes Jim calling her names now, she doesn't understand that in healthy families, this kind of behavior is not the norm.

The next step in Susan's educating Jim how to treat her badly occurs the first time Jim comes home angry or drunk, and Susan suddenly finds herself fearful of his temper (whether there is the threat of physical violence or simply emotional outbursts). Susan decides the best plan of action is to lay low. She thinks that by not "rocking the boat" Jim will calm down and the issue will blow over. She doesn't want to make a bad situation worse, so she doesn't stand up for herself. In some of these situations, Jim might even apologize to Susan for his behavior the next day, and Susan will breathe a huge sigh of relief, certain that the bad behavior won't happen again. After all, Jim promised her, didn't he?

By even after the second time Jim has demonstrated these behaviors without Susan standing strong within her boundaries, she has taught him that behaving badly is OK with her. It will not endanger their relationship. In fact, she is giving him permission to do as he pleases, as she continues to hope, pray, and not rock the boat in case things might get worse.

And guess what? Things usually do get worse. Once Jim realizes that calling her stupid and coming home angry is acceptable, his next step may be to add something new to the pile … like adding threats to his earlier behavior. "I'm taking over the checkbook from now on and don't you even think about asking me for it. I run this house and it's high time you learned that!"

As Susan's fear and confusion mount, she feels more and more isolated as well. Of course, if there are kids in the picture, she's got even more responsibility on her mind. She must do whatever she can to protect her little ones.

She may also pick up behaviors she never had before, things like becoming quiet and shy, and withdrawing from friends and family. Moreover, she is now spending every waking moment planning to do whatever she can think of to "keep Jim happy."

At some point Susan may realize that Jim's behavior is inappropriate, but by then she may feel she is in over her head. The first time he shoves her, she denies that this is physical abuse, since he didn't actually hit her. She may even draw the new boundary in her head: "The first time he lays a hand on me or one of the kids,

I'm outta here!" But unfortunately, as with the lesser boundaries, she probably won't stand strong with this boundary either, and the physical abuse may not be long in coming.

Do you start to see how we teach them how to treat us? It's painfully slow, hard to see, and we oftentimes miss it because we try to be compassionate, understanding, empathetic, and loving. We forgive easily … at least the first few times. And yet, after a while, we lose trust. And once trust is lost, there is no healthy relationship left, no matter how much we hope and pray it will return.

So how could Susan have set a new course? How could she have taught Jim differently about her boundaries from the beginning?

Well, the first time he called her stupid she could have said, "Jim, I really like you, but you have to understand something if we're going to be in a relationship. I am not stupid, nor are you allowed to call me that. I'm going home. Thanks for the dinner."

Period. No ifs, ands, or buts.

If Jim is smart and really wants to continue with the relationship, he will call Susan ASAP and say nothing short of, "Susan, I apologize. You're right. You're not stupid and I had no right to call you that. It will never happen again." Note – there should be no excuses attached like what a bad day he had, etc.)

Susan can then decide if she wants to give Jim one more try or not. So let's say she does. And let's say that he is now smart enough to never use the word stupid around Susan again, *but* he's smart enough to try another tack. Now he starts picking her up 20 to 30 minutes late. The first time he has a good excuse, so she just puts the incident in her memory bank. But the second time he's 30 minutes late, he offers no reason for his tardiness.

At this point, Susan would do well to realize that Jim is a late person. Now if this doesn't bother her, that's fine. And yet, by Jim being consistently late he shows her how her time has no value for him. Once again, he implies that he is more important than she is.

So, again, Susan can either let him know that her time is valuable and, if he's late again, she won't be going out with him, or else she can cut Jim out of her life and move on. He has already shown her in their early dating life that he is neither caring nor respectful of her or her boundaries.

But if she continues to cut him slack over and over, she will only keep giving away bits and pieces of herself in the process. And teach Jim that whatever Jim wants, Jim gets. And Susan will never have a clue about the role she played in aiding and abetting this behavior from the start.

Codependency

Another possible reason that Sally and others like her continue to stay in these turbulent relationships is "codependency." The psychological world has a variety of definitions for codependency but basically it is when someone stays in an unhealthy relationship, despite its horrors, because there is something that they get out of it as well. These victimized partners develop behaviors that not only deny the wrongdoings of their mates but oftentimes actually enable the mate's unhealthy behaviors as well.

Codependents rely upon others in their world for emotional support and validation. They do not believe in themselves and their own worth without others constantly giving them feedback that they are needed, wanted, and valued. Even when the feedback they receive is predominately negative, painful, or even dangerous, the intermittent positive "crumbs" (like *not* being abused today), seem monumental. They live with an overwhelming fear of abandonment and will do anything to maintain their relationships – even if those relationships are abusive, which they frequently are. They spend all their time focusing on everyone else's needs and issues, but the end result is that they suffer tragically themselves and can't figure out why.[6]

This can explain some of the issues behind what holds the targets of narcissism in their Victim Boxxes. They feel that their abuser really "needs and loves them," that these abusers don't really mean to do the terrible things that they do, that they will change with the victim's help – and that all can once again be the perfect picture.

People who fall into the role of codependency can benefit from work with an understanding therapist to help them reestablish their own boundaries and work on building self-esteem. Remember that it's important that a therapist in this situation is especially familiar with the ins-and-outs of narcissism (not all are), or the victim may end up being devalued further.

While malignant narcissism is a definitive personality disorder, codependency, on the other hand, is a learned behavior based upon an unhealthy emotional environment. The blessing is that with professional help, codependency can be unlearned. The first and biggest step to healing is for codependents to learn to say no to the person who is abusing them … and mean it.

To give you an insight into what a person with codependency might feel, this is what Jackie said:

"I like being in the position of looking up to somebody and putting them on a pedestal and serving them and all the things that go with them. I pick people to define me. I guess I play the role of martyr."

Gaslighting

Gaslighting is another reason that many victims have a difficult time extricating themselves from their web of narcissism. This is a psychological term that describes a technique of controlling people by making them doubt their own reality. Victims start to wonder if they are losing their mind and literally going crazy.[7] The term itself was originally coined from the movie *Gaslight* (1944) in which Charles Boyer's character (a narcissistic husband) went to great lengths to convince Ingrid Bergman's character (his rather vulnerable and naive wife) that she was going insane. Through little comments and suggestions that lead her to constantly question herself, he continually suggested she was forgetful, misplaced things, and wasn't "well." After a while, she began to believe she *was* going crazy. While this movie is designed around a criminal intent, the manipulation is priceless to watch nonetheless.

Another example of Gaslighting might be if a narcissist strikes his partner and yet denies doing so by claiming that perhaps she dreamt it or she remembered it wrong (because of course everyone knows he's not that kind of man).

> *The end result is a victim who is now even more confused about her true situation. She begins to question what she remembers as real or imagined.*

He might then begin to suggest to her that she's just depressed, or she's confusing him with someone else, or she's just remembered an event incorrectly due to her own stress or fatigue. In Sally's case, when Tom suddenly chastised her for cooking his eggs wrong, it only led to her doubting herself on one more level. Was she going crazy? Did she remember his instructions wrong? Or had he told her two totally different things?

Eventually, the game does what it's supposed to – it adds one more layer of uncertainty to the already uncertain victim. She's not sure what to tell her friends or therapist now, as she's not really sure herself. She may even believe that she needs her narcissist now more than ever. Of course, at this stage it's very easy to suggest that she may need medications to help her with her "issues" and if this becomes the case, it may only make the situation worse.

The end result: the narcissist has gained yet another layer of control and dependency over his partner. And of course, his Narcissistic Supply – the ongoing feedback that he is as powerful as he thinks he is – is safe for a while longer.

Narcissists are ever so clever at using Gaslighting techniques. Be on-guard for this behavior and keep your friends close to you. You may need them to help you determine truth from fiction. And although the film *Gaslight* is ancient, it is still available from a variety of places, from video stores to public libraries. I highly recommend that you pick up these films immediately to truly get this angle on how one person can very coyly manipulate another without that person even seeing it. It has opened the eyes of so many of my clients. Why one woman even called me to tell me that after watching 20 minutes of *Gaslight* she had to go vomit, as it struck her between the eyes just how the same manipulation had been going on in her own home.

While watching these movies may be a bit painful, I think seeing how this stealth behavior starts and grows is crucial to anyone questioning whether they too are living in an unhealthy relationship. Sometimes it takes a visual media to hit home … when all the words in a thousand books might not ever deliver the same in-your-face punch, so go get these films now!

The Stockholm Syndrome

Another possible reason victims stay with their controlling or abusing partners is known as the Stockholm Syndrome; an interesting phenomenon that was first labeled in 1973 after a bank robbery in Stockholm, Sweden.[8] For over five days the robbers held four bank employees in the vault with dynamite strapped to their bodies. The hostages suffered threats and emotional abuse, in addition to not knowing whether they would live or die. Yet, by the time they were rescued, they were actually protective of their abusers when overtaken by the police. Furthermore, one of the victims became engaged to one of the criminals and another established a fund for their defense.

In a similar situation, Patty Hearst, the heiress daughter of a wealthy newspaperman and upstanding social family, was kidnapped at gunpoint in 1974 and disappeared from sight for weeks. When friends and family had given up on her being alive, they were later surprised and confused to see her in a bank video surveillance film. She had been transformed from kidnapped victim to bank robbing accomplice, after being convincingly "brainwashed" to participate in her captor's cause. As a result, she was sentenced to seven years in prison for her actions after the gang was successfully captured.

So why did both of these situations occur? Actually, many psychologists believe it may be an unconscious safety position taken on by the victim – a type of survival strategy, so to speak. By learning to bond with the abuser or controller, the victim learns to understand his personality and anticipate his needs. This attachment may limit the abusive episodes, thereby putting the victim in a safer place. The longer the relationship lasts, the stronger these feelings seem to become.

In this phenomenon, four conditions are usually present in the victim's environment: 1) the victim feels that the abuser or controller can hurt her in some way; 2) there are occasional small kindnesses shown to the victim; 3) the victim has often become somewhat isolated from friends or family; and 4) the victim thinks she cannot escape the situation.[9]

While the first two examples mentioned above involve criminal hostage situations, these behaviors also appear to apply to "captives" of all kinds. From physically abusive relationships to subtle, emotionally abusive ones, the same patterns can evolve as the resulting feelings in the victims are those of helplessness and powerlessness. Controllers also like to keep their victims in a state of chaos, never knowing what might come next. They keep them off-guard with their inconsistent, arbitrary, and unpredictable behaviors, leaving some victims regressing into childlike patterns, eventually believing that their controller is a dominating or fearful parent figure.[10]

Unfortunately, victims may also fall into the destructive dance of rationalizing or justifying their partner's behavior. This may mean that by understanding the controlling partner they also justify the abusive behavior. "He only abuses me because he was abused himself – he doesn't mean to hurt me. He just can't help it. That's just the way he is." Or, "He only treats me like that on days when work has him stressed out." This kind of thinking does nothing to break the cycle of abuse and control, and the victim remains a victim even longer.

Remember, you don't have to be bleeding to be a victim. Falling prey to the mental games that hold you hostage can be just as emotionally destructive or more so. Learning to recognize them in your controller as well as identifying your own behaviors in the relationship are the first steps towards a healthier lifestyle.

Intermittent Reinforcement

Psychology calls it Intermittent Reinforcement and it's apparently the strongest form of learning in the universe. What am I talking about? The type of positive treatment or reward that happens just periodically enough that we *believe* if we hang around long enough, it will return with certain regularity.

> *I like to call it,*
> *"Of course I deserve love and respect ...*
> *at least one out of ten times!"*

Let me break it down a little further ...

If you're training a dog to fetch, do you give him a treat absolutely *every* time he brings the stick back? You certainly don't need to. He'll be motivated to fetch even if you reward him every fifth time. Maybe even every eighth time. Maybe, just maybe, after he's conditioned to it, you will only have to treat him with a reward every tenth time because he *knows* that, sooner or later, there's a treat coming. (History has proven it to him.) And he'll keep performing with the hope that he will get one again.

Now I suspect in days when we were hunter/gatherers, this was a response that may have kept many of our ancestors alive. If they saw game at a given spot occasionally, it paid to check out that site for game regularly, as even if they only found a reward once in a while, it may have been the only food they found. It may have meant survival.

However, while this form of conditioning and reward may have been useful in our primitive days or even now in training animals (or even children), it is *not* optimal in building healthy relationships. In fact, it's what keeps many of us in unhealthy relationships, sometimes long after we should have figured out just how unhealthy our partner is and moved on.

For example, Jane has been dating John for a couple of years now, yet he only treats her well periodically. Of course, when they were first dating, he treated her well all the time. He was attentive. Called her regularly. Listened to her when she had something to say. Shared equally in decision-making about where they would eat, what movies to see, or where to go out for the evening.

Of course things evolve and change in any long-term relationship. Jane certainly didn't expect John to bring her flowers every week or take her dancing every night. However, neither did she expect John to change dramatically.

It started out with little things, like not calling her when he said he would. Then he fell into the pattern of making promises that he ended up breaking … things like repeatedly making plans to spend the weekend in the mountains and then having a last minute excuse why he had to cancel.

Then he started becoming quite critical of Jane. If she would only do this or that, he would be happy. (She of course, tried to anticipate his needs so that she could *make* him happy, and yet things still continued in the pattern. Because, of course, she hasn't figured out that we can't *make* anyone happy except ourselves! John has to find happiness within himself and no amount of standing on her head to please him will ever make him happy, no matter how long and hard she tries.)

John even fell into dishing out the silent treatment; basically ignoring her, hiding behind his newspaper for hours on end, and treating her as if she didn't exist, whether at home or even if they were out in public together.

All of these changes in behavior left Jane completely confused when she remembers that wonderful, positive John she first met. Of course, perhaps if we asked Jane to look at her first interactions with John more closely, we might actually see where she allowed the Red Flag behaviors that should have given her plenty of warning signs that she wasn't being treated as an equal in the relationship to begin with.

Things like, just how often did he call her? Just how eager and needy was she to catch John to begin with? What signs did she show him that indicated she would accept less than stellar behavior in the relationship? And what behaviors did he show her, even then, that said, "I don't have to treat you nicely all the time. You've shown me that doing so just some of the time will work just fine!"

Yet whenever she gets fed up, threatens that she will pull out of the relationship, or doesn't call John for a few days, back he comes, all smiles; the perfect gentleman again. He might even resurface after disappearing for days on end … probably with flowers, or an apology, or a dinner invitation. Maybe even with a bottle of wine and a couple of glasses and a big smile on his face.

The "Old John" returns. The one she remembers. The one who treats her with respect and love. And of course, John promises that he will change and never treat her badly again, because he certainly loves her with all his heart!

And of course, Jane stays.

And of course, she's just as surprised when the negative, critical, promise-breaking John returns once again, now that he's won her back.

Why? Because she's fallen victim to that wonderful phenomenon of Intermittent Reinforcement.

But what does that truly say about Jane? That Jane believes (subconsciously) that she only deserves love and respect some of the time.

Remember, Intermittent Reinforcement is one of the most powerful entities in forming patterns of behavior. So, for as long as Jane keeps putting up with it, she also reinforces for John that it's OK to treat her reasonably only periodically.

Until Jane stands up for herself and says,
"I deserve better,"
she will stay in her roller coaster relationship with John,
or else will find other men just like John, because
she hasn't learned that healthy relationships mean that you
deserve to be treated well
most of the time, not merely some of the time!

So to return to the question that started this chapter, "Why Me?" the answer is simple: something in your past, within your beliefs, or how you were raised combined with the concepts of weak or non-existent boundaries, Gaslighting, the Stockholm Syndrome, codependency, or intermittent reinforcement to lead you right into the path of the narcissist. And kept you there as well.

In many cases, the narcissist actually chose *you*. But take heart – that doesn't mean you are destined to be stuck with narcissists your whole life!

Knowledge is power. So keep learning…

Chapter 7
The Sex Game –
When You Are the Pawn

"**E**ven bad sex is better than no sex," my friend Karen confessed to me one day as we were discussing the good, the bad, and the ugly aspects of sex.

I looked at her in amazement. "Not in my opinion," I countered. I had images of a frantic Lorena Bobbitt running through my head. She obviously hadn't believed that even bad sex was better than no sex – and had sliced her husband's penis off to prove it.

While some people may never have experienced such a thing as "bad sex," many of the respondents to my survey had much to say about sex as it pertained to the narcissist in their lives. Could it be that John Wayne Bobbitt was a narcissist and drove his wife to hysteria based on his extreme sexual demands? We can only guess. However, what we do know is that she did not appear to have found sex to be a "Bed of Understanding" and I would guess that it had something to do with a "Position of Power."

A Bed of Understanding – or a Position of Power?

For human beings sex is complex. We don't just have sex for reproduction; we have sex for so much more – for recreation, for pleasure, for feeling loved and secure, for discovering a connection to another person that just cannot be uncovered in any other way. We have intimacy. I don't just mean intimacy, as in the act of sex itself. I mean intimacy the way Dr. Phil McGraw recently described it: "Intimacy means trusting people enough to give them the power to hurt you." And that's where things get complicated.

Sure, there's sex just for sex. There's prostitution, or one-night stands, or any variation thereof, but that is purely the act of sex. There is nothing personal about it – not the intimacy involving trust. But what happens when two people come together sexually within the confines of a relationship? What do they want out of it? What seems to change for some couples between the time they begin dating and as the years slip by? Do they continue to enjoy sex throughout their relationship, or does something occur that changes what was once wonderful into something routine, boring, or even unappealing? What really happened to Lorena Bobbitt?

Sex has been used as a form of power for centuries, evidenced by rape throughout the course of history. Does rape really happen between a married couple or does the marriage license mandate that sex is allowable under all circumstances? And, if it is not physical rape, are there other types of manipulation put upon one or another in a relationship, whereby one feels pressured into submission by the other, perhaps psychologically as opposed to physically? Does it become a game where one person is the pawn and the other the manipulator?

In emotionally healthy relationships (gay or straight), where two people respect each other and share trust and intimacy, sex can be a "Bed of Understanding." Both partners attempt to provide what the other needs and desires, while still maintaining their own boundaries. Both need to feel safe in the other's care. Both should feel comfortable letting their partner know the things they particularly like as well as the things they are uncomfortable with. Each one expresses their care and love throughout the act of lovemaking. Intentional pain (emotional or physical) should *never* be an intended part of a healthy relationship!

However, being involved in a sexual relationship with a narcissistic person complicates normal sexual issues even further. It oftentimes becomes a setup for ongoing confusion, sadness, and pain – emotional and/or physical. Remember, narcissists do not know how to truly love someone. They do not have the ability to share the usual emotions affiliated with lovemaking. They do not understand or participate in true intimacy. For some who never experienced the physical love of touching and hugging that they so desperately craved as small child, sex may feel like a way to meet that unfulfilled need. The pure physical pleasure derived from it may mean "love" to the narcissist. Thus, frequent sexual satisfaction for these individuals is a necessity, albeit purely physical, with no emotional connection whatsoever. For some couples where both partners function this way, this may work well and yet, for others, it may mean excessive demands for frequency, which do not mesh with the other partner's needs.

On the other extreme, some narcissists find lovemaking is only another layer of emptiness. It means nothing. It is purely mechanical. They can do without it for months or more at a time. Or in some cases, they may prefer homosexuality, pedophilia, or unusual sex rituals. If they are homosexual, they may hide this side, as it may not be seen as acceptable in their business world or other peer group. They may need the cover of a heterosexual relationship to present a socially acceptable image to the outer world (in their ongoing search for perfection). They may withhold sex from their confused heterosexual partner at the same time they partake in regular sex with their same-sex partner. Or they may be straight and appear to have a low libido or be completely disinterested in sex with their spouse, while they have ongoing extramarital affairs with others.

Yet, the most insidious part of the sex game is that it can be all about control and manipulation through humiliation, withholding, abusing, overpowering, and/or literally dictating the behaviors of the victim. The submissive partner becomes the pawn – dispensable, disposable, and certainly destructible. The destruction may be slow and subtle, a constant chipping away at self-esteem, emotional health, and physical well being.

If your lovemaking during courtship seems absolutely fine to you – caring, attentive, compassionate, and passionate – the narcissist actor may be putting on his best mask to fool you into believing that everything is absolutely perfect. You may feel like he is the best lover you have ever found, yet once he has you securely in his game, he can feel quite justified in changing the rules, leaving you dazed and wondering what happened.

Narcissists can control the sexual relationships on several levels: First, by withholding or denying sex from their partner for weeks or months at a time. Second, by having abnormally high frequency and/or "performance" expectations. And third, through requiring their partner to perform sexual acts they are uncomfortable with. They may consciously do these things just to humiliate and manipulate their partner, or it may simply be that, as usual, their needs are the only ones they believe need to be addressed, and the need to control may be the biggest one of all. No matter the reason, the game is played and the victim can become one very confused pawn.

There are many facets to this sexual behavior; from turning every phone call into phone sex, to pressuring the partner into accepting painful positions or acts, to demanding breast implants, to requiring multiple sex partners, and more. No matter what the mechanism, the result can mean injury and lifelong scars for the victim – sometimes physical, but always emotional.

Here are some questions to ask yourself about your sexual relationship with your partner.

- ❑ Do I enjoy sex with my partner?
- ❑ Do I feel safe telling my partner everything about how I feel regarding our sexual intimacy?
- ❑ Has the act of lovemaking changed dramatically over our time together?
- ❑ How often do each of us desire to have sex, and are we understanding and able to compromise with each other's needs for frequency?
- ❑ Does my partner understand if I am not in the mood for sex, or does he or she act hurt, frustrated, or angry with me if I am not always a willing partner? Do I get frustrated for these same reasons with my partner?

- Does my partner enjoy giving me pleasure as much as he enjoys receiving it, and do I enjoy giving my partner pleasure as much as I enjoy receiving it?
- Do I feel pressured in any way to "perform" while having sex?
- Do I look forward to having sex, or does it make me feel anxious, threatened, or worried in any way?
- Can my partner and I enjoy physical closeness without it necessarily culminating in sex?
- Does my partner satisfy my overall need for sexual fulfillment?
- Does my partner respect my boundaries and not pressure me to do things that are uncomfortable for me, and do I respect his or her boundaries as well?
- Do either of us "keep score" as to how often we have sex?
- Is there ever anything painful involved, physically or emotionally?
- Am I unhappy with my sexual relationship and, if so, why? What can I do to change it?
- If I can do nothing to make the situation better, am I sacrificing myself in order to make my partner happy?

Alexis

The frequency of any sexual encounters rapidly decreased as soon as we were married. The few times that I attempted any type of intimacy, I was physically and emotionally pushed away. He didn't even want to kiss me on the mouth, but preferred that I give him childlike/motherly kisses on the cheek.

Sex became a fixture that happened once every four to five weeks on average, at his liking. As an expressive person, I tried to communicate with him the feelings and emotions that occurred for me during lovemaking, but he would put his hand over my mouth and tell me to be quiet. My talking was "distracting" to him. He usually closed his eyes and seemed to focus on his own physical sensations without any connection to me. Once the physical interaction was over, he would immediately push me away as he didn't want any further form of physical contact. Then as soon as he had recovered, he would immediately focus on the projects and tasks he needed to complete that day.

The overall physical connection was very poor. I tried to ignite his interest by dressing provocatively when he returned from a business trip, but his eyes usually went straight to the windows that needed to be cleaned, the picture frames that needed to be straightened, or anything else that seemed amiss during his absence. His need to control his environment was overwhelming. He demanded order in everything.

> *He said that he could not be attracted to me sexually without having an impeccably ordered house.*
> *He also let me know that I didn't meet the physical requirements to excite him. He told me that if I got breast implants he might be more interested in me.*

With time I saw that it really didn't matter what I did. He was just not interested in me sexually and withheld sex as a means of control and manipulation. While this was only one part of our dysfunctional relationship, it was a big one.

Claudia

Our sexual relationship seemed to start out fine. I felt attractive to Todd, and as I never felt particularly beautiful to begin with, that was an amazing feeling to me. I only had a couple of boyfriends in high school. They were losers like me, so I was particularly thrilled when Todd was so good-looking. I was convinced that he was probably the only attractive man in the world who would ever find me attractive as well.

We married and things seemed just fine at the beginning. Although he did have a rather unusual habit of measuring his penis every day, I figured it was just his insecurity, as he wasn't overly endowed in the size department. Then, as time went on things began to change. He started making suggestions that we get x-rated movies periodically. I didn't think much of it as I knew a lot of men liked those sorts of things. So, even though it didn't do much for me, I agreed.

Then he started showing an interest in doing some of the things they did in those movies. He wanted me to dress up in exotic lingerie. Again, I complied. For a while, I even felt sexy and excited about it. Then he got into some of the bondage things – nothing horrific initially, so I didn't object. At first, they seemed kind of fun, but as I watched the eerie look in his eyes begin to appear, I started to feel a bit uneasy. Sometimes he'd tie me up and place a gag in my mouth and that seemed to turn him on even more. I never felt in danger but I didn't particularly like it either.

Then he suggested anal sex – another thing he liked watching in the movies. I told him I wasn't comfortable with that, and tried to make my needs known. I was getting a little bit afraid and pain in the bedroom wasn't exactly what I had in mind.

He would pressure me then. Play little mind games with me. Say things like, "You know you want it, honey. Come on. Just try it once. Look how much pleasure they're having. Don't be a baby. Don't you love me? You'll do it for me if you love me. Don't be so selfish."

If I refused, he would act hurt and tell me I didn't love him. Then, I would get served the silent treatment for days. He would ignore me altogether or cut me off from anything other than superficial conversations. At first I didn't make the connection, but after a while the pattern became obvious. He wore me down until I couldn't take it anymore. I finally gave in and found that the pain of rectal sex was shorter-lived than the pain of the silent treatment for days on end.

He became very good at playing the game and I became a very good pawn. It was just easier to comply than to resist.

His strange sexual needs continued with things like urinating on my chest or ejaculating onto my face while pinning me down with his knees on my shoulders. It was humiliating and the look in his eyes at the time was downright frightening. While I never feared that he would physically abuse me with his fists, the emotional abuse was ongoing and exhausting. The humiliation and degradation were constant.

He demanded I perform oral sex on him frequently. He knew it was uncomfortable for me and that when he came in my mouth it made me want to retch. He knew how to play the pressure game well. Of course it was the same result – if I refused or begged off, the silent treatment would follow in due course, and perhaps last days at a time.

One day I will always remember, we were fighting about sex and I was trying to stand up for myself and what I had done for him sexually per his requests when suddenly he screamed at me, "Hell, when it comes to oral sex, you don't even do it anymore!"

I was confused, as only days prior I had performed oral sex on him for an extended time, but had changed the momentum of the direction it was taking and had climbed on top of him before he had a chance to come in my mouth. So my response in the argument was to mention the recent event. He said he didn't consider that oral sex, since I hadn't let him ejaculate in my mouth. Once again, I squeamishly protested that it made me very uncomfortable.

"I've told you how you can make it better," he bellowed. "You can put your panties over my dick to diminish the squirting when it happens! What's wrong with you, anyway? Why are you so selfish"?

That was the straw that broke the camel's back. It became clear to me that everything was about him and that I was just being used. I just couldn't take it anymore. I had to leave before there was nothing left of me. There was really no love in it. Instead, it was all a myth, a very ugly game.

Ally

Alan was anally retentive on every level, including in the bedroom. I started feeling like making love was all about keeping score. He had an extreme need for sex. It was almost like living with a drug addict. If he had his way we would have sex daily or more. If he'd had a hard day at work I could bank on him needing his sexual fix. It didn't matter what my needs were.

I was convinced that he recorded our lovemaking episodes in his calendar, like notches on a gun. At times he knew that I just couldn't handle it on a certain night and so he would let me off by rubbing his penis on my butt and coming that way. Of course those episodes didn't count on the list. They weren't having "real sex."

I don't mean to say that he didn't ever give me pleasure, because quite often he did. However, I wish I knew at age 19 what I know about life, love, and sex now. One of the Red Flags I would have picked up on at that stage in my life occurred during one of our first intimate moments. I was gently trying to show him with my hand, exactly which places his touch made me the most excited. I met with a bit of resistance during my guiding episode and wasn't sure how else to show him what I liked. His hand seemed to intentionally ignore my direction. I guess I must have continued in this manner, hoping that he would understand my tactile suggestions when he responded with a short, "Yes, Ma'am!" as though he was in the military responding to an order. I felt him get tense and angry almost instantly.

At the time, I did whatever I could to sooth his bruised ego, but it occurs to me only now, years later, that the issue was really all about him. In his mind, he was determined to be the one to show me what I needed! I was not to have needs of my own. He must have learned "what women want" from somewhere, and wasn't about to admit that he was amiss in his expert knowledge of *my* sexual needs. Therefore, I must have been the one who was wrong or uninformed! How telling that one incident was, had I been open to understanding its deeper meaning at the time.

Another issue was that he wanted me to "desire" him and be the one to initiate lovemaking more. I found this ironic, as he barely gave me time to breathe with his demands for frequency to begin with. I used to tell him I liked pizza too, but I wouldn't eat it every day or I'd grow tired of it. He didn't like that comment too much. However, there was one time when I felt particularly close to him. We had gone on a tropical vacation and left the kids at home. It was so freeing, knowing that we could have sex at any time of the day without the little ones barging in on us. I found myself desiring him in the worst way and dragged him off to bed three times a day for three days in a row. I thought he'd be thrilled, for that's what he had begged me to do for a long time. And yet, of course that didn't turn out to be good enough either. When I mentioned it to him some time later his response was, "It wasn't *that* great. Personally, I could have used a little more foreplay!"

I couldn't believe it. I doubted that most any man who had a wife begging him for sex nine times in three days, would remain unhappy and unsatisfied. It was absolutely inconceivable to me.

On another occasion, many months after that, we were lying in bed on a Saturday morning. Trying to please him, I began the motions towards lovemaking. As he responded to my touch I was already thinking how happy he would be that I was the initiator, and that hopefully it reflected that I did desire him in the manner he wished. Yet, the moment we finished and rolled apart, I knew something was wrong. He fell into silence and his body language was cold as he lay on his back, arms folded across his chest, his eyes cold and glued to the ceiling. I wracked my brain for something that I could have done to upset him but couldn't think of anything. He had seemed to enjoy our closeness and I hadn't sensed anything unusual, as my brain rehashed each moment of the intimate episode.

At last I couldn't stand the silence and coldness any longer. I took a deep breath and asked as non-threateningly as I could, what was bothering him. After a long pause and without averting his fierce eyes from the ceiling, he said, "The windows in this house are absolutely filthy and you haven't done a thing about it!"

I couldn't believe it! His compulsive need for cleanliness even reigned over our sex life. That's the day that confirmed for me that lovemaking had nothing to do with a sharing of two people's needs. No matter what I did, it still wasn't enough. Nothing was *ever* enough.

I wonder if he misses me. I certainly don't miss performing for him any longer. And sleeping alone for the last few years has been absolutely incredible!

Cammy

Max was a doting husband and wonderful father who always appeared to love to me, or so I thought. We were the perfect, successful couple with the beautiful daughter living the American dream of having our own business and living in the big house with all the nice things. Everything seemed so perfect. I thought I was happy except that we had no real intimacy. Max was never really interested in having sex with me. He seemed to prefer masturbating. It was embarrassing to him and to me when I found him masturbating on many occasions. I thought it odd, but I loved him and denied there was a problem. We never even made love on our wedding night or on our honeymoon. Although I was physically fit and outgoing, he was not sexually attracted to me and I lived in denial, thinking he just had a low libido and that was OK with me. I didn't expect too much. I could live without sex. I thought I had intimacy in just having a loving husband.

Obviously, ours was not a normal sexual relationship. On the rare occasion that we did have sex, he seemed disinterested and lacked passion. After a while I didn't have much for him either, after being turned down so often. There were times I thought he might be gay, but of course I never addressed that with him. He didn't have the typical male energy and sexual drive. He seemed almost intimidated by me at times while in the bedroom. He was certainly never open to trying new things. It was always just one way without exploring each others bodies. I loved him without sex and, in retrospect, I loved him in a very shallow way and he loved me in an even more shallow way. I turned my libido off for him and never expected him to have an affair of all things. (Although I sometimes suspected he was involved in porno stuff on the Internet, but was never able to prove that.)

When he suddenly announced he was leaving me for the woman next door I was shocked. That is what made this all so devastating. I still believed that we had the "perfect" life – albeit not in the bedroom. Then, as if it wasn't bad enough that he was having an affair and was leaving me after 18 years, he began to spread rumors with my friends and family that I was frigid. (How ironic.) After the divorce I had three friends who told me that he had tried to "put the moves" on them over the years. They had always seen him as a "player." I never saw it. I suspect he'd probably had several affairs throughout the course of our marriage. It leaves me totally baffled and confused how he could have the passion and energy for them and not one ounce of it for me.

Eleanor

I thought the first three months of our relationship were great, although by then I had already started to complain about Jack's demanding nature to my friends. I guess I should have listened to myself more. I kept asking him the question, "How do I win your heart?" to which he could give me no reply. Looking back now, I realize that his heart was never in it to begin with.

He had some strange sexual behaviors – like frequently watching pornographic movies, wanting me to play the role of his "sex slave," and make all his fantasies a reality. Sometimes he wanted to have a threesome. Most of the time he wanted me to perform oral sex on him. He started pushing my head down there from the very beginning of the relationship. He never outright admitted that he liked domination and control, but he hinted that a lot.

At times he called me names like sex addict, nymphomaniac, psycho, and crazy. He'd accuse me of hating men. I really started to doubt myself and my sanity and began thinking there must be something really wrong with me. I ended up seeing a therapist and taking Prozac after the devaluation continued for a prolonged time.

For Christmas he told me he would get me my favorite perfume. When I asked him what he wanted, his answer – "Sexual coupons for sexual favors" any time he wanted. That upset me enough to want out. I told him that I was sorry but I couldn't comply, and I ended things immediately. I just couldn't imagine spending my holidays on my knees.

Abbey

He was with me because I am an extremely small woman and he would comment often that I was built "like a little girl." He could never kiss me with his tongue and was statue-like during sex. I would later find out that he was into child porn and is a pedophile. He is in jail for Internet child porn now.

Remember, having bad sex is definitely not better than having no sex, because bad sex can leave you with life-long scars visible to no one but you. It can limit your ability to do your best and live life in a loving and intimate relationship.

It is a choice you make between enjoying a sexual relationship that is:

A Bed of Understanding or a Position of Power.

It's your choice.

> *"Love without trust is dependence masquerading as trust."*
> *Sam Vaknin, narcissist*

Chapter 8
When Abuse Is in Your Past

Some abusers are full-fledged narcissists, other have narcissistic traits. The bottom line is that they continually put their own needs above those of anyone else. Their lack of emotional feelings, empathy, and compassion make it easy for them to watch someone else in pain and not even react. As a matter of fact, some actually seem to derive pleasure through delivering pain to others and watching the results. It may be the only way they think they can feel.

Abuse comes in a variety of forms. As the slogan for the Anti-Violence Program in Colorado reminds us, "You don't have to be bleeding to be a victim." Certainly, according to the law, physical abuse is relatively easy to quantify. Broken bones and bruises speak quite clearly. Sexual abuse, when it involves a minor, has specific criteria. Rape is a capital crime. Yet, the emotional abuse that can occur outside those specific acts and behind closed doors comes in many flavors. It can be so nebulous that members within the same household might not even recognize it as abuse. And even if they did, they may not be in a position to stop it.

Emotional abuse can start out as ongoing, small "digs." Little comments meant to wound, such as, "You're just not smart enough to go to college," or, "You never were as pretty as your sister," and, "The Ayatollah says dinner's ready." These little cuts can eventually evolve into, "You're too stupid to even balance the checkbook," or, "You got a C in calculus again? You sure didn't inherit my brains," or, "Why didn't I have that abortion like I should have, instead of giving birth to you?"

After a while, the recipients of those messages begin to believe them and the negative brainwashing starts to chip away at their self-esteem. Listening to years of these types of comments builds such strong messages that the victims can carry on the conversation all by themselves. They don't even need their abuser to tell them anymore. The little voice in their head does the blaming and name-calling around the clock.

No matter what the format, emotional abuse is meant to be demeaning and degrading. There are other types besides just verbal attacks. For example, one respondent wrote how her very Catholic grandmother gave her enemas every day to cleanse away her "filth." Demanding oral sex of another person who is uncomfortable with it is instilling emotional abuse. Threatening a person with physical violence or harm, even though that violence is never carried out, is emotional abuse. Promising things and never delivering on them is emotional abuse. (Several respondents to the survey mourned over promised marriages that never came true after years of waiting.)

> *From a degrading comment to a demand for extreme sexual favors, the end result can be equally damaging.*

A history of abuse can definitely affect a person's relationships in many ways. One woman reported her husband throwing an entire cooler of ice on her when he was angry with her, and in front of their friends. When they asked her why on earth he did that, she simply replied, "That's just the way he is." If she had never been exposed to abuse of one form or another in her past, she probably would never have tolerated his behavior and certainly wouldn't have just brushed it away as "that's just the way he is."

Living through regular doses of physical or emotional abuse as a child sets a pattern of a tainted "normalcy," whereby other abusive environments later on don't seen abnormal to the victim. It's just an extension of something already familiar. As a result, physical and emotional abuse from a husband may feel just like how Daddy used to treat you as a child. How often do we see people attracted to a familiar, albeit dangerous or unhappy environment, over and over again?

A history of childhood sexual abuse also can affect one's adult sexual relationships. One of the dominant narcissists in my own life was the person who sexually abused me when I was 13 years old. He was someone in a position of trust, who fortunately moved away from the area shortly after the abuse occurred. I was lucky in the sense that I did not have to endure years of abuse, which many people do. However, as short-lived as my experience was, the long-lasting effects most definitely carried over into my own sex life as an adult, as well as into my personal beliefs about myself.

Abuse plays weird psychological games with your mind. For me, it colored my overwhelming feelings of my own value in every regard. I guess I believed if I had truly been valuable, then someone would have saved me, or the perpetrator wouldn't have abused me to begin with. I overcompensated my whole life to avoid the real me from being discovered, or having anyone ever guess my horrible past. I never felt attractive. I felt dirty and that no one would ever want me if they knew what had happened to me. Thus, when it came to setting my boundaries in the bedroom as an adult, I didn't. Having been abused, I had already sacrificed my needs for someone else – how would I have ever known to establish them in any other relationships? In addition, I certainly didn't want to rebuff someone who might actually want me, for what if no one else ever wanted me again?

As with some other victims, I repressed the memories of the abuse for some 30 years, yet still unconsciously dealt with the undercurrent of the aftereffects every day – I just didn't realize it at the time. When the memories engulfed me in my 40s, it was like being in a hurricane of emotions and was almost like reliving the events all over again. I can't begin to explain the emotional toll it took on me. Yet, I did get through it, but not without careful research into the subject of sexual abuse. I got my hands on every book and report I could find to help me understand the feelings and behaviors I experienced. Through a combination of self-study and research, and a good therapist (after firing a bad one!) I began to heal. I also learned to recognize which of my behaviors were helpful and which led me into trouble in my relationships. Most importantly, I learned to break the pattern.

I also had the distinct advantage of being able to confront my abuser many years after the fact. I had run across him from time to time over the years, but until the repressed memories had resurfaced, I had only known that I had a vague unease about him. I knew that I didn't like him very much but I couldn't say why. When at last I confronted him and he confessed his actions in front of others, I felt vindicated and free. I didn't doubt my memories any longer. I knew that he had been in the wrong and that I had only been a victim.

The interesting thing is that while I could forgive his behavior as a 21 year old perpetrator (I need only look at my own daughter in her early 20s now and realize how young and unknowing kids at that age really are), I have not been able to accept him for his current stance. He remains a staunch narcissist even now. (I continue to forget how they just never change, no matter what.) His first comment to me when I confronted him was how he had only wished we could have kept the "situation" between the two of us (I had told many others who knew him by then, much to his dismay). In addition, my only request of him to help me heal was that he would see a therapist, so that we could both better understand what had transpired so many years before and why. His answer was that he didn't need a therapist because there was "nothing wrong" with him. And besides, I was "just as much at fault" as he had been, anyway.

Looking back now, I am appalled to think that for years I was emotionally controlled, manipulated, and degraded by that man, long after he had thrown me aside as his temporary plaything. I *let* him affect me for years. I *let* the beliefs he left me with determine many directions of my life.

Well, let me tell you something …

I don't anymore and you don't have to either!

In cases like that of Marilyn Van Derber, the former Miss America who was a victim of incest for 13 years at the hands of her extremely wealthy and influential father, narcissism is obvious. Her father's needs were more important than anything else. Being the incredibly powerful businessman he was, his entitlement knew no bounds. No one *ever* said no to him – whether at home or at work. Yet, due to his uncaring, unfeeling personality, the results of the abuse he inflicted upon his daughter has left her with lifelong scars – scars she couldn't identify for decades. She too fought repressed memories until she couldn't fight them anymore.

Fortunately, Marilyn also attacked her difficult past head-on. She not only went public after her father's death and spoke out about what happened to her, she has also written her inspirational biography, *Miss America By Day*. (www.MissAmericaByDay.com). She not only describes her incestuous past, but also informs others how to look for the subtle signs of abuse around them and what measures to take to keep their children safe.

Marilyn and I have both taken our abusive pasts and made it our mission to educate others about ways to take better care of themselves in this sometimes dangerous world. While neither of us wished to be abused, we have both come to terms with our past and no longer let it dictate our future. We have let it teach us how to make good choices, how to set our boundaries, and how to never let anyone who isn't honest or trustworthy trap us again.

Many of my survey respondents replied that they had also been physically, emotionally, or sexually abused in their childhoods. Most, but not all of them, reported that their abuse (including sexual abuse) came from within the family – grandfathers, fathers, brothers, cousins, and even mothers, grandmothers, and sisters. Of course some were unrelated abusers, but most had been in some position of trust: the baby sitter, the neighbor man next door, a priest, or perhaps a coach. One thing the victims all agreed upon was that they did not know how to say "no" as a child, even when they were uncomfortable or knew that something was wrong.

Certainly a child saying no to a much older perpetrator is nearly impossible. Yet, indeed most of these adults started their pattern of compliance as children and evolved it over many years into adulthood.

> *As a result of their past abuse,*
> *many victims feel that these issues led them to*
> *missing the Red Flag behaviors involved*
> *in the many games of manipulation*
> *played by the narcissists in their lives.*

In fact even as adults, when they may have felt uncomfortable with situations they found themselves in, they still never stood up for themselves when things simply felt wrong. And thus, the abuse continued anew, just with a different partner.

Alexis

I was molested by a neighbor at age nine. He was in his 30s and was a friend/pseudo father-figure. I was later raped at age 15 by a boyfriend, whom I desperately wanted to have so I could be cool. I never told my parents about either incident, which disconnected my relationship with them even further. I think that these two events were precursors in my behavior of letting men take advantage of me, in the hope that they were truly interested in me and would show me affection. I never learned to develop healthy boundaries and say no with ease. And so I kept right on saying yes to things that were not healthy for me.

I met my husband during a time in my life when I was emotionally vulnerable and was seeking attention and affection from any male figure that seemed to fit my laundry list of qualities. I think that I so longed for someone to love me, and I feared rejection so much, that I subconsciously wrote off the abusive behavior. I allowed him to cross my boundaries because I had never established them or enforced them. I complied with my husband's demands in hopes that it would make everything OK and that he would love me and care for me. In retrospect, it cost me dearly in the long-run.

My family believed in the Christian idea that people should be loving and kind, which translated into being flexible and unassuming, always putting others' needs in front of my own. Yet at the same time I was also physically abused by my father. He demanded compliance to his daily religious routine. He forcefully spanked me from a young age up until I was 15 years old. It wasn't just big infractions – he'd spank me for small things as well. The last belting incident was because I wanted to wear knee-length shorts to a youth group softball game. When I was 12 years old, I actually had the nerve to call the police after a week of him holding me down and covering my mouth if I did not sit still for the hour-long evening prayer. I'm sure that my past has a lot to do with my reactions to sex and my behaviors with men in general, even all these years later.

Maria

My grandmother was a monster and had sole custody of me. She and my dad destroyed my self-esteem. She forced enemas on me every day. My grandfather chronically called me names because my mother abandoned me. I was such a mess that I sucked my thumb until I was 13 and of course there was name-calling that went with that. I was sexually abused by a cousin when I was a kid. He urged me to suck his penis like I sucked my thumb. My family didn't want to hear it. So I protected him and went on to have serial relationships with narcissists who either polluted me or wouldn't have sex with me at all because I am so very vile. I have decided not to have any more relationships. I am ruined in every way. It's all I know to be reviled. To be inferior.

Marianne

I was the youngest of three girls and was tormented as a baby and toddler by my sisters. From dropping me on my head on numerous occasions to harnessing me to my crib because I climbed out all the time, the abuse began early. Yet perhaps the most damaging abuse came from a professional. My mom sent me to a child counselor when I was 10 years old. After a few visits he began to touch me in an inappropriate manner. At the time I didn't realize that wasn't OK, but after a while I started to fight my mom whenever it was time for me to go. Finally, Mom gave up sending me after my ongoing protests but I never, ever told her what really happened.

Christy

I realize now that my father was narcissistic. He was often verbally and physically abusive to my sisters and me. This also included improper sexual fondling. I am sad to admit that I was probably drawn to my ex-husband (also narcissistic), because of some need to appease my unappeasable dad. I am happy to say that since I've moved on from my abusive marriage I have found a wonderful man who is the exact opposite of these two influential men in my history. I have come to realize that old wounds do heal. In my case, they just took half a century and substantial work on my behalf to face my demons and choose to move on.

Cammy

I'm uncertain whether there was sexual abuse in my past or not. There seem to be so many gaps in my childhood memories. I'm wondering if there is a strong tie there. It could be why I was comfortable with my husband's low or non-existent sex drive. It's probably why I stayed in a marriage with no sex or intimacy for years and that is why it felt safe at the time. Thank God I escaped and now know what real intimacy is.

Chapter 9
A Family of Narcissists

Narcissists are oftentimes family members. We are born into their midst and escape is nearly impossible – at least until we are adults and can choose to stay or leave. Unfortunately by that time, we are usually well enmeshed in the all-encompassing environment of the narcissist and escape is difficult at best.

As with many behaviors, narcissism may well be passed down from generation to generation. After all, as children we emulate what we see our parents do. We learn how to treat people and take care of ourselves, and we understand how people interact with one another. If our parents are kind, we are likely to learn kindness. If they are smokers, there is a good probability we will becomes smokers too. But if they are narcissists, we can learn to become narcissists as well, or even narcissistic victims (codependents) just as easily. Frequently, we can become both. For in childhood we are the victim, but in adulthood we can become the abusive controller when we have a family of our own.

Jan, a psychologist, shared a comment with me regarding one of her narcissistic patients. He said:

"When I was a kid my dad ruled our household as if he was king. I guess I grew up just waiting for the day when that was my right too."

This pretty much says it all.

A narcissist in the family can be the mother, father, grandparent, uncle, or anyone in a position of authority. Frequently, the other adults within the environment are passive or frightened themselves, and thus do not limit or inhibit the behavior of the narcissistic adult. The unpredictability, inconsistent behavior, and lack of empathy and compassion lead young children to live in fear and uncertainty. This instability can lead to self-doubt, confusion, depression, and many other emotional and life-long issues.

For yet another movie to watch and see how this manipulation looks from a third party view, pick up the film *Shine*, starring Geoffrey Rush (1996). The story is a true account of a young Austrian piano prodigy whose abusive father tortured him at such a level (emotionally as well as physically and verbally) that he literally had a nervous breakdown followed by years of psychological problems.

This film is an excellent view of just how destructive a family can be to its own members. The fear, distrust, and silent torture can leave deep scars that can affect children all their lives. While certainly not all families are as abusive as the one in this movie, the following stories will clearly demonstrate that family abuse is alive and well in various forms.

Samantha

I am a 43-year-old female just coming to terms with being the child of a narcissistic mother. Ironically, she is also a licensed mental health care worker! We haven't been in contact with each other for the past year after I finally escaped the stifling, sickening world she trapped me in. I have been in therapy off and on since 1992, but only started to look at my denial of her behaviors since the death of my stepfather last March. It has been a roller coaster of emotions: fear, rage, grief, and paralyzing depression. It still amazes me how I could go so long and not see her sickness.

My first steps towards enlightenment and freedom occurred when my current therapist told me that my mother was probably a narcissist. I began to read everything I could get my hands on about the subject. That knowledge changed my life, for it allowed me to see her behaviors for what they really were – abusive and controlling. I am still in therapy once a week, dealing with 42 years of repressed anger, rage, losses, and the ilk that goes with being trapped with a narcissist.

The realization that my environment was not normal came slowly. For most of my life I had always thought there was something deficient in me. I never felt good enough for my mother, no matter what I did. Nor could I ever receive her love or approval. To this day I continue to struggle with the painful realization that I am no more than a possession to her. She feels that because she happened to be the one to give birth to me, I can be treated in any manner she desires. She says, "It's my right, I'm your mother." Like there is an unending secret sin I am fated to pay for forever and must seek her forgiveness as a result.

When I was 18, I told her I had been sexually abused by my older half-brother. She responded with, "Oh, well I thought something like that had happened to you." She then proceeded to tell me about her own abusive history, totally discounting and ignoring what had happened to me. She never showed me the slightest inkling of empathy or compassion. It took me years to understand that her ongoing devaluation and criticism of me, in addition to her treating me like a child my whole life, was actually abuse.

> *I thought of suicide many times,*
> *as the only way to escape the pain.*

When I was 35 I had a complete breakdown, physically and mentally. I had never been on meds before that. I was in and out of a psychiatric hospital four times in about five months. She never came to see me once. This woman is a therapist, for God's sake, and she couldn't even come to visit her own daughter.

A couple of years later I had to move in with her due to another bought of depression. During that time I was hospitalized once. I had to drive myself to the hospital. While she did offer to visit me, her tone was that of, "if I have to." I told her no. I drove myself home again four days later.

While I lived with her for about seven months, she decided to sell her house and had me painting, cleaning, gardening, and landscaping. I do not ever remember her talking to me about my depression or about my feelings at all. When it came time to move, she instructed my half-brother and me to move the entire contents of her three-bedroom house by ourselves, while she and my sister-in-law went shopping. I also had to help her unpack and then depend on friends to help me move my own stuff into my apartment.

I not only fought depression but was later diagnosed with active chronic fatigue. Later she told me she always thought I was faking the depression, until she saw it first-hand when I lived with her. What a comforting comment from a mother to a daughter!

About two years ago I had to move in with her again at a time when I needed help. I paid her rent out of my disability ($200 a month), plus another $200 for a loan she paid off for me on a bad car deal. I knew she bailed me out of that because it would tie me to her forever. It was about $6,000, of which I still owe a little under $4,000. I also tore up all her carpet at her request, repaired the tile underneath, and re-landscaped her entire yard. During this time I was going to college full-time and still attending Alcoholic's Anonymous meetings regularly. (I am proud to say that I have been sober for 11 years.)

All the time I lived with her she would watch me like a hawk, like I was 15 years old. (I was 42.) She was nasty to any man I ever had a date with. Many first dates were ruined even before I left the house, due to her controlling, meddling behavior.

I remember thinking of killing myself constantly. The thoughts were so invasive, and got to be so intrusive, I had to be hospitalized again. As before, I had to drive myself there. She didn't come to visit this time either.

When I finally told her I was moving out months later, she threw a fit and kicked me out for the weekend. When it became apparent that I was serious about the move, she kept hammering at me as to why I was leaving, constantly questioning how I could do this *to her*. Things like that. I finally said, "Mom, you have to stop trying to live my life for me." With that, her face screwed up in rage and she told me to "Get out and never come back."

I tried to email her afterwards, when I hoped she had calmed down, but she just left me a message to pick up the rest of my things or she would throw them out. She ended up throwing away my high school year books and several other things that were important to me. Of course she kept the childhood mementos of mine that were important to her.

I have not spoken to her since. It will be two years next September. The confusing feelings I endured as a result of all of this, left me a mess. I self-abused for the first time in 13 years (cutting and cigarette burning). I had a drinking episode, but thank God that was a brief two weeks and I have been sober since.

I have gone through such rage, I thought I would explode. I found out later that she abused my younger step-siblings as well. I always thought it was just me she abused, since I am her only natural child.

At times I hate her guts, at times I pity her. Mostly I just want to stay away from her. I see a therapist once a week and my psychiatrist once a month. I attend AA meetings and try to help others. In spite of my mother instilling in me that I was a piece of crap and treating me like a slave or an object, rather than a human being, I know I am a good person. I love others and they love me. It still hurts. I have felt actively suicidal much of the time, but I wouldn't give that bitch the satisfaction of killing myself for her anymore. This may sound blunt, but it sure feels good to at last be able to say it, as opposed to feeling so many other negative emotions.

I will never contact my mother again. She is a narcissistic, abusive, bitter, spiteful, spiritless woman. I pray for her soul because she doesn't add much to this earth, at least not for me.

I realize how unhealthy she is for me, that she will never change, and that my life is at stake when I am around her. It's just not worth the risk.

I find the holidays are the most bizarre time for me. All the Christmas brouhaha they sell you. The whole "happy family" thing. Well, it has never been that way for me, or for many other people I know. Sometimes I would like to write Hallmark Cards and tell them to lay off the syrup and come up with some realistic Christmas cards for those of us who don't have family by our own choice or circumstances. Cards that say something like, "Hey, growing up was horrific, but now I can finally have my own Christmas."

Thank God at last I can.

Jay

I'm the oldest of three children. Before my younger siblings were born, I was the apple of my mother's eye – or so it seemed. However, when my two brothers were born in short succession, my mother apparently didn't handle the added stress well and seemed to change suddenly.

The biggest problem I began to face was that she became extremely unpredictable. One day I would come home from school and she would invite me to climb up on her lap to watch her soap operas with her and the next day she would be screaming over some perceived infraction that I couldn't even understand. I never knew if I was going to come home to a hugging or a beating. It left me in constant doubt and worry. I think I first developed anxiety during those years.

There were frequent occasions when she would be seemingly calm and collected and yet her hand would suddenly lash out and smack me across the face – so instantly that I would never see it coming and never even had the time to understand what had set her off in the first place. Even my dad was afraid of her and I think he started drinking just to hide from her constant criticism and wrath. I guess I wish that he would have stuck up for us more.

In addition to this instability, my father was a military career man and we moved every two years or so, adding to the stress and confusion we dealt with every day. I guess she didn't feel like she had much control over things and that made her angry as well.

As a grown-up, I still feel that I can do no right in my mother's eyes. For my forty-fourth birthday when she asked me what I wanted for a gift I simply replied, "Just please treat me like a grown-up for a change." That seemed to be one of the first steps I made in establishing my boundaries with her.

I hate my mother for her controlling mentality. She's got to control everyone and everything. I spend as little time with her as I possibly can. She just has this way of eating away at my soul. For so long I have dealt with guilt, anger, frustration, and anxiety regarding how she treats me that I've just had enough. I do what I have to with her and that's it.

Mother's Day and her birthday are a month apart and it's a grueling time for me. Ever try to pick out a card for a mother you still put up with in your life but fight your own inner turmoil about every single day? The task is absolutely torturous.

Andrea

My father was the ultimate authority in our household. He had a temper that would explode at the drop of a hat and my brothers and sisters did our best not to ignite it. He would fly into a rage over the smallest things – like when the house wasn't perfect or if anyone left anything out on the counter or there were any crumbs lying about. My older sister got grounded once for not lining his hats up correctly in the closet or another time because she returned the empty trash can and had the absence of mind to set it next to the wall with the insignia not facing out for everyone to see it.

He traveled a lot and it seemed like we could breathe a bit whenever he was gone. But the day we knew he was coming home, we all got tense and wondered what his mood would be the minute he walked in the door. It would take us about two seconds to "read" him and know what was in store for the rest of the evening. It made us all learn to be anxious, worrying about everything all the time.

My mom was like this mouse. She was always quiet and tried not to have anything out of place. She was not permitted to give us hugs and kisses, even if we got hurt or something, because he didn't want us to be "coddled." One time my brother got in a bad accident with his bike and came home crying and complaining about his ankle hurting. My dad told him to "quit crying and be a man." He was only about 10 years old, for pity sake, but he wasn't allowed to cry. As it turned out, he had broken his ankle, but no one took him to the hospital for about a week because he was too afraid to tell anyone how much pain he was in.

Dad criticized us all the time for everything … if our nails were dirty, if our hair wasn't brushed, if we had our elbows on the dinner table and weren't paying attention (then we'd get a fork jabbed in an elbow to teach us not to do that again). If Mom would cook something new for a meal, he'd tell her what she did wrong every time and never comment as to anything good about it.

Of course when we deserved punishment his belt came out instantly. Or even worse, he might send us out to the weeping willow tree where we were supposed to fetch him a proper switch to beat us with. No one wanted that because you couldn't sit down for a week. Imagine choosing your own weapon of torture! It's maddening to even think about. I suspect in today's society he could have been arrested for child abuse, as we carried bruises from those beatings for a good week.

The funny thing is that Dad was seen as a pillar of the community. We went to church every week and he was even one of the volunteers there. He was funny and told jokes all the time. He was very tall, so he stood out from the crowd. Everybody loved him but I bet nobody knew what he was like to live with.

Bette

I come from a family that not only has a mother who has suspected Narcissistic Personality Disorder, but a brother and two sisters as well. My father and my other sister, brother, and I are survivors. We have been able to track this disorder down through the family tree. It stems from my great-grandmother. We don't know if this is nurture or nature, but it's real. The four members of my family actually grouped together in their illness to form a cult-like association. My mother, brother, and sister joined together and committed acts of sexual abuse against my younger sister. My mother also physically abused us. But the public persona was squeaky clean. They stole everything from us and used it for themselves. My younger sister is the most dangerous of them all; she is pure evil. My other sister and I are both in counseling, and our therapist has assured us that we are not the mad ones.

Jordan

My mom was forever telling us that she had never wanted us in the first place. I realized early on that in her eyes my entire job was to meet her every emotional need. I was really raised by my sister until I was nine years old. Mom didn't see much use for me before that, I guess. I felt like I was always trying to keep Mom on an even keel, but of course it was an impossible feat.

By the time I went to college I had been a caretaker for so long that becoming a psychologist seemed a likely choice. While my mother touted my education to her friends, she ended up being jealous of me when I went beyond her education and attained my master's degree. God knows, I should never look better than she did. She just couldn't understand why I went back to school – after all, I was married and had children by then. What on earth did I think I was going to do – set the world on fire?

I remember one very telling moment in our relationship when I was being honored with an award at a university function. It was given to me during a big banquet and the entire evening everyone was telling Mom how proud she must be of my accomplishments. Mom seemed to be basking in the attention, even though it wasn't about her at all. I was sitting next to her and as they called my name to go to the stage to accept the award, Mom suddenly grabbed my arm as I stood up, saying "Are you going to go up there with your hair looking like that?"

Up until that moment it was about Mom being applauded for my success. I realize now that she just had to get the last word in and control me with fear of failing – of looking stupid right up to the end. She just couldn't be happy for me having a moment in the limelight that didn't reflect her.

Over the years I've come to realize and accept that if everything is not about her, she makes life miserable for everyone in sight. If she comes for a visit, I can spend eight hours talking to her and kowtowing to her wishes nonstop, yet the phone can ring and I will be tied up with the caller for five minutes and Mom will say, "Well, I guess I should just go home. You certainly don't have time for me!"

Yet the amazing thing to me is that so many other people see her as absolutely wonderful. She's a saint in their eyes. I always wonder what they would say if they knew the real story.

Angela

My whole family is controlling and narcissistic. As a kid I had to be perfect. I had to be "up" all the time. Shame, blame, put downs – those were the typical behaviors from my parents. They always told me that something was wrong with me, but I never knew what. I just felt at fault or defective somehow and that everything that went wrong was my fault. I felt I must be a terrible person because I could never do anything right.

My real father abandoned me at age eight. He was an alcoholic. My step-father was a West Point career man and as narcissistic as my mom. I have suffered from depression since he and my mom married back when I was nine. She's very masculine and is on a continuous mission to dominate everyone and everything. She's always barking orders at everyone and still calls me four times a day. I'm 42 years old. When is she going to let me grow up and live my own life? She tells me it's for my own good and gets really angry if I don't keep my cell phone on at all times.

I never know what I'm going to get from her whenever I answer the phone. She either jumps down my throat and begins criticizing me for something I may not have even done, or else she's condescending and sickly sweet. If I bring up something she doesn't want to deal with, she simply says, "Oh, darling, you don't know what you're talking about – it's all in your head. *We* don't need to deal with this right now. It's just your depression talking." If I try to talk about something emotional, she just finds an excuse to get off the phone. You can never win an argument with her – she's so quick! I learned early on not to even try. As I look at the mechanics of it all now, I can see where she's truly made me crazy. And I unknowingly let her. It's taken me years to understand it's a family dynamic that is the underlying problem – not just me. I kept thinking my family was supposed to be there for me, but they just weren't. I have had suicidal tendencies all my life as a result.

At last I now realize that my mom and my brother are only nice to me when they need something from me. I'm finally able to recognize the pattern now, but before I thought it was all my imagination.

Once you recognize they are narcissists it's a relief to some degree. I recognize how I can cope with it better but it never stops the pain. I have learned that it's not my responsibility to try to please everyone else all the time, nor is everything my fault. I haven't always done something wrong, despite all the accusations and blaming they do. Furthermore, I don't have to be perfect all the time. All my life I thought I did. It's no wonder I've fought depression for over 30 years, with the weight of the world on my shoulders.

At last I see that the control is about them, not me. It looks so charming, but in fact it's so manipulative. They always act like they're doing me these great favors but usually, whatever they're up to, it's about making their life easier.

My brother blames me for ruining his life with my depression. I'm not sure how he figures that but he tries to put me in guilt mode all the time. He will barely look at me and is so cold. He is emotionless. It used to tear me up inside all the time, but I'm just not taking it anymore. Recently I went to a family wedding and in an effort to start establishing some new boundaries with all of them I sat with people other than my family during the dinner. They accepted it and I felt great about it.

I'm recognizing that I'm only responsible for me and that they are each in charge of themselves. It's such a relief now, knowing that nothing has to do with me being irresponsible for everything and everybody's issues.

Now that I've been making huge strides in my self-esteem and establishing my own boundaries I've been doing a lot of things differently. I've been teaching kids to read at a local school. I like who I am now. I believe in myself. I don't have to believe what my family tells me anymore. There's no going back for me. I'm way too positive for this negativity. I feel like I have a choice in all I do now.

I'm changing the dance. One day I just got sick and tired of being sick and tired. I started to believe in, and take care of, *me*. But they don't like it when you start taking care of yourself. They like to lay on the guilt, etc. When I do well, my family takes all the credit for it. They make it look like they did all the work to make me better. They are heroes to all their friends, the people in the community. They get so much attention for this. The good thing is that now, I don't need the credit. If it makes them happy to play the role of the savior, I don't really care. I know I have moved past the darkness and have come out into the light.

Unfortunately for them, they'll be there forever.

"My therapist said that I should think of my narcissistic husband, John as "emotionally retarded."
If he were mentally retarded I would never expect him to be smart.
As emotionally retarded, she helped me to realize that I can never expect him to be able to understand emotions either."
Sheila – survivor

Chapter 10
Narcissists in the Workplace

Not all narcissists are people we are related to or in romantic relationships with. Sometimes they are people you work with, bosses, or employees you manage. Unfortunately they can be just as difficult to deal with in these roles as they are when they are your husband or mother. The stress, anguish, and abuse go on in just the same way as with any other type of narcissistic relationship, but now the number of people affected by these toxic bosses and/or employees can multiply substantially and the bottom line to the company can prove overwhelmingly costly. And, sadly enough, most never see it coming.

A Toxic Workplace

As companies weigh the costs of doing business, the easy figures to analyze and compare are the traditional black and white ones: salaries, overhead, cost of goods, etc. Yet, what are the nebulous costs that result from frequent absenteeism, lack of employee focus, increased use of insurance due to medical conditions, and even sabotage instigated by unhappy and/or vengeful employees, all of which can be caused by an emotionally hazardous work environment?

But just what is an emotionally hazardous work environment?

In the case of one created by management, it is a workplace managed by a leader who believes in demonstrating power and control over employees, dominates others through his or her constant attempts at intimidation, conveys no compassion or understanding for the individual needs and issues of employees, and frequently takes credit for the work of any subordinates.

Just as with those narcissistic types in romantic relationships, narcissistic managers are extremely famous for demonstrating God Complex behaviors: They think that others in the world believe exactly what they believe at the same time that they see themselves as omnipotent, untouchable, and feel that rules don't apply to them. They are frequently arrogant and conceited and have a sense of entitlement about them. And when they're your boss, your life is miserable.

Yet the worst part of their behavior is that they do not see others as equal human beings — employees might as well be robots or machines. These emotionally toxic leaders do not comprehend that others have feelings, needs, and thoughts, thus the reason they are incapable of empathy or compassion in their dealings with all those they perceive as "underlings." A vision of Scrooge comes to mind, constantly harping at Bob Cratchett to work longer, harder, and for less, and pouting like a child or having a temper tantrum when Bob asks to have Christmas Day off.

Despite his (or her) apparent lack of emotion when it comes to others, when the tables are turned it is quite another matter. When the narcissistic bosses get their feelings hurt, perceive they have been slighted in any way, or are threatened that an employee's abilities might be better than their own, they can overreact with a rage that leaves terror in their wake. Everyone knows when the boss is having a temper tantrum and they do whatever possible to stay out of the path of the hurricane. Unfortunately for some, they will always be stuck in the eye of the storm and will suffer from the emotional abuse that ensues.

In these days of extreme competition in business, it is common for corporate leaders to hire managers with vastly competitive personalities, who will work themselves (and their teams) like crazy to make it to the top. And yet we have seen in recent years how those same go-getters are sometimes oblivious of whom they walk over on the way up, to the detriment of everyone.

Take Enron for example. Top leaders of the once powerful corporation became so obsessed with their power, control, and omnipotence, they were blindsided to the devastating end result they were creating. In their God-like vision, how could anything possibly go wrong?

Of course, not all narcissistic bosses are as obvious as the infamous Mr. Scrooge. The more insidious, stealth type narcissists also can create an emotional living hell for all those around them. Name calling, talking down to employees, using sexual harassment, doling out the silent treatment to those who have slighted or mis-stepped around the boss, establishing multiple and/or unrealistic rules, prohibiting personal objects in the workplace (photos of family, etc.), and dishing out unrealistic job expectations are just some examples of the brainwashing and controlling techniques that gradually but consistently erode a once normal workplace into one that is downright cancerous. And just as with cancer in the body that can spread its malignancy throughout, thus can an entire corporation become victim to this "DIS-ease."

The Tyrant in the Cubicle Next to You

Narcissistic employees can make their coworkers and the environment equally toxic as well. While these people may not have the title to go with their grandiose fantasies of power and importance, they thrive on acting out the role anyway. Those in the crossfire can still suffer the same effects as if they were working for a narcissistic boss. By using bullying, persistent teasing, emotional threatening, name-calling, employing the silent treatment, filing false accusations and attempting to control others in a variety of ways, these powermongers can still leave the victims in their path exhausted, drained, and looking for work elsewhere.

So how do these abusive monsters gain access to a position within a corporation to begin with if they're so terrible?

I remind you again that one of the greatest abilities of narcissists is their incredible acting skills. They win the Academy Award for Best Actor or Actress, and can worm their way into any variety of positions. They know just how to be the perfect employee, manager, or partner for as long as it takes to become well entrenched in the system,. Once they have a strong foothold, their unhealthy real personality eventually surfaces. Again, Dr. Jekyll and Mr. Hyde do a flip flop, yet by then it's usually too late for human resources to pick up on their error. The probationary period is up. And to terminate the employee now becomes a tricky legal walk.

The Boss With Two Faces

Worse yet is the narcissistic boss who continues to look like the ideal employee to those he reports to, yet unleashes his terror on his underlings when no one's watching. When his employees go to complain to upper management, they are not believed, since the middle manager has convinced upper management of his excellent role-model behavior and talents. He or she has become a member of the "Good Old Boys" manager network and no amount of proof or explanation from others will de-throne this demigod from his pedestal … despite any pain or even mass exodus from the worker bees in his hive.

A War Zone

So what is the hidden cost of employing narcissistic individuals in your work place? Is it high turnover? High absenteeism? Employees on Prozac? Or could it be that people now hate coming to work and are giving a halfway job?

Just as it is for those living in a home with this same unhealthy and unstable environment, working in a toxic workplace can be compared to living in a war zone as well: the instability of a situation that can change without notice, the constant strain of living under high tension, the ongoing worry of being under the gun, the desire to stay out of the line of fire for fear of being attacked. This is indeed how many employees report feeling in these extremely unhealthy environments.

If you were living in a real war zone, what symptoms might you see? Depression, sleep disorders, anxiety, chronic fatigue, anger, inability to concentrate, gastrointestinal symptoms, blood pressure changes, headache, backache, changes in appetite, agitation, hysteria, Post Traumatic Stress symptoms, and so on.

So what is the real cost? Unfortunately, until someone studies this work phenomenon closer, these emotional sweatshops will more than likely continue to exact their toll on those who remain in them. If we could quantify the cost of the dollars and cents that affected the bottom line into black and white, I suspect we might be more careful whom we hire to be members of our production team.

Instead of a huge percentage of our populace being drugged with antidepressants as a means to cover up the root of the problem, they would do well to better understand that their symptoms may be coming directly from the environment they subject themselves to for eight hours a day, 40 hours per week, and – in a full-time job – 2,000 hours per year!

With today's laws regulating hiring and firing of employees, getting rid of employees who cause trouble in the workplace can be very difficult. Yet it becomes crucial to the health of the workplace to find a way to move out these bad eggs, these destructive people, in order to cleanse the work environment for the rest of the staff.

And if they don't move on, maybe it's time you do. What's it worth to your health? Is any job worth it? Personally I found a few that simply were not ...

Little Man Syndrome

One of the narcissistic bosses I had years ago really left me emotionally distraught for a while. I didn't know about narcissism at the time or I might have at least understood my feelings and his behaviors better. Ted was the president of the company I worked for and he had only been promoted to that position a month or so before I began working as a medical sales rep for the company.

He was a rather short man – probably about five foot five inches – and I always just thought he suffered from what I always called "Little Man Syndrome." Like Napoleon or Caesar, it always seems like so many short men have an inferiority complex and have to overcompensate by screaming and hollering at everyone in their environment and throwing their weight around whenever possible. I don't think it helped that at nearly five foot ten, I towered over him! In addition, I had just come from the nursing field and my clinical knowledge often exceeded his.

The end result? He had to let me know my place.

The most horrific memory I have from that time was being the new kid on the block, having only worked for the company for a matter of months. I was brand new to the business world and to understanding the games one had to play within the company, to get the pricing I wanted for my clients. I had to call in to his office and give him the scoop on the hospital I was working with, why they needed a certain pricing, why I thought I would be able to close the sale, etc.

Well, he read my vulnerability and my lack of knowledge about how the financial game was played, and he went for the throat. He had several people in his office the day I called in to talk with him about my account. As I hesitatingly began to give him the necessary information, he began to quiz me about every little detail under the sun. Not knowing what the process would involve, I didn't have much of the information he was grilling me for and he could sense I was beginning to become a bit anxious. That's when he went for the kill. He told me to hold one minute while he put me on speaker phone, then proceeded to ream me out in front of everyone in his office.

Of course none of that was necessary. He could have conveyed the same message and taught me a more useful lesson by being patient, giving me his full one-on-one attention, and asking the people in his office to leave. But that wasn't his goal. His mission was to show me that he was in charge. That the world revolved around him … and I'd better never forget it.

For weeks I dealt with anxiety and fear whenever I had to think about my next phone calls to him. (This certainly did nothing to foster an environment where I wanted to give my best.) When at last I established myself as a "worthy" employee, who closed deals and made the company money, he finally quit testing me and moved on to someone else.

He was also an avid member of the "Good Old Boy network." He loved rubbing shoulders with the board of directors, kissing up to them regularly and looking important to everyone. Unfortunately for us lower employees, he used sarcastic teasing and constant criticism to taunt us whenever possible.

> *Looking back now, I guess he reminds me of those infamous college football coaches who lead by intimidation.*
> *Hasn't anyone ever explained to them that most people usually perform better with positive reinforcement, than when motivated by fear?*

In this day and age of enlightenment, I am still amazed when those methods are not only allowed to continue, but are often sought out and implemented by choice, by some companies and schools.

In reality, the emotional turmoil I dealt with for so many months working for my little Napoleon probably cost me in productivity in the long run. Yet, he thought he was inspiring us all with his threats and intimidation and that we would be more productive as a result of his God-like leadership! If only he could have seen how wrong he was.

Sainthood

Several years ago I worked for a woman named Carmen, who could get an A+ in her narcissistic skills. Carmen was a 50-something Hispanic woman who had worked her way up in the corporation for 30 years and had eventually made it to the top of the pile – a feat by any corporate standard! In addition, 10 years before I came to work there, she had cleverly calmed down a group of employees intent on striking and had been revered as a savior by upper management due to her quick thinking. Because of this, she knew she was untouchable. Even if she blew up the building, it would have been almost impossible to fire her. Between her minority status, the fact that she was a woman, and her history of saving the day, she walked on water. She may as well have been sainted.

She would drop by our department unannounced and while there, she pranced around like the Queen Mum herself, mostly looking for the employees to adore her and pay her homage. She rarely arrived alone, but rather, had an entourage of her own sub-supervisors in attendance, rather like her ladies in waiting.

As long as I recognized that she was the Mistress of her Kingdom, all was fine. But the minute that I questioned policy or brought up a new idea, her eyes would grow dark and she would glare at me in disgust and rage. How dare I question her intelligence and authority?

I quickly became confused, since one of the biggest reasons they had chosen me for the job was that the particular department I headed up was not the company's specialty. They had no one to guide them in the development of bringing that unit up to speed with the others. They claimed that they longed for an outsider to bring in new ideas for growth. Yet, each time I attempted to offer a change that could do exactly what they were hoping for, I was shot down.

One day at a management retreat, I saw the totally irrational side of her personality. As we all entered the hotel conference room, we were to find our nametags on the table and put them on, so that new employees on the management team would know who the players were. As she found her name on the table, I was shocked to see her pick it off of the table and violently throw it across the room. She then began screaming and hollering something about how her "official title" wasn't on her name tag. How dare anyone not identify her with the correct status!

It took the president of the company to take her aside and tell her to shape up and quit acting like a spoiled child. Yet no matter what her behavior, she was still sainted and none could touch her.

I guess I must have been one of the only people who ever stood up to her. I continued to implement the necessary changes to bring the unit out of the Dark Ages, yet, by doing so, it cost me dearly. She would call me in her office or send her underlings to give me threatening lectures about my behavior. By the time they left I was filled with fear, confusion, guilt, and self-doubt. The sleepless nights I had while manager of that unit were too numerous to count. I can tell you that when I did sleep it was filled with relentless nightmares.

What I didn't understand at the time was that my holier than thou boss was simply acting out her own narcissistic view of life. She kept hoping that by intimidating me, she would get her fix; her necessary homage. And if she could leave me feeling totally demoralized in the process, she was so much the happier. A saint can never be wrong, of course. She was no exception.

Perhaps I should have realized that there was a reason the managers in the department I managed had turned over constantly. I once calculated that there had been 13 managers in that department over the course of 10 years. That's ridiculous in any organization and certainly speaks to poor leadership from above.

When I finally couldn't take it anymore (I lasted 18 months), I inadvertently threw my sainted boss a curve. I tendered my resignation but with an unexpected twist – I gave her two month's notice. In my mind, I was giving the company time to recruit a new manager, which I knew would be a lengthy process. I remained a conscientious employee and didn't want to leave them in the lurch. I also knew it was annual budget time and that leaving with a two-week notice would have caused added stress to some other poor person who would be handed the budgetary issues, and I just didn't feel that was fair to do to anyone – no matter how miserable I felt.

My poor Saint! She was thrilled that I was leaving, but furious that she couldn't get me out from her hair in the usual two week's time frame! I inadvertently held her ransom!

How she finally regained her control and won the battle was quite clever, actually. She told Human Resources that they were to pay me a full two-month's severance, but that I had to leave immediately. She thought she won! While I was initially devastated that I was actually being asked to leave, the end result was that I had two month's pay and didn't have to go to work! I completed my master's degree studies without the added pressure of a full-time job, at the same time that I received full-time pay. She actually gave me a gift and had no idea she was doing so.

She remained the proverbial saint for several more years before she retired. I didn't envy the others who stayed behind. To me, my health was worth more than any job could offer.

Jelaine

I am 33 years old and have worked in the hospital industry in one capacity or another for over 14 years. After I obtained a Masters Degree in Administration, I got a job managing an admission department for a community hospital in a small, university community. I was excited for a chance to bring my big city hospital background to a growing environment that seemed to be seeking to broaden their horizons. I had always loved working with people throughout my career, and had moved up the managerial ranks quickly.

In my new job I would be supervising 12 employees who provided around-the-clock coverage, as patients were admitted to the hospital any time of the day or night. At the time I started this job, most of the employees had been there for a few years, but Charmaine had been there the longest – some 25 years.

I jumped in with both feet, and with all the optimism and hope in the world. I saw so much potential in the department and the employees. But I was stymied by Charmaine from the first week. She was in her 40s, a divorcee, and had been second in command without a title for several years, and under several managers. She had neither the educational qualifications to apply to be manager, nor apparently the inclination. Managers were on salary and I think she preferred the ability to still receive overtime, whenever it was available. At first I thought she was charming and civilized. She was born and raised in Georgia, so her accent definitely added to that impression. She rather liked everyone to think she had been quite the Southern Belle. As I learned from the other staff members, she'd had breast cancer the year before, and had a bilateral mastectomy as a result. She had also undergone chemotherapy, lost her hair, and had persevered and apparently won the battle with the disease. Everyone sort of treated her with kid gloves, due to her situation.

As her manager, I quickly took great steps to work with her, if there were any issues that came up related to her health. As a good friend of mine had gone through the excruciating ordeal of breast cancer, I was keenly aware of the issues involved ... frequent doctor's visits, chronic fatigue, issues with self-image, etc. My heart went out to her. I wanted to do whatever it took to help her through the recovery. As such, whenever she needed time off for doctor's appointments or to stay home to rest after an extra heavy work week, I supported her 100 percent.

She was both very clever and had a sharp (and sometimes wicked) sense of humor. However, she also showed great hostility toward me from the start. I was used to the typical adjustment any department goes through with a new manager at the helm and I expected some awkward moments. Yet it seemed like she had it in for me from the beginning.

For example, when my supervisor asked me about a memo she had sent out within two weeks after my arrival, I told her that I hadn't received any mail yet. She was surprised, and suggested that I check with Charmaine, who of course knew where everything was. As I hadn't even thought about getting mail yet, I really hadn't given it a second thought that I should be missing any. I asked Charmaine where my mail might be, since I didn't have a mailbox on my door and my office was generally locked if I wasn't in it. She claimed ignorance. I kept asking around for a few days and finally one of the newer staff members said she'd overheard Charmaine telling some of the others that she had deliberately withheld my mail from me. Yet, when I confronted her on it, she blatantly denied doing so. Fortunately, someone found it within a day or so, and my mail magically appeared on my desk from then on with no explanations. I tried to ignore it as my right of passage as their new manager, yet things seemed to continue.

Early on, I noticed she tried to brand me with negative qualities. She'd say things like: "You folks from the big city must think we're just 'hicks' out here." I was startled by that comment as I had no such feelings for the small town I had moved to, the company I worked for, or the people I worked with. In fact, I was enjoying the safe, cozy feelings I was evolving living in a close-knit, slower-paced community than I'd come from. Yet she seemed to like to throw out little digs regarding this situation as often as possible.

I experienced another Charmaine irritation when I implemented a change in how a certain procedure was done within the department. I explained my rational for the change and requested that everyone follow the new procedure. Charmaine's first reaction at a staff meeting was to roll her eyes and say, "But we've done it this way for the last 20 years. Why do we have to change it now?" Again, I explained the changes in the hospital industry and how it would bring us up to standard with other hospitals, yet she acted like a hurt child and pouted the rest of the day, at the same time she gave me her Cheshire Cat grin when I stopped by later to see if she was comfortable with the new procedure. Her condescending tone was icy and, combined with her cat-like grin, it was almost hysterical. Rather like a spoiled three-year-old child who didn't get her way, but would get revenge later through some temper-tantrum at a least opportune time. The icy look she gave me said, "You may be the boss, but I hate your guts." I just smiled back, trying to ignore the situation.

One of the most frustrating situations was when we had two of our usual night staff out with emergency situations at the same time.

I was frantic! Getting people to work the night shift was always difficult, but with our two regulars out, even for a short time, we were in a real bind. All of my staff understood the predicament we were in and when I asked each of them to pick up a handful of night shifts to help out during the crisis, they understood the concept of teamwork, and all went to bat for me. I even scheduled myself to work some as well, which put extra work on me to still cover my daytime responsibilities, but I figured that was part of the joys of management.

As I looked at the schedule, there was only one night remaining that was not covered. I had hesitated to ask Charmaine to cover it, both due to her recovery situation, and as she was most senior member of the staff, she hadn't been asked to work nights in years. But I had no other alternative.

As I approached her, I knew that she was well aware of the situation, and how everyone was taking on whatever they could to help. I told her how I hated to even ask her, but that I'd had to schedule her for one night shift during the six weeks of shortages.

She suddenly turned her back on me, walked away, and muttered "I don't do nights." She simply dismissed me.

Of course the entire thing blew up into a battle I had to bring my supervisors in on. The long and the short was that she worked the one night shift, but not without becoming the poor victim in the whole affair. She played up her cancer once again, although she had been out of any therapy for over 18 months. She was sure to inform the other staff of my disrespect for her seniority, how I was trying to get her fired, how I hated her from the first day, and how tough I was making it on her with all her cancer issues. She was the biggest cry-baby I had ever seen.

Fortunately, most of the staff saw her game. If they had worked there any time at all, they knew what a bully she was. Most employees working in the department were scared to death of her. She was great at playing the silent treatment when she didn't like something you said or did, or else pulling out her famous cat grin whenever she was letting you know that she was talking down to you. So, for the most part, I wasn't too worried about the majority of the staff. They were on my side. Yet, the frustrating part was the necessity of bringing in my supervisors to settle the argument to begin with. I felt that my authority had been undermined and that she knew she had caused a chink in my ultimate armor – not to mention dozens of sleepless nights over that issue and wondering what other issues she might have waiting for me in the future.

The hope and excitement I'd had when I first started this job several months ago have long since disappeared. While I realize that entering a workplace as a new manager who is quite a bit younger than the current employees can sometimes be a bit awkward, I have never found these issues in other places I've worked before. I have always gotten along well with co-workers and have been praised for my efforts along the way.

> *I ask myself every day why I put myself through this. Am I kidding myself the situation will get better all by itself? It certainly isn't likely.*

Am I trying to see which one of us gives in first? If so, that could be a long fight, as the benefits Charmaine receives at this job would be hard for her to replace. There are days I wonder if her illness will recur and will reach a point where she will no longer be able to work here and I win by default. Yet, what damage can she do to the attitudes and feelings of the others in this workplace in the meantime that will remain long after she's left? I feel like she's holding me hostage and no matter what I do, I'm the one left suffocating.

Why am I killing myself like this? In this wonderful, big country of ours, there's bound to be better working environments than this. There just has to be. I don't know how much longer I will last.

If only narcissists had to identify themselves with a big "N" on their foreheads, it would help everyone make more informed decisions about the temperatures of a workplace before they jump into the deep end of the pool.

Coaches, Teachers, Priests, Playground Bullies and More...

While I have been speaking directly to environmental workplace issues, there are others that while not considered employers, are none-the-less equally dangerous to our children. After all, it is our children's full-time job to be students, so those they interact with in their world have just as much impact upon their development as does your Mr. Scrooge at work. I am talking about the wide variety of caretakers whom we entrust our kids to for several hours a day … teachers, coaches, priests, daycare providers, and more.

It becomes even trickier to spot these dangerous people because we have to balance their intelligent and mature adult persona with those of our children who may often have their great imaginations or other issues to sort through. Yet, if your child's behavior starts changing in ways you don't understand (at the same time that they have inherited a new teacher, coach, or other new adult in their lives – including your new boyfriend), they may be giving you signals that while they don't understand exactly *what* is wrong, something most definitely is.

Certainly we have all become educated about the sexual abuse so many boys and girls have suffered at the hands of priests and even teachers. Not to mention the sad stories of new boyfriends or step-parents taking advantage of vulnerable children who don't have the ability to speak up. For, of course, abusers are incredibly good at intimidation and manipulation and many children keep quite because they feel they will be subjected to even worse treatment should they tell of their plight.

Parents must stay sharply attuned to their child's non-verbal behavior, as it may be the only clue they get that something is dreadfully wrong. A change in personality, clothing styles, behaviors, interactions with others, slipping grades, and so many other Red Flags are sometimes the only clues you will have that something's just not right.

And don't forget the playground bullies who may be children the same age as yours and not an adult at all. Kids can sometimes be the worst abusers ... especially emotionally and/or verbally. Being aware of whom your child hangs out with as well as being a careful listener to what they say (or don't say) about their day at school, can lead you on a path to becoming Sherlock Holmes about something unhealthy or unsafe in your child's every day environment. While overprotecting your kids can be unhealthy as well, no child should have to endure abuse and not be able to tell anyone else about their circumstances.

The emotional abuse that can occur to kids at the hands of a narcissist can stay with them for a lifetime. Remember, it doesn't need to be caused purely by physical or sexual abuse. Verbal abuse, neglecting, ignoring, and more all leave a child feeling vulnerable and unsafe at a time in his or her development when these serious gaps can lead to a lifetime of "baggage."

So remember, whether Mr. Scrooge is at your workplace, your child's classroom, or in the coach's box, he or she can be a ticking time bomb for everyone's health.

> *"To react emotionally to a narcissist*
> *is like talking Atheism to an Afghan Fundamentalist."*
> *Sam Vaknin, narcissist*

Chapter 11
When They Are Your Friends

*N*arcissists don't have to just be your intimate partners, family members, or your co-workers. Sometimes they are just your friends you spend time with. However, they have the same behaviors and can leave you with the same scars as those in the other relationships. The important thing to remember is that while we can't necessarily choose or leave our family members, we *can* choose to keep or leave our friends.

Friends or Frenemies?

Have you heard the word "frenemy" tossed around recently? I heard it discussed on one of those morning TV news shows and I thought it was a perfect label for narcissistic friendships. According to Wikipedia:

The term "frenemy" has become increasingly used to describe two (or more) people who are apparently friends, but are actually enemies. Such relationships may occur due to the desire (of either) to keep a close eye on the actions of their close rival (i.e., keep your friends close, keep your enemies even closer).

The term seems quite fitting. In reality, very little difference exists between a narcissistic relationship with a friend and one with an intimate partner, except of course for the sexual intimacy. Otherwise, the dance is the same. The narcissist leads his or her partner on the frantic roller coaster, through the eye of the tornado, or down into the depths of despair without even a second thought.

Christy

Joan and I both had boys the same age. We met when our kids were in 4H together and were preparing for the year's dog show events. The boys immediately hit it off and became best friends even outside of the 4H world.

I found Joan to be very quiet. Not shy really, just one of those people who didn't really open up about much. Pretty private, I guess you might say. Yet, she seemed to want to be friends with me and always went out of her way to "do the right thing." For example, if I drove us all to the dog show, she insisted on giving me gas money, yet she would never let me pay her when she drove. She would take me to lunch to thank me for something extra I had done for the kids, but again, wouldn't think of letting me pay for her lunch at any time.

Once I took her boy with my son and me, when we attended a big convention out of state. Joan couldn't get away and I was thrilled to take Tommy and Jake together, since Jake would certainly have more fun with a friend along than just going with me. When we returned it seemed as though Joan felt obligated to me for life for taking Tommy, while I didn't feel that way at all. She had certainly paid for all his expenses and all I did was chaperone.

I loved the fact that Joan and I had the boys and our love of dogs in common. We would get together periodically to take the dogs on an outing when the boys were in school and while it was always nice to have someone to get together with, I began to realize over time that I somehow always felt inferior to her. I could never put my finger on it, exactly. It was a nagging apprehension I felt, just the same.

Joan was a perfectionist in every aspect of her life. I suspect now that it all had to do with being in control of everything. Getting in her car I always felt like it was newly off the showroom floor. Not a speck of lint. Windows sparkling clean. Certainly no piles of stuff all over the place, like in my car. It didn't take me long to start worrying if I hadn't cleaned up my own car before I would pick her up, if it were my turn to drive.

Then I started realizing that she had a way of throwing out little comments that would nag at me. If I'd suggest we do something a certain way she would quietly say, "Oh, come on, Christy, nobody does it that way." And she'd look over the top of her bifocals at me with a message that said, "Must I teach you everything?" After a while I started to doubt my own ability to make smart decisions.

If I would have a tough day and need to talk about something on my mind, she would say things that let me know she really didn't think anything in my life was a big deal, and quickly blow off whatever I was concerned about. I soon learned that she was not going to be a sympathetic ear, no matter what my circumstances.

By the same token, she didn't share much of her own private life. I never felt like I really knew her. It was such a missing link in our friendship. I felt like she knew everything about me, but would never let me know her on any deep level.

I got to be more and more tentative about spending time with her, as I realized I was developing anxiety about each little thing I did or said in her presence. The little cutting comments were always there. Never anything huge. Almost intangible. If I let Jake go to a movie that she thought wasn't appropriate for a 10 year old, she would let it be known that Tommy wasn't allowed to see "such trash." When I let Jake talk me into letting him take Karate lessons, Joan just let out a big sigh when I told her and then informed me how children shouldn't be exposed to violent environments – didn't I understand that? She wouldn't say another word about it, but the comment would leave me thinking hard about my decision for days. While I could justify all the positive attributes of Karate – the strength, self-discipline, agility, and others – all I could think about was that perhaps I was jeopardizing Jake's emotional well-being.

Once she stopped by when Jake had another little friend over and the boys were rough-housing in the living room. I could just see her get tense and even more quiet than usual, just watching their behavior. When I asked her if anything was wrong, she just said, "I didn't realize you let Jake behave that way in the house."

Just one more jab to the fact that my parenting skills were not what they should be.

At last I just couldn't take it anymore. I was emotionally drained whenever I knew we were going to get together. I started backing down from our usual activities, claiming that I was more busy than usual. While we were still involved in the 4H activities, I quit volunteering for all the extra activities I used to enjoy doing, just so I could extricate myself from the situation.

One day she emailed me and asked why we weren't spending so much time together anymore. I tried to give her a response that I thought would sound OK, but she saw through it and sort of called me on the carpet for the infraction. I guess I reached a point of no return and told myself if she really wanted to know, then I'd tell her the truth about my distancing behaviors.

I wrote her about the many feelings I had, being her friend. I explained how all the little off-hand comments made me feel. How I had almost become paranoid about keeping my car and house spotless, when I knew she might be by. How the anxiety I was feeling each time I knew we were going to spend time together had begun to outweigh the warm feelings I used to remember in other friendships I had experienced over the years. How I felt inferior to her and I knew I had no reason to. How her thick, outer shell that she hid behind had never allowed me to get truly close to her to begin with. How I just couldn't take it anymore.

Her email back to me was scathing. She told me that all my feelings were in my imagination. That I was paranoid. That I must be the one with the problem.

She denied any of the incidents I had described from our times together that had left me feeling uncomfortable. And she closed the email with, "It's no wonder you don't have any real friends."

That was it. There was no further communication. It was one of the most uncomfortable things I have ever had to do, but once the crisis was over, the relief was so intoxicating! I didn't spend so much of my life worrying about myself each time she was coming over. I didn't have to keep wondering what I might do wrong whenever we'd get together. I didn't keep second-guessing myself about my role as a parent.

The best part is that in leaving Joan behind, I made room in my life for other friends who have since filled the space. Real friends. People who give and take, support and listen, help without judging, and share their personal fears and hopes without strings attached. It is so refreshing to find the difference and realize how wonderful true friends can be. I look forward to getting together with them without anxiety. I can't wait to be with them. They are the first people I run to with my successes as well as my failures and I know they will accept me either way.

The best lesson I learned was this: Don't let your friendships be anything less than equal and caring. If you do, you're only cheating yourself in the process.

Stacy

Susan and I had been friends for a long time before I began to recognize her behaviors as narcissistic and not healthy for me. She would bring her muddy dog over to my condo all the time and expect me to open my arms and my house to the animal's destructive behavior. After tiring of cleaning up after him on more occasions than I can recall, I finally suggested she leave him home when she came to visit. She became furious with me and said, "If you don't appreciate my dog, then I guess we just can't be friends." For the longest time I gave in.

She was a great one for coming over all the time and crying on my shoulder every time something didn't go right in her life. I had no problem giving her a safe place to vent, yet whenever I was having difficulty with something and would try to share it with her, she would blow me off, as if I didn't exist.

She'd make promises to me all the time and then break them at the last minute. "Let's go to the coast this week, Stacy," she'd say. "We can spend the weekend at my parent's house and have a great time." So, I'd get all excited about the upcoming weekend, be packed and ready to go, and at the last minute she'd always call and cancel. There would never be a crisis or some earth-shattering event that had made her cancel either – she would simply have changed her mind.

Worse yet would be the times she'd call me on Tuesday or so after the weekend we had been scheduled to be away and she'd end up telling me what a great time she'd had with an old boyfriend she'd gone out dancing with instead. One time she cancelled on me and ended up going to Hawaii at the last minute with another friend, then spent hours telling me all about it later.

I lent her $400 to pay her rent a while back. Months have gone by and not only has she not returned it, she hasn't even mentioned it, nor did she ever really thank me for bailing her out to begin with. I know if it had been me needing to borrow from a friend, I would have felt tremendous guilt until I could pay it back. It was almost as though she saw it as my obligation for being her friend.

She'd tell me how she and her family would love to have me over for Christmas dinner and about the fabulous gifts she had bought me for the event, but neither of those things would ever transpire and while I'd turned down other offers for my holiday dining, her last minute cancellation left me with few options left for the day.

By the time she approached me to lend her rent money again, I was starting to understand that this was not a good friendship for me, and I refused to lend her the money. She wasn't happy with me and tried to "educate me" that friends do these things for each other. I held my ground.

Shortly thereafter my grandfather died and I went into a depression that left me totally overwhelmed and non-functional for the better part of a week. She stopped over to use my computer one day and while I agreed, I told her she'd have to help herself, as all I was able to do at that time was sleep. She barely noticed my condition and certainly didn't offer any help, as she jumped onto the computer to do her business.

Days later, I was still in an emotional fog walking down the street in our neighborhood. I was so grief-stricken and lost that I could barely see. I noticed Susan walking towards me. Much to my surprise she walked right past me – completely ignoring me! I couldn't believe it. Here I was, in my darkest moment in years, and she couldn't even speak to me. When she finally called me days later and I asked why she hadn't talked to me, the bottom line was two-fold: Basically she was still angry at me for not lending her the money. ("Real friends help each other out when they need it, Stacy.") In addition, she told me to "get over it," referring to the death of my grandfather, who had been my primary caretaker for most of my life.

I realize now that I used to enable her. Now I don't call her anymore or engage in her conversation. If she calls me, I get off the phone as soon as possible. I just don't need her sucking the energy right out of me. I understand that she's only using me. I gave and gave and gave of myself and received nothing in return. I felt it was my job to be the caretaker and make everybody else happy, but I was so very wrong!

What I've come to realize is that it's all a crock. These people will just use you until there's nothing of you left. No one needs a friend like that in their life.

If you find yourself in a "friendship" with a narcissist, get out as soon as you possibly can. They're like leaches. They'll just suck you dry and toss you out when they've finished.

Nobody deserves to be treated that way. Nobody.

> *"I was constantly under the fear of rejection, criticism, and angry verbal attacks."*
> *Simone – survivor*

Chapter 12
A Word About Women Abusers

The usual picture of the abuse victim from newspapers to the big screen is most commonly a woman. Stereotypically, a small, weak, low self-esteem, and lower socioeconomic woman at that. Generally, someone who can't defend herself and has been taken advantage of by a brut, a cad, or a villain much like the monster of a man in the 1991 movie *Sleeping With the Enemy*, starring Julia Roberts. (Although, I dare say, Julia's role broke a bit of the stereotype itself, as she was married to a very wealthy and respected member of the community whose friends would never have dreamed of his abusive behavior behind closed doors.)

Yes, women have been abused (physically, sexually, verbally, and emotionally) by men for centuries. However, women can also be the abusers. As I mentioned earlier, women narcissists are out there as well, and in huge numbers. Trust me, I get those stories too.

Would you recognize one? They don't all deliver cuts, bruises, or broken bones, and thus may remain unnoticed by society. Yet the injuries they inflict can do more long-term damage than most would ever believe.

In fact, women oftentimes can wreak about as much havoc on those in their environment as their male counterparts. Some are even clever actors who can morph from June Cleaver to Cruella De Ville in a moment's notice. They can be manipulative bosses, name-calling mothers, cunning grandmothers, caustic wives, nightmare employees, and, yes, condescending friends.

They come in all walks of life, all socio-economic groups, ages, and races. And they can deviously trap their hostages in a living hell before the unsuspecting victim has a clue what's about to happen.

What do narcissistic women look like?

While they can look perfectly sweet and innocent on the outside, in actuality they can be as treacherous as the deadly Nurse Ratched from the famous 1975 film, *One Flew Over the Cuckoo's Nest*. And they can use the exact same methodology as their male counterparts. They can employ physical punishment, beating and/or torturing children or anyone less capable than they are (aging parents?). They can demand or withhold sex, using it as a weapon, or can cheat on their spouses without apparent conscience. They can name-call to the point that the victim is left feeling vile, unimportant, and as though he (or she) doesn't exist. They can deliver the silent treatment as punishment for perceived wrongs. They can even hold all the purse strings, not allowing their husbands or family members to have so much as their own allowance. And they can prohibit their loved ones from even interacting with friends and extended family.

Want some real examples?

✓ The woman who never takes responsibility for anything that goes wrong in her life and blames everyone else around her for her unhappiness.

✓ The 94-year-old mother with a senior citizen son, who is still calling him demeaning names. His ongoing attempts to win his mother's approval (even after all these years) has left him feeling like a failure at most things he tries and wondering why she still believes he is such a loser.

✓ The mother who constantly tells her grown daughter in front of her grandchild that she wishes she'd had an abortion instead of giving birth to her. That the daughter is, in fact, the worst excuse for a mother she's ever seen. (Now there's the pot calling the kettle black!)

✓ The woman who never has a kind thing to say about anyone and yet is quick to offer criticism to all in her path.

✓ The woman who continually "forgets" to give birthday or Christmas presents to her "loved ones," yet expects substantial gifts and attention lavished on her when her birthday and other holidays roll around.

✓ The wife of a decent, kind man whom she constantly belittles about everything he does, from how he dresses, to how much money he makes, to how he makes love, to how he bathes the children.

✓ The female employee who makes everyone feel as though they must walk on eggshells around her, as she in fact ignores everyone else, refusing to engage in conversation or even acknowledge anyone else's presence or value but her own.

✓ The mother who teaches her children to be shameful for any misbehavior they might experience, and then proceeds to remind them of their shameful selves as long as possible, ensuring the development of their low self-esteem.

✓ The condescending adult sister who loves to tell her grown siblings how they are terrible parents, undermines everything they do with their kids, and then attempts to guilt trip them about why they don't visit her more often.

✓ The mother of a 12-year-old child who punished her for misbehaving by submerging her in a tub of scalding water. The child needed hospitalization and skin grafts.

✓ The woman who hides behind her religion and uses it as her power base, threatening the wrath of God and being quite happy to lay guilt on anyone else in her world who does not follow Biblical teachings to the degree that she does.

I could go on and on ...

Reading the Victim Signs

Yes, women can be incredibly caustic and clever narcissists. And because society more generally expects women to be the victims, we may miss reading the telltale signs of abuse these women impose upon their victims on a day-to-day basis, slowly chipping away their very souls, bit by painful bit. For who would suspect some five foot two, one hundred pound female as being treacherous?

Just as with victims of abuse from male perpetrators, victims of women abusers may show increasing signs of depression, anxiety, gastrointestinal symptoms, sleep problems, Post Traumatic Stress Disorder, or a wide variety of other illnesses as a result of the nightmare environment they live in. Unfortunately, they may not recognize this emotional war zone that may be at the root of these problems.

John

I was married for 28 years to my high school sweetheart, and God knows how I made it that long. I should have seen the danger signs way ahead of time, as there were certainly enough of them to make me pay attention, and yet I ignored them all. Least of which was at our wedding rehearsal dinner when Betty got mad and dumped a can of soda on my head in front of everyone! You'd think I would have gotten a hint then that things to come were not as I was hoping. Of course, by not immediately standing up to her for such behaviors, this only started my unhealthy pattern of continually accepting inappropriate and abusive actions on an ongoing basis, both emotionally and physically.

Over the next few years she even managed to alienate me from my family and friends and I just kept letting her. Somehow we had four children, and she became more highly controlling over my time as well as theirs. I had no time for myself, working all day, and the moment I came in the door the kids were dumped on me. She continually wanted more and more of me.

She had an insatiable appetite for owning material things and began shopping as her outlet, hobby, and lifestyle. She filled up every nook and cranny of our 7,000-square-foot house with shopping bags. Rooms were impassable as the merchandise was overwhelming. She bought things she had no use for. Her goal was possessing things and spending money we didn't have. Floors were piled high with unopened shopping bags, beds were unusable with piles of wet towels and dirty clothes which were mixed in with brand new clothing. There were tables stacked feet high with newspapers, leftover food, and old pizza boxes. There were even partially eaten hamburgers shoved between the stacked bags. The cats ran through the house urinating on everything. Mice were all over the house. It was atrocious.

> *She actually bought a pillow that said, "Spend more than your husband makes, it will keep him motivated."*

If the children or I ever touched or moved "her" stuff she would go ballistic. Her temper was out of control. She would grab the steering wheel of the car, scream obscenities in public, run out into traffic … whatever it took to totally manipulate the family into getting her way.

Unfortunately I was laid off three times over the duration of our marriage and she would throw it in my face that I was an inadequate breadwinner, when I actually made a very good income as an engineer. She bent over backwards to be a socialite and she started running with the rich and famous, volunteering for charity events and other such activities, just to be mixing it up with the wealthy. She desperately wanted to get noticed and accepted in their world of diamonds and money. Although I was reluctant, we went to every function with the elite, spending hundreds and thousands of dollars for top seating at these "privileged" events. She even insisted that the whole family wear the same color outfits and that the girls be decked out in matching dresses. Everyone just had to look perfect!

My voice was never heard and I was told over and over again that I was insignificant. The relationship was also based on the "her way or the highway" principle. Our public façade of substantial wealth and happiness came crashing down after the ongoing credit card debts exceeded $200,000 and the house went into foreclosure. I was left to mop up Betty's mess as the judge who decided our divorce told me to, "Take care of all the debt"!

I'm still picking up the pieces, emotionally and financially, years later. God knows what unhealthy issues my kids gleaned from all of this. If only I'd heeded the Red Flags she showed me from the beginning.

Helping Male Victims

When women are the victims of abuse, they may be open to discussing their feelings and situation with others since this is one of the key ways that women solve their issues – by communicating with their gal friends and/or therapists to help find clarity and understanding in confusing situations that may leave them feeling lost, confused, or in pain. Although some women seem to stay stuck in abusive relationships (for many reasons), at least it seems to be more the norm that they still share their problems and pain with someone they can connect and converse with.

With men, however, coping skills are often quite different. Men don't often chat over coffee about their relationships and many simply don't easily share their feelings with their buddies, much less a well-meaning therapist.

Of course, in our macho culture, admitting that one's wife is a husband abuser just doesn't make a man a "man's man" either. Admitting this situation to male counterparts (or others) may seem like emotional suicide to some. And admitting that they've seen a shrink may be a bigger fear to some men than simply "taking it" from their narcissistic wives and girlfriends at home.

In addition, since the majority of support groups for these types of victims tend to be comprised of mostly females, men might not be made to feel welcome (or in some cases even at ease) because some female members may feel uncomfortable with any male presence in their midst. Thus, any unlucky males who are trapped in these abusive nightmares may find it even more difficult to explain their situations, feelings, and concerns to anyone they can trust, let alone take the next steps to safely extricate themselves from their unhealthy situations. Many feel lost and confused and simply don't know where to turn for help.

Educating men about the intricacies of these abusive, narcissistic individuals and, specifically, Narcissistic Personality Disorder, may be the first line of defense for many who are walking in the dark, questioning their own sanity.

As I've said over and over, knowledge is power. Enlightening these frustrated men to the wealth of knowledge available regarding this subject may be their first hopeful step towards determining their future course and plans. Realizing that they are not going crazy, (nor are they all alone with their feeling of being lost and confused as victims of narcissism), can give many the first keys to unlocking the doors to emotional freedom and healthy change. And it can finally allow the formation of new paths to healing.

Educating our communities and getting the media to recognize and talk about the fact that abuse does not just involve the typical male brute, but can also include the covert stealth manipulations of the female of the species might just make the difference for so many who feel trapped in these unrecognized emotional nightmares.

In addition, educating our society that abusive women can be as pathological as men and may cause vast destruction to those in their path (including their children who generally have no say in their situations), is vital to protection of all. For no matter what their sex, a narcissist can cause tremendous pain and suffering to absolutely everyone – even their own kids – as hard as that is to believe.

With this in mind it is also helpful for lawyers, judges, and child advocates to remain open-minded about whom the best caregivers are for children in divorcing families. While mothers seemed to have traditionally carried a strong influence as the natural caregivers in our culture, automatically handing custody of the children off to a woman just because she's a woman can, in cases involving women narcissists, mean sending them off to unhealthy environments filled with horrific emotional destruction.

This is where psychiatric evaluations of both parents can be a key in determining the welfare and best placement of the children. They can sometimes be the only tool in uncovering the otherwise hidden, unhealthy behaviors of whichever parent may be the narcissistic one; especially when their outward demeanor may be sickly sweet.

Remember, women can be great actors too and can fool the courts, the psychiatrists, and everyone else involved. There is no gender discrimination among narcissists.

> *So the next time you see on TV or in film*
> *those wickedly funny women (like the character Jane Fonda*
> *plays in the movie **Monster-in Law**), don't laugh so hard.*
> *These women are as real as the men we see*
> *in mug shots and in the news each and every day ...*
> *but too many times we just don't see them*
> *through their pearls and lace.*

Part Two
The Victims Tell Their Stories

"It's almost like they sit in the eye of the hurricane
and enjoy watching the total chaos they create,
as their loved ones go whirling around them.
Whenever there's a lull in the storm
and the winds die down,
they simply find a way to get things
all stirred up and turbulent again."
Monica – survivor

Chapter 13
When Things Change

Many things seem to change dramatically when you're in a relationship with a narcissist. Sometimes we just miss the Red Flag behaviors from the start, or circumstances change that seem to only enlarge the narcissist's view of himself. If you thought things were bad to begin with, there is still room for them to become horrific. Living with "God" isn't an easy road to travel.

Jordan

Randy and I married right out of college. We had been high school sweethearts for years. Being from a small town in Montana, I was pretty naive about the ways of the world. Since I had known him for years and had felt like I had almost been part of his family for so long, the marriage seemed to make perfect sense. It's ironic as I look back now, at all the Red Flags that should have stopped me in my tracks.

During our premarital counseling with the minister of our church, one of the questions he asked was how Randy might feel if, five years down the road, I was in a horrible accident and it left me severely disfigured me. Would he still love me?

Randy's immediate answer was, "It depends upon the disfigurement."

I think he took both the minister and me off-guard with that one. If either of us were thinking straight, we should have stopped right there and dug a bit deeper into his motives and feelings about love, marriage, and the rest. Instead, we both just bit out tongues and went on. In hindsight that was probably the first true look I had behind his mirror to see the real person he kept all of us from seeing.

Getting on the marriage preparation roller coaster seems to make your vision blur about a lot of things! We went ahead with our wedding. There were still plenty of Red Flags screaming at me but I continued to ignore them. The night before the wedding my sister sensed my apprehension and told me that if I wanted to back out, there was still time. To which my narcissistic mother said, "Of course she can't do that now. It's too late."

I remember thinking about all this again as I was walking down the aisle with my uncle on my arm. He actually turned to me and said, "Smile, you look scared to death!"

We started out as any young married couple – broke, but full of hope and energy. I had always admired Randy's passion and dreams of getting ahead. He pursued what he wanted but how he went about it was disturbing. He took excessive risks. He mowed people over along the way. As a psychologist, I observed his behavior with mixed vision. On the one hand, he was my husband and I just figured that's how married life was supposed to be. Yet, on the other hand, my friends in my profession would question me and speak up about his rather ruthless, risk-taking behavior.

Our sex life was very convoluted. He developed a habit of throwing little, subtle cuts my way all day – you're too skinny, too fat, you didn't make dinner right, and things like that. He would even tease me that he was planning on trading me in for a younger woman someday. Then at night I was supposed to jump into bed with him and make passionate love. Once he had gotten me into bed, I always felt like I was with an awkward, little kid. All his big talk about his sexuality and virility were really just an exaggeration of the truth. He really wasn't a particularly good lover.

On the other side of the coin, whenever I was ready and excited to make love, he wouldn't have anything to do with me. He would leave the house and not return for hours. It left me totally confused and filled with self-doubt. I was always unsure what to expect on any given evening. Little did I realize then that it was all about control.

Our marriage was very rocky. We even separated several times throughout the years. He would just come home unexpectedly and tell me that he was moving out and he would leave me for months at a time. Sometimes he wouldn't actually tell me first – I would just see a "for rent" sign in our apartment window and I would know that he was off again. I would grieve and get depressed and mourn his loss for weeks. Then, about the time I would get resettled and rebuild my self-esteem again, he would show up on my doorstep and beg me to take him back. We'd make up, plan a new start somewhere else, and get back into our old ways again. This pattern seemed to go on every few years, although I could never figure out what triggered it.

Eventually he fell into an extremely lucrative job and the money came in by the carloads. We moved to Chicago where he became famous in the business world and he was in the paper and on TV all the time. They even came and did photo shoots with him and our four young sons.

As we began spending more time with the jet-setting, affluent crowd, Randy was sure to tell me not to tell anyone that I was a psychologist. I guess he didn't see it as a proper role for the wife of someone so important.

In addition, he was a great one to flirt with all the women in his circles. He is very handsome and they hung on his every word and glance. He ate up all the attention and thrived. But he showed no interest in me. The more successful he became at work, the more difficult he became to deal with at home. He wanted me to be the perfect wife for his new perfect world and if I didn't meet his expectations, there was obviously something wrong with me.

Of course, we had to move up to a fancier house and have all the proper looks and toys that went with his ever-increasing power position in the Chicago business community. I found it almost funny when he started applying for memberships in country clubs and the one he wanted into the most wouldn't take him – his money was too new! That set him off in a rage for some time.

> *He loved to refer to everyone around him as "idiots."*
> *There were only a select few individuals that he felt were*
> *equal to him, and they were mostly people he needed*
> *in one capacity or another.*

People he secretly had to admit were more knowledgeable than he was in a given area. He believed he was the King of All Knowledge in his world, while he turned into the King of Hell in mine. His expectations of me soared right along with his expectations of himself. My ability to do anything right fell in his eyes, as he continued to be admired and glorified by colleagues and the press.

During all these years together he was less than a loving dad. He was almost like a politician ... he had to have that ideal family image to get him where he wanted to be. When he was with the kids in public he appeared to be the best dad anyone could ever ask for. He threw them in the air and made them laugh. He bought them expensive toys to win their favor.

Yet, he never knew how to show them real love. He could never make time to attend their soccer games or Boy Scout events. I can count on less than all ten fingers how many times he showed up at their activities and even then he'd make an appearance and need to leave right away. Of course his competitive nature did overflow into this area, however. He would get furious with the boys if they came home and said they'd lost the game. Once, he even told our oldest son, Dan, he'd pay him five dollars for any kid on the opposite team that he could "take out" of the game – meaning do injury to – so that the other boy was unable to play! Talk about leaving a child confused. On the one hand the Boy Scouts were trying to teach him good sportsmanship and on the other, his father was attempting to pay him to hurt other little boys he competed against in soccer.

I remember he used to break our youngest son's heart all the time. Adam was the most sensitive one and at age 6 he still enjoyed hugs and kisses regularly. As Randy was on his way out the door each morning, Adam would say, "Bye, Dad. I love you." All he wanted was to hear his father echo that sentiment back, but Randy just couldn't do it. Poor Adam used to ask me all the time if his father loved him. What could I tell him?

To add insult to injury, when his dad would walk in the door at the end of the day, Adam would run to him to give him a big hug, but the first words out of Randy's mouth, as he grabbed Adam's hands before his could touch the expensive Armani suit was, "Are your hands clean?" After a while, Adam quit offering to hug his father at all.

There were other demeaning, devaluing little comments that just kept adding up over the years. I'll always remember one Christmas Eve as we were driving to the family Christmas party. We were all in the car and had Christmas carols playing on the radio. It was about 6 p.m. and the snow was beautiful, gently swirling around us in the black, night air. Everyone was excited about the holiday festivities and it was all the boys could do to stay reasonably composed on the 30-minute drive to their grandmother's house. The kids and I were all vigorously singing along with the carols when Randy suddenly boomed, "Can't you all be quiet? How can anyone hear the music, if you're all singing?"

The mood in the car changed instantly. My little one secretly reached his right hand up to grab mine.
It was our usual pattern of recognizing when Dad was upset when we were in the car.

Randy never once noticed that Adam and I were comforting each other with our hands near the door of the car. The other boys stopped talking altogether and just looked out the window for the rest of the drive.

I was both angry and confused. Randy always knew how to throw us a curve when we least suspected it, and Christmas was no exception. When we finally parked the car, the boys ran ahead and I did my best to hurry in as well, when Randy interjected, in a hurt tone of voice, "What, isn't anyone going to wait for me?" He was oblivious as to how his demand for silence in the car had pulled everyone back into their shells with the hopes that they wouldn't have to interact with him any further.

It was like that all the time. The instability. The manic-depressive fluctuations of mood. The complete inability to empathize with anyone else's feelings or needs. The world only revolved around Randy's daily needs. He could never see beyond his reality.

Of course, for those on the outside looking in, we looked like the perfect family. Tons of money. Great house. Great kids. Husband with notoriety and a great job. People must have thought we were like the Kennedys in Camelot. Surely they saw that Randy provided us with the best in anything money could buy. The kids all went to private school. He even approached me about sending them to boarding school at one time, but I wouldn't hear of it.

If only onlookers could understand how it felt to live behind those closed doors. It was like walking on eggshells every single day. The emotional ups and downs were chronically draining. The self-doubt, depression, anxiety, and stress I developed only grew worse each year. The guilt that I took on was a constant companion.

I always kept thinking that everything was my fault. That if I would just try harder, be a better wife, a better mother, a better support system for my family, that everything would be fine. But none of it was true. It took me years of therapy later to realize that Randy would not be happy no matter what I did or who I was. No matter how old he lives to be, he will just never be satisfied with himself, therefore how can he be satisfied with anyone else?

One of his other problems came in the form of a bottle. He was a great lover of beer and could go through a 12-pack on a Sunday – especially if it was a hot summer day. He never considered it a problem until he was arrested twice within a handful of years for driving while under the influence of alcohol. Of course he blamed everybody else but himself for the problem. It was the cop's fault. It was the judge's fault. He was just fine, "Thank you very much!" The fact that the blood levels came back well within the intoxication levels meant nothing to him. The only thing that had meant anything was that he'd been caught. Of course he was able to pay for the best lawyer in town who handled alcohol-related cases and got off with community service. So once again he beat the system without much pain or damage.

Of course, the damage he did to our sons the night he was arrested for the first DUI is hard to quantify. They were excitedly waiting for him to come home to help them carve their Halloween pumpkins, after Randy had attended the Sunday football game with his buddies. Instead, in celebration of some coup they had pulled off at work, the guys went to the local girlie bar after the game and that's where he had too much to drink, got arrested, and then completely missed the pumpkin carving activities as a result.

Once again, his needs took precedent over theirs. My heart broke for the kids when he never showed up, as promised. What was worse was when one of them answered the phone when the police called to notify us of Randy's arrest. It was all so sad.

As life went on after the DUI, I became the designated driver whenever we went out together. That was fine with me, as I wasn't much of a drinker. However, by the time we would drive home Randy would be quite full of himself and would lecture me all the way home about my driving, the route I chose, how fast I drove (never fast enough) – everything. I bit my tongue and tried to ignore it most of the time, but once I almost lost my cool. There was a driver behind me who insisted on tail-gaiting me – his brights glaring in my rear-view mirror. While I was driving the speed limit, he apparently didn't think I was going fast enough and I felt like he was climbing up my butt. After a few minutes, I decided to just pull over and let him go ahead of me. Yet, as soon as I did, Randy flew into a rage. He chastised me for not sticking my ground. "Let the bastard sit there. He can just wait!" he growled at me. I heard about how stupid I was for giving way all the way home. Ah, the vision and knowledge of a drunken, back-seat driver!

At last I filed for divorce. It was bittersweet for me, as I really didn't want to break up our home for the sake of our kids. Yet I just couldn't take the Jekyll and Hyde behaviors every day. I couldn't take the continuous pressure to be perfect, to perform as if we lived our lives like actors in a movie. And I didn't think it was healthy to let our boys go on living like that either.

> *Everything had become about Randy's image to the world. There was no depth to anything. And there were certainly no feelings, no sharing, and no love.*

The divorce was ugly, as I should have expected. He blamed me for all of it. He agreed to allow me to move back near my family but it cost me in dollars and cents. I got much less of the divorce settlement as the compromise. I guess you could say that he sold off the rights for his children in order to keep more money in his pocket. I didn't care. I wanted to get as far away from him as possible. I was an emotional wreck and I just needed space and a safe place to heal.

The custody arrangement allowed for the boys to fly out to visit him on regular occasions, or for him to come see them here. For a while they found it exciting to fly to go see Daddy, but over time they were less inclined to want to visit. He was busy with his many girlfriends, his new big fancy homes, and staying in the limelight. He had a favorite bar he frequented often and had no qualms about taking our oldest son Dan, who was 16 at the time, out with him for the evening. At first Dan was impressed but soon discovered that young women not much older than he would hang on his father for hours, sometimes going home with them at the end of the evening to spend the night with him. He started seeing another side to his father he didn't much care for.

One time I took the kids for their visit with him, as I decided to see some friends in the area while he was spending his time with them. One day during their week together, my oldest boy called me all upset and wanted to talk to me about something important. I called Randy and suggested that I take Dan out for the afternoon, as he was obviously concerned about something. He agreed and although I never exactly figured out what was on Dan's mind, he seemed to feel better just getting together with me for the afternoon.

I knew Randy was having a party that same day and figured I should get Dan back before the party was over. By the time we arrived Randy was in an intense rage for my tardiness in returning my son to him. Yelling at me at the top of his lungs, with spit flying in my face, he didn't seem to care that he was carrying on that way in front of all his friends and colleagues. He was even furious with Dan for not obeying him and being present for the entire event.

Dan told me later that Randy then proceeded to totally destroy Dan's hockey sticks and other athletic gear in front of him, as retaliation for his tardiness. He carried on like this for 10 minutes while some of his friends tried to calm him down. As he was destroying Dan's things he shouted at him, "You have no respect for me, you pathetic excuse for a man. You embarrassed me in front of my friends." Dan was so frightened and confused that he had no idea what to do. One of the neighbors kept pounding on the door asking if he was alright and he didn't even know whether or not to respond. Needless to say, he hasn't had an interest in more visits with his father and fortunately, he's old enough to say no. He's not a child anymore. He knows he's beyond the court dictating his time with his father at this point.

At the same time Dan refused further contact with him, he kept begging me for answers as to what was wrong with his father. Dan recognized my education in psychology and didn't understand why I had no magic wand to wave to make him better. I finally went to see a psychiatrist for my own sanity. I didn't last long with the first few, as they each told me everything was all my fault. The recurrent answer I found from them was that "we all need a little healthy narcissism in our life." I knew they were wrong and so I kept looking for someone who could help me identify and understand the problem.

Finally, I found someone who was educated about the depths of this disorder. After I spent only 15 minutes with him, explaining the situation, he diagnosed Randy's problem as Narcissistic Personality Disorder. The incredible thing is that I was a psychologist for years and never knew about so many of the subtle signs and behaviors involved in this complicated disorder. Sure, I understood the diagnosis and had seen a few narcissistic patients, but they had been overtly abusive people who had other psychological issues as well. I had no idea that the behaviors involved in this disorder could be so insidious, all-encompassing, and so virulent. I was dazed when I started investigating the information my new therapist gave me. Suddenly everything made so much sense. Yet I hadn't ever recognized it. Just knowing about the ins-and-outs of this disorder has given me better ammunition in dealing with it. It's also let me stop blaming myself for so many things that were really never my fault to begin with.

I think the best analogy I have come up with when I think of Randy is this: It's like he has a parrot on his shoulder constantly reminding him that he's no good.

> *I remember him occasionally saying, "With everything I have accomplished, why do I still feel like such a failure?" When his needs aren't met it's like he's just being re-injured over and over. It must be awful to feel that way all the time.*

Unfortunately, when you have children together, you can never completely remove yourself from the weird world your ex lives in. He continues to try to control me in every way imaginable. Even hundred of miles away.

While he dated much younger women immediately and eventually remarried, he had his lawyer inform me that I wasn't allowed to have any relationships as long as I had custody of the boys. He even threatened me if I dared consider getting involved with someone. I guess the rules he makes up for his kingdom are designed to suit his needs and the rest of us "idiots" simply aren't entitled to be happy. I'm hoping that since he has new children with his young wife, that maybe he'll cut the kids and me a bit of slack now, but I won't count on it.

Now she has to put up with him on a daily basis. I hope for her sake that he'll treat her better. I'm glad that I escaped with my self-esteem a bit scarred and wounded, but completely repairable.

My advice to people getting married now is, "Listen to your inner voice! Look for and heed the Red Flags. They're there for a reason!" If it means saying no at the last minute at the altar, that's better than making a mistake that you will pay for the rest of your life! I wish someone would have told me that. Many years of my life might have been so much different.

Chapter 14
Who Is This Person?

The Dr. Jekyll and Mr. Hyde phenomenon that occurs in relationships with narcissists is a regular theme among those who sent me their stories. Soaring with the extreme highs of new love with the most incredible, romantic, unbelievably perfect man or woman of your dreams is tantamount to a romance novel or soap opera. So many of us pray and hope for such a relationship, but we never truly think it can *really* happen. Then, when it does, there is such fear of losing such bliss that many are blinded when Dr. Jekyll behaves like the deadly Mr. Hyde. They ignore the Red Flags and the gut feelings that keep trying to tell them something's wrong because they know "Mr. Perfect" was not a figment of their imagination. He was very *real*. And so, if he's suddenly Mr. Hyde momentarily, they are convinced it is a temporary situation and that their perfect partner will return any minute, if they are just patient enough.

In addition, victims keep going over and over in their own minds what they did "wrong" to sabotage the relationship. They convince themselves if they just figure out what *not* to do, that they can make everything "go back to normal" when all was magical, wonderful, and utterly perfect.

If only they knew just how wrong their belief is!

Another prevalent theme among victims is the feeling that when the perfect partner leaves (or she leaves him), that he will treat his next significant other differently. They envy the new person in the narcissist's life and are convinced the new love is being treated perfectly, or at least better, than they were. Of course the new partner will know better than to *ever* do anything that might upset Mr. Perfect. She will live the life of the fantasy world that the discarded victim once held. She wouldn't *dream* of making the same mistakes that the first victim did. She's probably smarter, more beautiful, thinner, or more understanding than the first victim. Isn't *everyone*? Isn't that what he told his first victim over and over? They remain paralyzed with guilt, confusion, and sorrow and continue to blame themselves for the loss.

Despite the fact that most of us realize people don't change easily and that logic would dictate if someone behaves a certain way with one person, he will also behave that way with another, the fantasy of the lost, past *perfect* love now seemingly given unconditionally to another, permeates their minds like a malignant cancer. Many just don't seem to be able to irradiate their cancer and move on to a clean bill of health.

Perhaps Marti and Erica's accounts will help illuminate some light on this subject...

Marti and Erica

Marti and Erica didn't know each other last year, yet this year they sit with me and we talk of how they were both involved with the same narcissist. The fact that they even fell upon each other is remarkable, as they live several hundred miles apart. Yet when they found each other and began sharing stories of the same painful dance, their laughter and tears merged in a unique sisterhood.

Marti: A bright, beautiful, red-headed gal in her late 30s, with long, flowing locks and stylish professional fashion was well-educated and mature in the ways of the world. She had worked in business for years as a savvy sales rep and was very comfortable with both men and women. She had never been married and longed for a lifetime mate to start a family with.

Erica: Fresh out of an almost-19-year marriage and a bit cautious and still healing her wounds, she was none-the-less a strong woman with conviction and an independent streak. Her blonde hair and snappy, blue eyes sparked a spirit that was longing to get out, yet one that appeared a bit defiant and untamed.

Neither of them ever guessed they'd be swept off their feet by one very manipulative man.

Marti

I first met Gus online. While I'd done the Matchmaker scene for quite a while, it usually took a lot to get me to actually take the next step to meet someone. I was in the early stages of running my own small business, so time was a commodity and the thought of wasting it on meaningless coffees and dinners with guys who were nothing like what they appeared to be online, just didn't excite me. I would periodically reply to an email, take a phone call and meet someone, but was more often frustrated than excited. Sometimes I'd just walk away from the whole dating process for months at a time.

For some reason Gus was different. Once we connected, it was like we couldn't stop. After only 24 hours of emails and phone calls, I just *had* to meet him. Our first obstacle was that we lived six hours apart, but we knew we had to get together as soon as possible. We agreed to meet in a town halfway between us for a dinner date.

As his email had led me to believe, he turned out to be absolutely charming. He just "got me" instantly. Dinner was fabulous! We had this intense connection – a chemistry that was indescribable – both intellectually and physically. Two days later we rendezvoused for the weekend and we both knew what we were anticipating. I knew something special would happen once we connected overnight and of course it did. It was indescribable! I stayed three days more than I had planned. I barely thought about my business and even cancelled a speaking engagement just to stay with him. I was so caught up in his charms … in the magic. It was like I was hypnotized. All I could think about was him … and *us*.

By the end of seven days he asked me to marry him, and I had to say yes! How could I ever find someone like him again? I wasn't about to let him go! I sincerely believed there couldn't be another man like him in the world.

We immediately went ring shopping because Gus insisted that he didn't want me to go home without "proof" of how serious he was about us. As we excitedly hurried into the jewelry store, Gus, grinning ear to ear, announced to the clerk, "Today's our anniversary!" She smiled and said, "That's wonderful! How many years?" To which Gus replied, "Seven days!" I was flying. I guess I must have completely missed the quizzical look she gave us. We got a ring with seven stones to always remind us of our life-changing seven days together that had sent us in a direction we knew would last a lifetime.

While my rational mind kept sending me caution signals that no one got engaged in only seven days, my optimistic nature couldn't get over the wonderful gift God had given me. In fact, when friends (and even strangers) learned of our whirlwind romance they often told us their stories of love at first sight, quick engagements, and dozens of happy years of marriage! I could not imagine anything going wrong in this relationship because it was so absolutely perfect! Nothing could be so terrible that we couldn't possibly work it out. One of Gus' strengths was his incredible ability to listen, understand both sides of any issue, and to remain calm and compassionate no matter what the situation (even when I spilled red wine on his carpet). His demeanor was gentle, kind, and so polite; opening the car door for me each and every time, even buckling me into my seatbelt, which he made a big deal about doing so that he could "keep me safe," at the same time he'd sneak a kiss.

I felt so adored. It felt like he hung on each of my words and knew just what to say every second we were together. He made me feel like royalty. It was hard carrying on a relationship with a six-hour drive between us, but we were so in love we knew we could do anything necessary to keep it alive. He was so romantic. He would write poetry that swept me off my feet. He even bought a Webcam for my computer – a device rather like a video camera – so we could see each other while we emailed or chatted by phone. It was so great just to see him and hear his voice when I couldn't be with him. We were grateful to the latest technology for keeping us connected.

He was attentive to every detail; every word I wrote, every thing I said. It was like he lived just to make me happy. He even insisted on buying new tires for my car, as he was concerned that if I was going to be driving to see him very often, that he wanted me to be on the safest tires available.

Then came the flowers. I was hosting a big event one evening and he was unable to make the trip. I understood completely and didn't give it a second thought, so imagine my surprise when I arrived at the conference center and there was the largest arrangement of flowers I had ever seen! The note said, "If only I could be there with you tonight … All my love, Gus."

Romance, flowers, love letters, planning our future … He was my Prince Charming. He could do no wrong in my eyes. He had won my heart.

And then I started noticing subtle changes …

Quite honestly I really didn't get it at first. It started with little comments that seemed a bit quirky and out of place. For example, he told me one day that my actions spoke more to him than my words and he gave the example that he knew my favorite color was yellow, even though I'd told him it was purple. I laughed and said, "Actually, it *really is* purple."

"Of course it's not, Marti. Just look around your house. You have yellow things everywhere," he replied, almost speaking down to me as a parent might scold a child.

I agreed that, yes, the bedspread we were sitting on was yellow, but there was far more green everywhere, purple in some places, and even red. All decorating choices I liked, but truly if I had to pick a favorite color, it was purple … even in my company logo.

"No, it isn't," he countered. "I can see that plain as day. But if that's what you want to believe, you go right ahead and believe it. I know better."

I thought that was really odd, but harmless. Not so harmless, in reality – as I would later realize. He would say, "I will watch your actions, not what you say, to determine what you really mean."

On his first visit to my home I was overwhelmed with work, and as my office is in my house, it showed the effects of my stress by looking as though a tornado had struck. Although the rest of the house was in perfect order, I figured I'd just close the door to my messy office and not worry about sorting through the stacks of papers to tidy it up before he got here.

Well that idea didn't fly with Gus at all. He pressured me to let him see my office. I brushed off his request a couple of times, telling him that the room wasn't fit for man nor beast, but he became defensive and told me I was shutting him out of a part of my life. I must be keeping secrets from him. What was I hiding?

I promised him that I wasn't hiding anything, but that I was very embarrassed to have him see my office in such shambles. I finally gave in and opened the door. Of course there were no secrets or anything of particular interest other than the mess, but he became very quiet and withdrawn for the rest of the day. I thought this behavior a bit odd, but again, was so overwhelmed with the deep and incredible love we shared, that I just figured it wasn't a big deal. If he didn't mind my messy office, I guess I didn't mind showing him. Only now have I begun to realize that what he was showing me by that behavior was that he had absolutely no respect for my boundaries. By giving in, I never told him "no" and meant it. Thus, he just kept pushing my boundaries further and further – always testing the waters to see just how far he could go. He often said things like "I'm going to be your husband, so I have a right to …"

One particularly busy day he was back at his house, so many miles away, so we'd check in with each other often via the Webcam; longingly looking into each other's eyes, wishing we were together.

After talking for quite a while I told him that I really had to get some work done, so we said goodbye and I shut the Webcam off. He called back instantly and insisted that I keep it on so he could see my "beautiful face" any time he wanted. I smiled that he was so passionate and interested, but I told him I really found it hard to concentrate and I'd get nothing done knowing he was so close and distracting. He really insisted, but I stood my ground. So we said goodbye and agreed we'd talk later in the day.

When we got on the phone that night he was cold and silent. I couldn't figure out why he was angry. After much coaxing on my part, he confessed that he felt "hurt" that I wouldn't leave the Webcam on all day so that he could watch me.

I held to my earlier points about needing to focus and kept the discussion light, but I was really uncomfortable, even creeped out by what felt like voyeuristic and controlling behavior. He tried to make me feel that his interest was caring and romantic, but the little pangs of nausea I was getting didn't seem to be related to any foods I ate.

Most of the time things were great – *amazingly* great! Overwhelmingly great! Beyond description great! But over time, things became stranger and stranger. Our plan was to spend a few months dating, decide what changes one or both of us would make to bring us closer together geographically, then marry and move within a year. I began to learn that his grandiose plans were wishful thinking at best. It also became clear that if I gave up my business and life here to move to him, he'd never value or appreciate that I did so. He seemed to have great respect for my work unless it took me away from him for even a minute. While he wanted to know every minute detail of my life, it turned out that he didn't always like to share his. Sometimes he'd share with great depth, even on difficult issues and I'd feel really connected to him, yet other times a seemingly superficial question would make him furious. Several times he abruptly ended a conversation (not an argument) by saying he refused to talk about that subject any longer, period. Also, when I'd get a business call from a male colleague during business hours, he would instantly become jealous or cold and demand to know all about the person who called, yet a woman would occasionally call him at 3 a.m. and when I asked him about it he would get defensive and angry at my curiosity. Although his feelings were easily hurt, he was indifferent when mine were.

He appeared to care less and less about my needs and my life. All those first nights of listening to every word I said seemed to disappear. One night he called after I'd just found out that my stepfather had died. He was very sympathetic for about three minutes, but then he asked a question that made it obvious he wasn't listening. He admitted he was distracted and I nicely asked him to call me back when he was finished and we could talk. I really needed to feel that I had his full attention in my time of need.

There was a sudden chill at the other end of the phone. He icily said "fine," hung up, and never called back. I was stunned. In my darkest hour I was looking for a comforting partner and he suddenly turned into a cold, uncaring stranger. Then for the next several days we exchanged emails and voice messages whereby he chastised me for suggesting he call back when he was distracted. He said I was rude in pointing out his lapse of attention. "It's like pointing out to someone when they've farted," he quipped. He even said I should have been grateful for his "generosity," as he had called knowing I'd be hurting and I should have just kept talking even though I knew he wasn't listening. Never, not once, did he ask how I was feeling about my stepfather's death.

I couldn't believe the words coming out of his mouth. This mouth that had kissed me like no one else in my wildest dreams. This mouth that had whispered romantic poetry to me for hours on end. This mouth that had tasted my body and all its crevices. Who was this person attached to this mouth?! Certainly not the person I was choosing to spend the rest of my life with. Where did that man go?

These are a few of the "choice words" he emailed me after this incident:

Dear Marti,

I will be guarding my heart and emotions from this point on. I feel I have opened myself up prematurely to your personal attacks and therefore must protect my own feelings. The Bible says "it is better to have only a crust of bread to eat upon the rooftop than to feast with many in a house of contention" and I believe that to be true.

I have listened to your voice mails and am disappointed with your efforts at communication. I am growing weary of what I perceive to be a pattern of nitpicking over my phone etiquette. You must acquire a more effective method of conveying your thoughts...I am not stupid.

I believe about you what I have observed about you. I am not swayed by words to believe something I have not seen demonstrated, regardless of the frequency with which I hear the explanation. If I believe, after observing your *behavior*, that you are irresponsible, then I will not change my mind when you simply *say* with words that you are "a responsible person." In this regard you will only sway me with your *actions*. Furthermore, the continuous droning of statements not backed with observable behavior or perceptible intentions, only serves to shut me off.

Perhaps if you were to recognize these communication failures on your own *I would not have to hang up on you* and wait for your emotions to subside. Even better would be for you to restrict these intense emotional diatribes to written words in an effort to limit your verbosity and to focus on the important points and issues.

On another matter, you still play hide and seek with secrets only you can know. The fact you hesitate to allow me into certain areas of your house when we have promised to spend the rest of our lives together, is quite disturbing to me. This is not how a loving relationship should look.

Please be assured that I am standing by to help in any way that I am able, in spite of the impression I may have given by words or deeds, up until this moment.

Love always, Gus

I physically wanted to throw up. I had just returned from a visit with him and was still "under the ether" – madly, crazily in love and thinking of every way possible to be with him. There was no contention in my words or my heart. The intense coldness of his email and the unreasonable reaction to our conversation was so confusing. It just didn't make sense. In fact, one moment we'd have a loving phone call, then I'd check my email and there'd be a hurtful note that he had to have written before we talked! Then he'd send a note about a house we should buy together. Talk about Dr. J and Mr. Hyde!

Although my worries increased, I was still convinced that my perfect partner would return if we just understood each other better. I blamed the distance and limited time together and decided not to address certain issues until we were together, for surely it would be easier in person. I found that if I just dropped a tough subject, so did he, yet I felt more and more distant from him. Things sort of fell into a pattern of Gus getting upset and me being confused about why.

Then came an interesting weekend where I was being honored at a banquet for my work with the non-profit community. Gus was coming and I looked forward to including him in a special moment in my life. However, one of my growing worries was related to his heavy drinking. It wasn't uncommon for him to pour himself a vodka at 9 a.m. and I worried that alcohol could become a problem between us. I gingerly shared my concerns with him and he promised that drinking wouldn't be a problem because of his love for me. Of course he was in the limelight at the dinner, being on the arm of the guest of honor. He basked in my glory and I even introduced him to the audience as the man I was going to marry. Unfortunately, my fears were realized when he embarrassed himself and me by getting drunk after all. I was hurt and fearful that I was going to have to leave my perfect love because of alcohol, but in the morning he lovingly apologized, saying he never wanted to see that look of disappointment in my eyes ever again and he thanked me for not giving him a hard time. Once again, I melted.

Then one night, the Red Flag got bigger. It was past midnight and I was getting ready for bed. I had put on a cucumber mask, slipped into my flannel PJ's, and was about to fall asleep when the phone rang. It was Gus, and I was happy to hear his voice before falling asleep. After nearly an hour on the phone he surprised me by telling me that he was a mere four minutes away from my house! (He had been driving nearly six hours and hadn't given me a clue he was coming.) He wanted to talk all the way to my driveway, but I begged off in order to wipe the mask off my face and look presentable when he arrived. I would have to scramble to get it all done in four minutes!

He suggested I leave the door unlocked for him, but I said I'd just meet him at the door. (Living alone I wasn't comfortable leaving my door unlocked and I was racing for time as well.) He rang the doorbell and I opened the door within seconds, but when I saw his face I was startled. He was furious. He had transformed from my sweet, romantic man into someone I didn't recognize. His eyes shot bullets at me as I held the door opened for him and I softly questioned, "Gus, what's wrong?"

"It was extremely inconvenient for me to have to wait outside your door!" he cursed.

"But Gus, it was only a few seconds," I countered.

"It's just not right that you treat me that way, Marti. I'm your fiancé, for God sake!"

We argued and by that time I really didn't care if he stayed or went. In fact I remember saying that I was aghast that he would say he was inconvenienced when he was the one showing up in the middle of the night.

"I'm outta here," he bellowed, and then turned to go, but I could tell he didn't really want to. We talked it through and as it turned out, his sister had passed away and he told me he was on the way to her funeral. Of course my heart softened immediately. As we were making up, he shared with me how he had hated his sister and was torn about even going to the funeral. In the end, he didn't go and said it would be a "lesson" to his other siblings that if they didn't "straighten up" he wouldn't show up at their funerals either. (Can you say huge Red Flag?) He could never give me a reason for the intensity of his hatred, and although we made up once again, that Red Flag stayed with me and was perhaps the one that eventually began to get my attention. As of weeks later, he still hadn't even called his mother to see how she was handling the death of her daughter! I couldn't help but wonder how he'd treat me if he ever really got mad at me. For the first time I allowed myself to wonder what the truth was about why his children hate him – a fact that he had shared with me early-on.

Somehow, we spent a blissful weekend once again and then came the final straw. We were having such an incredible time together that I decided to cancel everything for the next week and drive back to his home with him. I was going to miss some huge meetings, but had decided it was worth it. I told him I'd go, but that I would need to get a little bit of work done before leaving. He agreed. While Gus waited for me to finish up that morning, he got bored and went to the store. When he came back he announced, "Clearly spending time with me is not important to you, so I'm going to take off." And he made motions to leave … right then.

I was totally shocked and taken off-guard. We'd discussed and agreed to the plan only a couple of hours earlier. So where did this angry response come from? I just didn't get it. Couldn't he see that I was canceling meetings, rescheduling work, printing paperwork to take along? I was totally rearranging my life and business to spend time unscheduled time with him. Didn't he appreciate all that I was doing? I was expected to understand when he had work to do.

On one hand I wanted to talk it through and work something out, rather than give up on our week together. Yet on the other hand, his irrational behavior made me actually fearful that his anger would lead to something I couldn't handle.

What if he drove like a crazy person and we ended up in a wreck? What if he just decided to throw me out on the side of the road? Or worse, what if, once we got to his house he decided he just didn't feel like driving me all the way home again? We had planned to take my dog and the thought of having to buy a plane ticket and bring my dog back in a crate on a plane made me think twice.

The caution signs started hitting me over the head. I finally recognized that I no longer felt safe and didn't know what to expect from this man.

At the same time I struggled with my own sense of integrity – I was wearing his ring and my word had always meant a lot to me. Knowing that if things were this chaotic so early in the relationship it would only get worse, I decided to hold my ground. When I told him that it just wasn't working out between us, he was astonished. Then, in defiance he asked, "Are you really breaking up with me?" Interestingly, he never asked why. He just stated that he was in this "for the long term" and that clearly I wasn't as committed.

Fortunately, a knowledgeable friend had begun to educate me about narcissism during the few weeks before that awful moment. She knew I was head-over-heels in love with Gus, but had seen the terrible signs in our relationship, so had been careful to feed me little bits of information whenever I had called her in tears and confusion. Her support and information gave me the strength to know that the situation would never change. So, instead of torturing myself with doubt about the "what ifs," I was able to end the relationship with certainty and the reality that a better future was waiting for me elsewhere, once I let go.

The education she gave me about this serious personality disorder literally saved my emotional well being. I started to understand the roller coaster ride I was on and see his behaviors for what they really were – controlling, manipulating, and outrageous. My "Perfect Gus" was just an act – nothing more than what Brad Pitt or any other movie star was capable of. One minute a knight in shining armor and the next minute a heartless, blood-sucking vampire. It was all just a wicked deception.

The sad difference, I realized, was that Brad Pitt knows he is acting. Gus doesn't. I felt terribly sad for him, for I knew he would never change nor understand who or what he really was. Yet, I understood my empathy for his illness didn't mean I had to marry him. That would have been the biggest mistake of all. No matter how incredible the good stuff was with us, the bad stuff wasn't tolerable.

If you do not feel sane or safe in your relationship, get out. Listen to your gut. Don't ignore the warning signs. I was lucky. It only cost me 12 weeks of my life. It could have been so much worse. Now

I'm a bit hypersensitive to potentially narcissistic behavior, which makes dating even more challenging, but I'm so glad to have a healthier perspective and I'm sure that I learned this lesson with Gus for a reason. Perhaps it was just to enable me to develop the even stronger bond I know have with my girlfriend who educated me about this terrifying disorder.

Erica

I met Gus on the Internet as well. I was new to the online dating scene, after having recently divorced my husband of nearly 19 years. I was cautious but hopeful. It actually took Gus a while to respond to my email and when he did reply he apologized and said that he had just experienced a tough break-up (with Marti, I realized later), and he was pretty melancholy about the whole thing. He explained that he was taking his time before he stuck his neck out again. Of course, I felt sorry for him immediately. "The poor guy must be sensitive and emotional for him to react that way," so said my heart. I loved sensitive guys! I just always thought they were a myth.

We emailed for a couple of weeks and then he suggested we meet for ice cream on Saturday. I apologized, but said that I had already made plans for the weekend. "No need to apologize, dear," he wrote. "I understand you have a life. We'll get together in time, if this is meant to be."

I was so impressed. He respected my boundaries and needs, and that was rare in my past relationships with men. We kept the email doors open and kept chatting, learning more and more about each other in the process.

As with Marti, Gus and I lived hours from each other. While one of the joys of living in quiet, laid-back New Mexico is the slower lifestyle and the friendly people, the vast emptiness between towns makes going anywhere a lengthy ordeal. The logistics of a long-distance relationship had its ups and downs in my mind, but I wasn't ready to rule it out.

He kept offering other times when we might be able to connect, but for the longest time I was busy with my teenager's sporting events or school schedules, in addition to my own work schedule at the credit union during the day and the local pub at night.

"Is there ever going to be a time I will get to meet you?" he wrote. I felt guilty. He had shown himself to be so patient and understanding that I finally gave him my phone number so we could at least talk.

Our first phone conversation ended up lasting for hours. It was like we had known each other for years. Maybe even all our lives.

There were no tentative opening lines or worries that either of us wouldn't meet the expectations of the other. It was fabulous.

When next he asked me if we could meet, I was still hesitant. Talking with someone over email or on the phone was one thing – in the flesh was quite another. I was still new to this dating thing, after being married so many years, and I didn't want to get in over my head. I asked him what his expectations were.

His answer was perfect – Absolutely no expectations. Lunch only. Friends for as long as necessary. Purely platonic was just fine with him. He would get a room at a hotel and whatever time I could give him around my hectic family and work schedule, he would accept. No questions asked.

We agreed to meet for lunch on Thursday and on Wednesday afternoon he surprised me by waltzing in to the credit union where I worked. I didn't know he was there and when a co-worker told me there was a man asking for me, I was completely amazed. He told me that he just wanted to be early for our lunch date the next day and would it be OK if he stopped at the pub where I worked in the evening and had a few beers while I was stuck there?

Of course I didn't object at all. I was so impressed he had gone out of his way to come early to spend as much time with me as possible! I had never expected it. What a wonderful surprise! He obviously was a man who cared a great deal.

My friends were overjoyed for me. "Oh, Erica – he's adorable," they said. I had to agree.

When I walked into work that evening, he was already at the bar and had a big map lying open on the counter. I asked him what he was doing and he said he was looking to invest in some land and was studying the map of the area to get a better understanding of the big picture. Of course, I was immediately impressed that he must have enough money to invest in anything. (Little did I know the truth was he didn't have a dime in his pocket.)

We chatted a great deal while I tended bar throughout the course of the evening and I found him to be delightful. By the time our lunch date came around the next day, I couldn't *wait* to see him again. He mesmerized me, without a doubt. He was like a drug. I would sit and look at him for hours on end. It was like I was a different person when I was with him. He kept encouraging me to tell him everything about myself. He listened so intently. He shook his head compassionately if I spoke of something painful from my past, then would pat my hand gently in understanding. He eyes grew teary in sympathy when I discussed an extremely difficult moment during my divorce. As he'd been divorced too, I felt he knew my pain first-hand.

He was so polite. He held the doors open for me. Kissed my hand. Even wanted to buckle my seatbelt for me, which was the only thing that left me feeling a bit uncomfortable. Yet, at the end of that first date when he said, "Would you mind if I give you a kiss on the cheek?" I knew I was hooked.

The minute I left him to go back to work, all my mind could do was figure out how to spend every possible moment with him. Just as we were about to say good-bye, he had an idea. He was attending a birthday party that evening back in his small town and on impulse he suggested I join him, and if I wanted, I could spend the weekend.

My mind whirled! I had just promised my ex-husband I would take care of our 16-year-old daughter while he was out of town, but I instantly considered possible alternative options concerning what I could do with her. He could see me hesitate and he said, "It's all about what's important to you, dear. Do this only if you're comfortable. There's no pressure."

Within seconds I had made up my mind to go.

The weekend turned out to be something out of a dream. Romance. Scented oils. Tender kisses. Incredible bliss.

> *I wanted to marry this man after only knowing him 48 hours!*

I took him home to meet my mom right then and there. I guess I should have thought something was a little out of the norm when he walked in her house and said, "Should I call you Mom?" when he hadn't even officially met her yet. Hindsight is a marvelous thing and I realize now that my mother had been in a relationship for 19 years with a narcissist and the first thing she commented was how much Gus reminded her of her ex-husband!

Fortunately the reality of an instant marriage was not possible for us, as I already had a life plan I was working around. I was due to move to Phoenix within a few weeks, where I was registered to begin a two-year court reporter course. Nothing was going to deter me. Not even Gus. However, I swore to him that if all remained the same, I would promise to marry him at the end of that time. He was thrilled!

I look back at that momentary lapse of sanity and wonder how the heck he pulled me into his web so easily. Was it the charisma? His great acting job of being such a knight in shining armor? What? To this day, I can't even figure it out. The fact I so quickly farmed out my daughter to friends without hesitation, just to spend the weekend with a man I had only met 12 hours before, still boggles my mind to this day.

He was very good at what he did.

We were instantly boyfriend and girlfriend. I would drive several hours to his house to be with him every weekend I could possibly get away. Of course we had endless phone calls and emails that were filled with romantic language and love poetry he wrote for me.

However, the Red Flags started showing up by the third weekend I spent with him. By the time I had driven to his house I realized that I had forgotten some necessary toiletries and knew I needed to stop at Wal-Mart to pick them up. I decided to go to Gus' house first and figured we could stop and get the supplies when we went out.

He agreed we should stop at the store on our way to dinner and kill two birds with one stone. We had a great conversation on the way and I figured I'd just rush in and out of the store so we could be on our way. With that in mind, I jumped out of his truck once we parked, and hurried into the store. He seemed to lag behind and I just figured he'd stroll around until I got my things and we'd be out of the store in no time. Yet, once inside the store I could feel his personality change like a light bulb flickering out. I shook off the weird feeling, but there was no denying it. He had suddenly become very angry over something and I hadn't a clue what it could be about.

I tentatively asked him what was wrong and he jumped down my throat. "How dare you not let me open the truck door for you?! You know that's my job. You absolutely ignored me on your way into the store!"

At first I thought he was kidding. Like he was playing the hurt little kid who had tried to do something right and no one had noticed, but I quickly realized he was dead serious. His eyes were cold and seemed to throw missiles at me. I had never seen him like this before.

My gut told me this was terribly wrong and I decided right then to return home that evening. I made him take me back to my car and I left. It had become quite clear to me that we just weren't compatible and I told him that.

As I drove the many hours to get back home I gradually started doubting myself. I kept going over and over the situation, trying to decide if it was a figment of my imagination or if it had really happened that way. It seemed too ridiculous to be real. Then I remembered this lovely man that had swept me off my feet and I blew the entire episode off as a complete misunderstanding.

I decided to call him up and apologize. It wasn't worth throwing away all the good we had over some silliness. He accepted my apology and we went on as though nothing had ever happened.

The next weekend it was his turn to drive to my town. I was all excited to have him meet my friends and was sure they'd like him as much as I did. We were all meeting at the pub I worked at and I could barely contain myself all day awaiting his arrival. When at last he showed up, I was shocked. He was wearing tattered clothes, a beat up old cowboy hat, and had a cigar hanging out of his mouth. I knew that he understood that it was a non-smoking bar, and yet he flaunted his cigar like he was above the rules. I didn't know which surprised me most – the fact that he looked like a homeless person for his first appearance with my friends, or the fact that he thought it was OK to push the rules of the bar with his cigar. When I reminded him that he wasn't allowed to smoke inside, he said, "That's OK, honey. I'll just hold it, okay dokie?"

Now I realize that growing up in New Mexico I should be used to the cowboy look, but it has never really done anything for me. I had shared that with Gus in one of our first days together, so I was mildly surprised that he would wear his cowboy hat, knowing how I felt about it. Much less not take the time to clean up a bit for my friends. At first I was a bit disappointed and angry and then I said to myself, "Come on, Erica. You're being a real bitch. He just drove four hours to see you and you're going to get upset over this?" I tried to let the whole incident go. It wasn't worth it. I was looking forward to our time alone together, and that was worth everything to me.

Yet, the next day when he insisted I accompany him to the local ranch-wear store to buy a new cowboy hat and clothes, a little bell started going off in my head. That little bell rang even louder when he made me take a picture of him in his new outfit which he knew I disliked. I just didn't get it.

We continued to take turns driving to each other every weekend. The next weekend we decided to meet at a small restaurant I had never been to before. I got there before he did and had a couple of beers before he arrived. When I asked him what was good on the menu, indicating I'd never been to the restaurant before, he insisted, "Oh, come on, you know you've eaten here before."

I thought that was a strange statement and I reaffirmed that I had indeed not ever been there before.

His eyes suddenly grew cold and the conversation ceased. As the silence hung between us like a brick wall, I couldn't believe what had just transpired. Apparently my disagreeing with him had sent him into "angry land" and now I was being punished for it. In addition, I realized that he was playing the cowboy outfit again. All I could think was where did my REI outdoorsman go? And what is he trying to prove with the cowboy stuff?

I asked him if he knew where the bathroom was and he wouldn't answer me. So, out of spite I fought back in a rather defiant way. Still wearing my dress and heels from work, I walked over to a table of men sitting near us and asked them where the bathroom was. They were most happy to tell me and Gus' rage only multiplied.

Needless to say the evening was a disaster and the end result was that he blamed it all on me drinking too much.

The Red Flags had begun to wave furiously and I was refusing to see them.

The roller coaster pattern had begun. Wonderful days. Terrible days. Passionate lovemaking with candles and scented oils. Cherry wine with chocolate on the rim. (Come to find out, Marti had taught him that one!) Angry nights with hours of the "silent treatment," for infractions I wasn't even aware of. Moments of rage, with eyes so black and deep, I feared I might get sucked into them.

I think part of the reason I stayed so long is that I'm a caretaker by nature. I love doing things for other people. Helping them. I have spent so many years putting other people's needs before my own that it just came naturally for me. And of course there was always that deeply imbedded memory of Mr. Perfect. I knew he had to be in there somewhere, if I only knew how to get him to come out and stay out. I guess that means I kept looking for his *potential to change*, which I've since learned is one major mistake. *Never* enter a relationship looking at someone for their potential. Look for what *is*.

Then he began with the ongoing sermon about my actions. He would tell me how it was his observations that told him who I really was. "I will watch your actions, not your words, Erica," he used to taunt me. Then there was the other sermon about his "needs."

"I have independence and you *will* acknowledge that." I never was entirely sure what he meant by that one. I would go crazy with the mind games he played with me. Yet, every time I considered leaving, he reeled me back in with his charm. It was an amazing phenomenon, now that I look back on it.

The beginning of the end occurred one night when he was going to meet me at the bar for a drink before we went home. I knew an old friend was coming in that night and I told Gus that I'd love to have him meet George, a 60-something-year-old friend of my mother's. Gus said fine and showed up a bit before I was finished. He jumped into a conversation with another guy at the bar and by the time I clocked out, the only empty stool at the bar was one seat away from Gus and next to George. Since Gus was obviously deep in conversation, I sat next to George and waited for my opportunity to introduce the guys to each other.

When he finally finished chatting and walked the three steps over to us, I could barely wait to introduce him as my "boyfriend" to my dear friend George. They shook hands and then Gus threw me another curve. He turned to me and said, "Hon, I'm really tired. I've got a long trip ahead of me. I'm going to head on home. It's OK. You go ahead and chat. Take the time you need. I'll let your dogs out when I get home."

All at once I realized what was up. He was jealous and was playing the hurt little boy. He was punishing me for talking to my old friend and not dropping everything for him. So he was going to leave without me and I would have hell to pay later.

I was livid. This was too much. I didn't need a child having a temper tantrum in my life. I had already raised three children of my own. I simply didn't need another one.

So he left and I stayed.

By the time I got home an hour later, he was nowhere to be seen, nor had my dogs been cared for.

I called him on his cell phone to be sure he was OK. After all, he had been drinking for a couple of hours and that, combined with his anger when he left, caused me concern. I certainly didn't want him to be off the road in a ditch somewhere. But he wouldn't answer his phone.

I drove around looking for him and at last saw his truck at a local motel. I called his room from the lobby phone and asked him what was going on. In a cold, calculating voice he simply said, "I'm going to bed. Why does it matter to you? You were obviously more interested in your old friend than you were in me."

> *I replied that I hadn't done anything wrong and he assured*
> *me that if I would just think about it longer,*
> *I'd realize just how wrong I was.*
> *After all, I was a smart person, he reminded me.*
> *"If you just look at it from my side,*
> *you'll know you're wrong,"*

What was I supposed to do? I loved this guy. I blamed myself. I sucked up my pride and apologized if I had done anything to hurt his feelings. He acted wounded for quite a while and once again, we made up.

The next day he fell into reeling me in again. He fixed my car, which I was so grateful for, as I really didn't have the money to pay a mechanic. He took me to lunch. He bought me flowers. I hoped that whatever stress had caused him to lose himself, that it was moving out and the "old Gus" was returning.

My ex-husband and I lived in the same small town and still shared custody of our children, so that mandated we still communicated on a regular basis. At times things were pretty emotional for me and Gus suggested that I might benefit from taking some time off. "Why don't you move in with me for a while? It will give you some time to rest and put a little space between you and your ex too. Might be just what the doctor ordered." He also highly suggested that I really had no reason to ever talk to my ex again. I sort of blew the comment off, not believing that he really meant it. How could he? We still had joint custody of our kids.

It was the Tuesday before Thanksgiving when I moved in with him. I had to borrow my ex-husband's truck to move my big items and was on the phone with him arranging the details when Gus called and I picked him up on call waiting. I told him I was on the phone with Brian and Gus agreed that I should call him back when Brian and I had finalized all the details. When I called him back he was cool and distant. I didn't figure out until much later that he was furious with me for not taking his call over my conversation with Brian. I later paid for that mistake with several hours of the "silent treatment."

On Thanksgiving Day I cooked a huge dinner for Gus and a bunch of his friends. The day seemed perfect and he bragged to his friends about what a good cook I was. Yet, after they all left he immediately returned to giving me the cold shoulder. Except for one thing…

Since I was a new member in his household he took me by the hand (literally) and walked me through all his expectations. How he wanted his laundry washed and the clothes folded. How I should clean the toilets. Exactly how the food was to be stored in the refrigerator. I couldn't believe that he was treating me like a child who knew nothing when at age 41 with nearly 19 years of marriage behind me and raising three kids, I thought I had learned a few things by now. My gut was screaming at me that something was drastically wrong, and I was finally starting to listen.

I decided to go to bed and think about it with a fresh mind in the morning. Gus wasn't tired yet, so decided to stay up and watch some TV before he joined me.

I felt emotionally and physically drained. I kept remembering his suggestion to move in with him so that I could rest. Somehow I didn't see that happening. My mind kept reliving all my "transgressions," trying to make sense of it all. I finally couldn't deal with it any further and fell asleep in sadness.

About an hour later Gus came to bed and started screaming at me, wanting to know where his cell phone was. In a groggy daze, I realized he must be talking about his extra cell phone he had lent me after he had accidentally driven over mine and broken it. I told him I thought it was in my car, all the while wondering why it was such a big deal in the middle of the night. When he insisted I go get it, I refused and rolled over to go back to sleep. Well, that was entirely the wrong thing to do. "By God, you go get it right now!" he bellowed, as I lay there wondering, "Who is this man?"

Again I refused to get out of bed and at that point he grabbed me and physically threw me out of the bed, insisting he would not sleep with me. "I refuse to sleep with a contentious woman!" Then he began screaming scripture to me, "It is better to have only a crust of bread to eat upon the rooftop than to feast with many in a house of contention."

I looked at him in amazement one last time while he yelled, "Why do you insist on defying me and not showing me respect?"

I left his bed and slept in the guestroom, knowing full-well that I was leaving in the morning, never to return. I was scared, confused, depressed, and full of self-doubt. What was so wrong with me that he would treat me this way?

I had moved in on Tuesday and I moved out by Friday. It still amazes me when I rethink the whole thing.

How did the man I wanted to marry within 48 hours of meeting him become a Frankenstein monster who destroyed everything in his path? And furthermore, how did I fall for it?

The one thing that saved me from thinking I had gone completely crazy was finding Marti's business card and an old email of hers that Gus had left lying about. As soon as I got to a safe place I summoned up all my nerve and called her. It was like finding a life line.

She told me about the turbulent relationship she had lived through. (She lasted 12 weeks – I had only made it 9.) But the pattern was exactly the same in both of our relationships.

We laughed together and cried together. We compared stupid details and stories of his behaviors that left us amazed. We realized how he tried to parent both of us in his own way. "Now, darling, if you'd just realize I'm trying to help you," he loved to tell us. In my case he always told me how he just viewed himself a little further along in the divorce education than I was and so he could "teach me the ropes."

In Marti's case he attempted to be the all-knowing businessman. (He had no credentials or background in business – he was a plumber by trade.) Yet he insisted on showing Marti how to run her business and her finances.

The behaviors relating to him having control were absolutely like déjà vu. We marveled at how the whole, pathetic process had evolved.

After I left Gus he didn't try to contact me. About a week and a half later I emailed him and said I was sorry things had turned out the way they did. He blasted me back with a scathing email, blaming all our problems on *my* drinking. (This from a man who used drugs and alcohol freely.)

All I can say is thank God I discovered the issue I was dealing with was NPD. Understanding the behaviors and motivating factors behind his actions has helped me quit carrying the guilt that seemed to follow me like a stalker. I kept believing that everything had been my fault. Now I know better.

The sad thing is that both Marti and I know he will find another victim and we just wish there was a way that innocent women could be warned. It's easy to spot loud, rough, pushy men. You know to stay away from them. But these actors are another matter. They're so insidious. They're like quicksand – you don't know you're in danger until it's too late and then it seems close to impossible to get out …

Closure

As I finished the interview with Marti and Erica that night, I mentioned that since I had never met Gus, I could only use my imagination as to what he must look like. Erica instantly pulled pictures of him out of her wallet. Marti and I were surprised and asked her what on earth she was doing, still carrying his photos with her. She honestly couldn't say. I also found it interesting that I saw a rather plain looking man when they both commented on how "handsome" he was. The photos obviously stirred deep, emotional responses in both of them.

I suggested they burn them ceremoniously right there..

They each took one and lit a match to it, watching it melt and shrivel up symbolically into the ashtray, as the bartender curiously watched the powerful event unfold.

Hopefully, the imagery will translate into moving on for both of them. It can be done. It just takes time and a belief that they can.

> *"Narcissists have no feelings of any kind.*
> *You must remember that above all.*
> *They are simply actors on the stage,*
> *pretending with all their might. Yet, it is all a lie.*
> *There is no real emotion of any kind. Any actor can act and*
> *these folks win the Academy Award in that category."*
> *Michael – survivor*

Chapter 15
It Must Be My Fault –
If Only I'd Tried Harder

*W*omen can dish out just as much emotional or physical pain to unsuspecting victims as their male counterparts do. The controlling behaviors of a woman can be just as spiteful, hateful, angry, and humiliating to a male victim, leaving them equally devastated in the end, wondering what hit them.

Steve

I had loved Emily since high school. She used to appear suddenly and sit beside me in the school hallway. I was the thoughtful, shy one and I appreciated her attention. "Read to me," she laughed. And I did. After swim meets I'd go to the sub shop where she worked and order something, just to see her. She was a sprite that brought joy to my heart. I thought I knew and understood her.

We went on a few dates in high school. We'd go to a place to sit and talk, or to a movie. We had photography, psychology, and journalism classes together. I brought a daisy to class for her one day. The way she appreciated it and the way she looked at it, I remember it now. It was so entrancing and beautiful. I brought her little gifts from places I went, such as tiny cans of soda that could be purchased only in Canada. She seemed to relish my attention as much as I cherished hers.

I loved her.

Melville writes that there is a "Catskill eagle in some souls that can alike dive down into the blackest gorges and soar out of them again and become invisible in the sunny spaces. And even if they forever fly within the gorge, that gorge is in the mountains; so that even in their lowest swoop the mountain eagle is still higher than other birds upon the plain, even though they soar."

A Catskill eagle is what I felt I'd found in her. Even in her moods, no other girl compared. I hadn't even kissed her yet, but I felt she was the one for me. I didn't date much or very seriously in high school. I saw a few girls here and there. I know now that's because I had already given away my heart in my mind to Emily. Yet she dated others regularly and I had to watch her from afar. I took another girl to the prom. She was pretty and friendly. I liked her and she desired me. Yet I dreamed and yearned for the love of a Catskill eagle.

Our lives went different ways during college and beyond. We stayed in touch over the years and after she had seemingly chased many men and had almost gone down the aisle with one, she at last allowed me to woo her for my wife. She was mysterious, funny, imaginative, sexy, and aggressive. She had boundless ambition. No one could tell her what to do. Yet despite her independence, I also loved the moments when she seemed vulnerable and unsure of herself. I wanted to take care of her forever. The first night we made love was fantastic and in the morning she told me that she only had sex with those she considered "future mates." I thought my prayers were answered when she agreed to marry me.

It wasn't long after the wedding day that I began to realize Emily had a dark side...

Living with her turned out to be like living on a roller coaster. At times she seemed to be the perfect mate, but other times she turned into someone I didn't recognize. Little things started to become a pattern of bigger things. One morning she woke me up and angrily accused me of taking her socks. "Where are my socks?" she screamed at me repeatedly. I was half asleep and had no idea what she was talking about. I guess she found her socks, but no apology was ever offered. It was like the entire incident never happened.

Then she began a pattern of always demanding more from me, no matter what I did. She started telling me I was weak. I wasn't strong enough for her. Why didn't I work out more? The worst thing was when she began discouraging me from following my heart in the work I did. While I fully supported whatever career direction she wished, mine was meaningless to her. She quit teaching, was fired from other jobs because she couldn't get along with others, and finally quit working altogether. I continually supported her in her endless search for happiness in her career; in obtaining a graduate degree, financing her failing business, and encouraging and helping her as best I could. I did all the housework, grocery shopping, and cooking at the same time that she mercilessly kept telling me just how worthless I was.

She was envious of the other women in our neighborhood. "If I had her clothes I'd look as good as her," she complained. Other women, according to her, were only pretty because they had face lifts or fake breasts. She wanted what they had, telling me I was foolish and cheap to desire her as she was.

She wasn't following her heart, only her image. But her image was never, ever good enough. When the weather or circumstances appeared bad, when attention wasn't focused on her, when my brother had a new baby and everyone stopped paying attention to her in favor of the infant, or when things didn't go as she planned, I became the lightning rod for her discontent.

I blamed myself constantly for causing the problems in our marriage: for not earning enough, for not providing a home, for raising my voice, for not being a better mate, and for not having children when she wanted them. I thought forgiveness was the only way and thus I just kept forgiving her for her behavior and I promised myself that I would do better next time.

She was verbally abusive throughout our relationship. It increased in frequency and intensity as our relationship progressed. She threw glasses, pans, dishes, and gouged a hole in the wall with a chair, but never hit me. (She is 5 feet 4 and I am 5 feet 11). All I could do at those times was cower in a corner or walk away.

She was very active sexually and towards the end of our relationship she turned abusive in this regard. She always said "I love men and they love me." She had her hands on other men all the time, including her male high school students, who she said called her "Nipples." She seemed to especially enjoy that kind of attention and yet would become enraged if I just talked to a pretty woman. She taunted me for not having sex with her enough, saying she'd had sex with other boyfriends a few times each day, but would refuse me often enough when I was in the mood. She had sex with another man during our marriage, primarily to punish me and isolate me so I'd be better under her control.

Later in our marriage she became increasingly arrogant. It got to the point where I couldn't do anything right in her mind. She often told me I was worthless, that I was without pride, that I didn't "know how to treat a woman." She'd sternly correct any little mistake I made: mispronouncing words, taking a wrong turn, spending money, breaking eggs. Any little mistake was tantamount to incompetence in her mind. She treated me worse than a fool when she corrected me. Yet even when she slept with another man while she was angry with me, it wasn't something I should bother her about. She certainly didn't refer to her infidelity and I was prevented from even bringing it up at all.

The beginning of the end came when we traveled to our cottage for the holidays with my extended family. Noticing that my two year old niece's bathing suit was hanging on the clothesline, my mother made the comment that it "must be Emily's bathing suit," since no one else in the family was as incredibly petite as my wife. What happened next took me completely off-guard. Emily was enraged! She completely turned on my mother over the comment, imagining some trivial slight was meant. Even a week after the incident and my mother's return home, Emily was still tearing into me. She accused my mother of hating her and she offered the bathing suit comment as evidence. She maintained she would never be in the same room with my mother again. She accused me of not understanding how women feel and said if I didn't straighten my mother out (how I might do that wasn't very clear), then she would never see my family or come to our cottage again.

Everything she said hurt me a great deal. She wouldn't let the matter rest. Day after day she ignored all the beauty around her – the loons calling in the distance, stars in the sky, the rising and setting of the magnificent sun. But most of all, she ignored me. Yet when she wasn't ignoring me she was concentrating on "straightening out" my mother and threatening that I'd be punished severely for my part in the drama.

I got on my knees, half crying – half laughing, in frustration and begged Emily to see my mom didn't mean it. Even if she had, it was no matter because she was hundreds of miles away and I could get her to apologize. But, no, it was "too late." She forbade forgiveness. She insisted my mother hated her, that nothing would improve, and that I was a terrible human being for not doing something about it.

I cried. I begged. I tried to make her laugh. We had sex. We went hiking and swimming. I even tried yelling and screaming, but nothing worked. Day after day she told me how terrible I was. How she was never doing anything with my family again. Was never going to our cottage again. And was certainly never trusting me again. All because my mother gave her a compliment.

Of course the bottom line was that she really just wanted complete control of me and everyone else. She saw all of us as "goats." In desperation and without hope, I ended up walking to a cliff, the same formation of rock that Niagara Falls plunges over, and considered jumping. I couldn't believe my wife, the woman I loved all my life, could treat me this way. But somehow I mustered up the courage to go on. Being comforted by our yellow lab Max beside me, the forest surrounding me, and Hudson Bay extending into the distance, I found the strength to return to her. I tried as hard as I could to hold our marriage together and find the right way to go. But it was so frustrating. Eventually, no matter what I did, it was never good enough.

I found her up late one night typing on the computer. "What's wrong? Please come to bed", I pleaded. She growled, "Go to f___ing sleep." The next morning she sat me down in a local cafe and told me she was leaving in two days. She said the divorce papers were ready and she had a lawyer. She told me she was taking our bed, stereo, thousands in cash, dishes, TV, and, most hurtful of all, our dog. The new Ford Expedition she ordered, which I put $10,000 down on, had arrived. That was the moment she had been waiting for. Months earlier she wanted to order it with a trailer hitch. I asked, "What for?" Suddenly I knew why. She needed a get-away vehicle to haul her stuff off to another part of the country.

I begged her not to go. I helped her pack because that is what she wanted and she told me if I didn't help, she'd get some guys who would. She told everyone that I was divorcing her. She told each person, depending on their personality, what they wanted to hear. So no one helped me. She drove away with our dog. I slept as I could on carpet and concrete, in my sleeping bag, in despair.

Months later she emailed, writing that it was Easter and she was thinking of me. Could I send her another $2,000 for the Expedition? If I didn't, she threatened to derail our divorce settlement and ask for more. I sent her the $2,000 and haven't heard from her again.

It has been about two years since she drove away. I've since learned about Narcissistic Personality Disorder. I'd like to reach out to her. I love her, but I can't reach her. I write letters to her that I never send. I believe she is lost in a forest of her mind. I call out to her, I reach for her hand, but she is beyond my reach. I don't know who she is. She doesn't either. To go any farther I would lose myself again. She alternately holds onto people then lashes out at them. It is a roller coaster. Passion sways her towards people and then fear makes her run. Inside she is still a child whose parents claim her and continue to abuse her, never allowing her to be who she is inside or to ever truly be loved. Her mind takes over where her parents left off.

Even though we were only married for two and a half years, I lived with her for five, and knew her for 20. I still think about her now, years later. She's the only narcissist I've ever been in an intimate relationship with and I hope it's the last. And yet, I'd take her back in a blink of an eye. She's a siren. She's irresistible. At no point did I ever say I didn't love her. I love her still. Yet I can say in confidence that this day will never come. My boundaries are too strong. I've done all I can do. I can't carry the load (of life and our relationship) when she not only does not help, but actively creates obstacles and chaos that get in the way. I can't love someone who won't love in return. Nor can I let go of who I am or let go of my heart to follow an image, as she does. She knows this. She won't come to my door now.

The saddest part is that at age 34 I feel like I've wasted my best years and that no one attractive will love me or be available now. Loneliness burns like a fire in my heart and mind and remembrances of her haunt me every day.

I never really considered divorce or that someone who said they loved me could hurt me so badly. I never understood until now that someone could actually be so in love with their own image to the exclusion of everyone else. Now I know.

No one can love an image.

Nor can anyone be happy as an image.

It's just impossible.

> *"I learned early in life that compliance was
> the best method of survival."*
> *Barry – survivor*

Chapter 16
It's All About Humiliation

Webster's dictionary defines humiliation as follows: "to reduce to a lower position in one's own eyes or others."

Personally I think it has to do with one person trying to become more powerful than another through instilling in the victim a belief that they are lower in value than the perpetrator.

There are a few situations where there seems to be a genuine purpose to intentional humiliation. Certainly military boot camp could be a stage for this type of behavior. Letting everyone know "who is boss" supposedly leads to a cohesive team and an understanding of the power of the whole, versus the power of one. Yet, in the military it is absolutely necessary that the chain of command be followed, for there cannot be more than one leader in moments of battle. No one has time in war situations to debate the pros and cons of the enemy attack. The strongest regiments believe in their leader's authority and command and obey unconditionally.

Notorious cases of extreme humiliation have been reported in some college fraternities accused of "hazing." These stories however, have nothing to do with survival under wartime conditions. The narcissistic individuals in positions of power in these situations simply seem to feel entitled to bestow humiliation on their fledglings because they can. The newcomers, hoping to please their leaders and gain admission to the fraternity, will oftentimes stoop to some incredible lows to "pass the test," when under normal circumstances these otherwise rational people would never dream of participating in some of the behaviors they are expected to perform. One difference in this situation from that of an intimate relationship is that the new fraternity pledges can see a time when it is their turn to be in the power position – when they are no longer the new guys on the hot seat. This alone may restore a fragment of power in their minds while they endure the rights of passage.

However, when humiliation of any kind enters a relationship of friendship or love, it is all about power and it is *not* OK. People who truly love each other give their partners respect, compassion, empathy, understanding, and above all, trust. We should always be able to trust those we love (and who claim to love us) to provide a safe environment for us at all times. For if they don't, who will?

Certainly we all have bad days, lose our temper, and sometimes do things we regret later. We are not perfect. In healthy relationships when we do something that hurts someone we love, the best course of action is to go to the person we hurt, sincerely apologize, ask for forgiveness, tell them how much we love them, and vow to ourselves and them that we will not repeat that behavior again. And then we learn from that behavior. We do everything in our power to avoid the harmful behavior again.

For example, you come home after a particularly tough day. You're tired, short-tempered, and feel like you're going to blow if the least thing goes wrong. You walk into your house and find your 14 year old has left the stove top on and has macaroni and cheese pouring all over the top of your range. You find yourself suddenly angry for the mess as well as the danger involved. When you hear him outside with his friends you race into the yard and begin screaming at him at the top of your lungs about how irresponsible he is, how the house could have burned down, his little brother could have gotten burned, and on and on. All the while his friends are looking on, feeling terribly out of place. However, what you find out later is that your son was called out in the yard unexpectedly upon hearing his little brother scream when he fell out of the swing. Thus, the macaroni mess was secondary to his concern for his younger brother.

So, how do you handle this situation after the fact? Do you apologize to your son for blaming him unfairly? For screaming at him in front of his buddies and humiliating him? For not asking him his side of the story first? Do you give him a hug and tell him how proud you are that he is so responsive to his brother's needs? Above all, do you tell him how much you love him and ask him to forgive your rush to judgment? And do you think twice about jumping down his throat quite so quickly next time before you know the facts of a case? Hopefully that is exactly what you do. Might you approach a similar situation a bit differently next time, even if you are having a rough day? If you are a healthy, loving person who cares for your son unconditionally, that's exactly what you do.

Yet, if you were a narcissistic mother, you would more than likely not do any of those things. You would have probably continued to rage at your son, telling him how stupid he was, what a big mess he'd made, how you can't trust him for a minute. As your son looked on in confusion and despair, you would see the hurt in his eyes and you would sense the power you had over him. You would remember that feeling and you would plan to use this tactic again in the future; for you discovered that it was very effective in achieving what you ultimately desire – more power and control of those around you. More Narcissistic Supply.

There is a fine line between yelling at your child and intentionally humiliating him in order to cause pain or to make him feel bad about himself.

> *Intentionally repeating a behavior that you know will result in pain is not OK. And that's where narcissism stands out differently from someone just having a bad day.*
> *It is a pattern of behavior that can be predicted to repeat itself.*

There may be an apology involved, but if there is it will sound something like, "I'm sorry, Bobby, but if you hadn't looked at me that way, I wouldn't have gotten mad at you in the first place." This is not an apology! This is still blaming others for the narcissist's behavior!

Intentionally humiliating someone is *not* healthy, loving, or meant to help you in any way. There are many ways to teach people about life and the world. "Teaching you a lesson" through humiliation is not one of them. Do not kid yourself that the narcissist in your life is giving you this treatment because he loves you. It is all about him meeting his own needs. As soon as you can see through the mask, the easier it will be to avoid falling into his web.

So many of the stories I received from survivors and victims had to do with humiliation. Name-calling, belittling, beatings, criticism (especially in front of friends), demanding sexual behaviors that left the victim uncomfortable, and so many other forms of humiliation were rampant throughout these first-hand accounts. Unfortunately, the result was always the same: The victim's self-esteem continued to chip away, bit by bit. Eventually, little if any was left. This, of course, is the hope of the narcissist, despite what he might say or do to the contrary.

This roller coaster ride seems endless. The pain and torment is ongoing, yet sprinkled with the occasional moments of kindness perceived as "love," victims feel confused most of the time. Just about the time they feel like they've reached the last straw and can't take the misery any longer, their narcissist seems to sense the changing wind and does whatever is necessary to hold them in place. Like the Indian enchanter, he plays the magic flute to the cobra that climbs out of the basket at his bidding. Mesmerized. Hypnotized. Obeying without question, while onlookers wonder just what spell he has over the empty-eyed victim.

Brenda

I am 43 years old and work as an administrative assistant for a small business. My life has been emotionally traumatic since childhood. I was the oldest child and adopted, after which I had two natural siblings who could do no wrong in my parent's eyes. For most of my life I felt like some adopted children do – as though I couldn't have been very valuable if my birth parents had simply given me away. I was often emotionally abused in my childhood as well. My parents told me that I was stupid my whole life, when in fact I later found out I had a genius IQ. I wasn't tall or blonde like my sister and never felt as though I fit in. I always thought there was something wrong with me. I had trouble with self-esteem for years and as a result, turned to alcohol at age 16. By 21 I was married and already a full-fledged alcoholic.

I never considered myself a very attractive person. I'm just a cute little brown-haired person. Petite. Just average. I was nothing like my pretty sister or later, like Chad's first wife – a blonde bombshell with huge breasts. I could never stack up to people like that. I drank myself out of my first marriage after 11 years. I was lost in an alcoholic dream world and floated between men when I fell upon Chad. He was my savior. My rescuer from alcohol. I was at the lowest possible point I could have been in my whole life when he found me. When I saw a copy of the Alcoholic's Anonymous "Serenity Prayer" framed on his mantle (his mother was an alcoholic), I was impressed. I knew he understood me. Unfortunately, what I didn't realize was that he had already figured me out – I was prime meat for him. He knew I was vulnerable to begin with.

At first he made me feel beautiful and loved, although my friends said I became a child whenever I was around him. He helped me get sober and get involved with AA. For that, I felt forever in his debt. He seemed so genuine. So kind. I could see him protecting me for the rest of my life. He dangled marriage in front of my nose for five years – yet he was never going to marry anyone. He had just divorced his first wife and had walked away with everything. He left her nearly destitute. Yet, I never saw the warning signs and just kept hanging on to the dream that he would put a ring on my finger and we would live happily ever after.

He was such a great looking man. I was overwhelmed with his appearance and the fact that he wanted me. As I look back on the situation now, I would tell you he looks like the devil, as I know him for what he really is.

He touted his Catholicism as if it were life itself. As I wasn't Catholic, he frequently reminded me that I would spend eternity in hell and damnation. I couldn't officially move in with him since we were not married (it was "against his religion"), but I stayed with him most weekends and one night a week. Just enough to do his laundry, cleaning, cooking, and anything else he needed. I loved him so desperately that I would do anything for him. I never realized when things were going bad. Although some things he wanted me to do made me uncomfortable, I did them because I wanted to please him. More than that, I didn't want to risk losing him.

It didn't take long before things started getting bad. Every time he called me it became prolonged phone sex. Every weekend was all about sex. I was his sex slave. He insisted we watched porno films regularly. Then he progressed to tying me up and sticking things in me. Toys, dildos, you name it. He caused me pain and didn't even care. He even spent $1500 on this sex contraption that was like a horse with dildo attachments. For years he wanted to make a sex video of me, like he had done with his first wife. After three years of him hounding me I finally gave in. It wasn't long before he threatened to use it against me as a method of blackmail. At one point during the relationship, when he didn't feel I was giving him enough sex, he even bought me Viagra and said, "I want you to be the sexy little slut you used to be."

For Christmas or my birthday he could barely acknowledge my existence – he might give me a roll or two of coins, or one year he gave me the "Therapy Game" and thought it might help me! Too bad he couldn't see he needed it himself.

My self-esteem was so low I didn't think I could do any better. So many people told me to get away from him, but I would never listen. I believed that he loved me – I could see nothing else.

We broke up many times over the five years I was involved with him. Once, when he flew into a rage about something, he put his hands around my throat and started shaking me. Then he told me to get out or he was going to kill me. He even bragged to me that, "I bury all my women in the back yard." (As I think back on it now, it seems that he said that to me the first time I spent the night with him.) My sobriety at that time was very fragile and it was fortunate that it was so late that all the liquor stores were closed. Somehow I made it back to my apartment and prayed.

After that night, I cut myself off from him. He retaliated and started calling me and calling me, referring to me as "Ms. Smith" on voice mail, oftentimes leaving threatening messages, so I blocked his number. I contacted the police and then he started leaving stuff outside my apartment door, and that's when he left the extortion letter. He threatened to show the sex video I had made with him to everyone I knew. I contacted the police about it and they told me to file charges and get a restraining order on him. Then we went to court where he was charged with extortion, which he could go to jail for. He had all these character witnesses and I had no one, but I still won. I agreed to drop the charges if he agreed to never contact me again. Of course he never apologized for anything and still blamed me for everything.

After that, two months passed and I hadn't heard from him. I thought I was in the clear. I had started to calm down and piece myself back together. Then, a priest called out of the blue and told me that Chad was suicidal. This was his weapon. I had become a Catholic by then myself and had been taught that everybody deserves forgiveness. He sucked me back into my role of victim for two more years. Don't ask me how – you'd think I'd know better by then. Even after we got back together, it was always this "bank account" of good and bad. Always, if he did anything for me it was in exchange for sex or some other activity that he thought he needed as payment. He kept telling me that I always did nice things for everyone else except him. I got to the point where I didn't want to do anything for him and I didn't want him to do anything for me because I never knew what price I would have to pay.

What finally broke me out of this self-destructive trap was discovering information on narcissism. I devoured everything I could get my hands on. Armed with my new knowledge I broached the subject with him, thinking that perhaps if he got help he could heal. I should have anticipated the reaction I got – he flew into a rage, denying that he might have any such issues. The violence erupted once again and I finally had enough. I told him to get the f___ out of my life.

It took five agonizing years for me to see the light. Five years of pure hell. I just know I'd be dead if I had stayed there much longer. The best thing I can say is that I've found God. I'm sober. I'm actually starting to live like a real human being, although I'm terrified to get involved with men again. Chad was one of many narcissists that I had allowed to manipulate me for most of my life and I choose not to allow anyone that opportunity again. I know the warning signs now. I'm armed with knowledge. Fear keeps me from going near another man again. But that's OK – sometimes fear can keep you safe.

Yet, I have to admit, I still miss those first wonderful weeks with Chad, before things went so bad. I'd take him back in a heartbeat if I knew that he could change because the wonderful times were so much more than wonderful. Unfortunately, I know the truth. I know he can never change. I know he isn't healthy for me – or for anyone else for that matter. The hardest thing for me is constantly wondering why God makes people like that? I keep praying to understand the answer to that question.

I know I'm healing but I still worry a lot. For one thing, I used to be so cute, now I look ten years older than I am. I keep hoping I will look OK again. Living in an environment like that is a stress that you can never imagine. It's constant. Draining. Exhausting. And so damaging in all aspects of your life.

I'm praying very hard for this year to be the one where everything finally gets right for me. Certainly being sober and away from Chad is a good start. My life is good now. I have a nice little house in the country, a neighbor that I walk with and can talk to, and family who love me. If Chad were still around, I would not have been allowed any of this.

Emotionally Held Hostage

The humiliation that Chad used on Brenda kept her hostage. The more humiliating the activities were, the more Brenda's self-esteem disintegrated. After a while, she started to believe that she was so damaged that no one else would ever want her. That's exactly what Chad had in mind.

Understanding the workings of narcissism is so eye-opening. Finally starting to understand that the feelings you may have are part of the brainwashing phenomena that you have experienced can help you to start to see the light at the end of this very long, dark tunnel. The role you may have played was determined for you, just as the director of a movie tells all the actors where to stand and how to say their lines. Your narcissist directed your life as well as your responses. What you didn't understand at the time was that you *let* him control you. Hopefully now you will see that you *do* have choices available to you and that you are equally as important as he is.

When I sent out a request for personal stories from anyone who wanted to contribute to this book I was overwhelmed at the response. Yet the message that came loud and clear from all who wrote me can be summed up with Michelle's words...

Michelle

If by sharing my story, I can do anything that will help bring clarity and education to the general public and can help even one person from becoming a victim of this modern day vampire, it would give me great pleasure and a sense of accomplishment. This horrific behavior seems to be in epidemic proportions here in this country, where power and selfishness seem to mean everything. I am appalled at the lack of public knowledge, not only about narcissism, but also other personality disorders that leave their victims traumatized. It seems to me that every child should be educated to watch for the signals, the danger signals. Then again, who listens when they have found their prince or princess?

Narcissism is insidious, but the destruction these monsters leave in their wake is nearly criminal. Yet it is only *we* who can control what others do to us and how much we take ... is it our own lack of worth that holds us in there for the final blow? Or is it that they somehow twist and manipulate us so that we don't know if we are coming or going that is the problem? I am still in the throws of the blowup and the confusion. I go back and forth between knowing that he is disordered and still blaming myself, wondering "what if?"

It's a tough thing to get over. In my group of friends no one seems interested in the technicalities. It's only about moving on. Well, moving on is definitely the goal, but when you have been wounded so deeply, healing is a prerequisite. At least it has been for me. Maybe I am weak and spoiled as my family seems to think, but I can't help but know I have never been weak before this. I am 54 years old and have raised two children on my own and have never felt this way my whole life. In fact, I had no idea I could feel so terrible ... it's hard, hard, hard.

I thought at first that these people were just random assholes, when in fact they really are a breed – like pit bulls. They know how to get their jaws locked onto something when biting and they just continue to shake their victim until they shake the last breath out of them. Or maybe instead, they are more like the scorpion who hitches a ride across the river on the back of the frog. He promises not to sting the frog, as they would both drown, but he cannot help himself and he stings the frog anyway. The horrified frog asks,

'Why'?!

And the scorpion replies,

"I cannot help it ... I am a scorpion."

"You don't have to be bleeding to be a victim."
Colorado Anti-Violence Program

Chapter 17
Death by a Thousand Cuts

The slow, chipping away of a personality comes in many forms. In some of the stories you've read, the abuse was so obvious and so large that it screamed to outsiders. Yet, the slow, torturous taking of a life through constant cuts at self-esteem also can be like Chinese water torture. The victims never even feel the pain until they realize that their body and soul are in shreds.

Worst of all, they have absolutely no idea how they got there and continue to assure themselves throughout the entire ordeal that everything is their own damned fault.

Mike

She used to manipulate my mind.

I didn't know it at the time. I just believed what she told me. Things like, if only I would do such-and-such differently, things would be perfect. I even believed her when she told me that she had a lot of male friends who were just "friends." I am a pretty trusting person. I guess that's why I let the situation go on for so long. It just never occurred to me that she would lie to me.

I first really began to suspect things were definitely wrong while we were on a family vacation. We were in Mazatlan with our teenaged kids and staying in one of those great all-inclusive hotels. They had every amenity known to man. It was almost like being on a cruise ship with daily activities in addition to the sun and surf. Of course, the staff hired to keep the guests entertained were mostly young, vibrant, attractive men – well, boys actually. Barely out of their teens. There were a few young women employees as well, but it was the guys who stood out. Of course all the teenaged girls on vacation drooled over them, as I guess was intended.

Little did I know that my wife was doing the same thing.

She would disappear for lengthy periods at a time, telling me that she was going to take a walk or stretch her legs. I would offer to go with her, but she would refuse my company and suggest I stay with the kids. At first, I didn't think anything of it. I enjoyed the time with our teenagers and busied myself having fun in the sun. Little did I know that she was off with one of the young studs, doing God knows what.

It wasn't long before I began to learn the truth ...

One night we decided to go into town to the disco. We both loved to dance, although she would never dance with me, as she said she didn't like the way I danced. I had grown accustomed to her dancing with other men and it worked out so that I could find an occasional dance partner myself. I really hadn't given much thought to how uncommon that behavior might be. I just blamed myself for my inability to dance the way my wife needed me to.

At one point I realized that one of the young studs from the hotel had also arrived on the scene and before long, he and my wife had both disappeared. When it seemed like she had been gone for quite a while, I went looking for her. About the time I saw her, she was coming back inside the disco from outside, climbing the stairs with the young man following her, but separately – as if to make it look like they had not been together.

When I asked her where she had been she became enraged. "Who do you think you are, turning this into something I did wrong?" she demanded. "I can't believe you're so jealous! You're making something out of nothing." Ultimately she made *me* feel bad. I ended up being the one to apologize to her and explained that her disappearance under those circumstances had looked highly unusual, and thus the reason for my question. My apology did little good. She remained "offended" for the rest of the evening.

We decided to try out another club, despite the emotional chill in the air. Much to my surprise, the same young man suddenly appeared at disco number two as well. My gut told me that this wasn't just coincidence, but after the tongue-lashing I'd received earlier, I just kept my thoughts and feelings to myself. Yet, I also decided to see where this played out.

Once again she danced with every man in sight while I watched, berating myself again for my poor dancing skills which left her unwilling to dance with me. It wasn't long until I grew tired of the entire thing and told her I'd like to go back to the hotel and go to bed. I'd really had quite enough for one night. She thought I was a party pooper, but suggested that since she was still having a wonderful time, that maybe I should go back to the hotel ahead of her.

> *I had always been very trusting in my marriage, but at this point I decided to trust my heart for once. I didn't exactly leave. I waited around the corner and hoped I wouldn't see what I suspected I would.*

Within minutes of my departure, she left with the guy from the hotel. At the time I didn't know where they went. But she finally returned to our hotel room 5 a.m.

The next morning I said, "You got in awfully late. What did you do all night?"

Her response was that she had just danced. Nothing else. As usual, she always had a way of putting everything back on me. I was so confused and filled with self-doubt that I didn't know what more to do. She acted as if her behavior was completely normal for any middle-aged woman on vacation with her family. And for some strange reason I kept trying to convince myself of the same.

When it came to having sex with me during our marriage, she would withhold and use it as a tool to get what she wanted. It was like a punishment if I didn't "behave." Everything was always about her needs and no one else's. I suppose I thought that everyone else played the same power games in the bedroom. You certainly hear enough stories about it on TV and in the movies, so I really didn't think her behaviors were particularly abnormal there either. It's amazing what we can convince ourselves of when we don't want to see the truth.

I guess what finally opened my eyes to reality was the day I had the radio on to a talk show program. The topic was, "How to Know When Your Spouse Is Having an Affair." When they started listing off the warning signs, I stopped in my tracks. The behaviors they mentioned were all hers. It was like a sudden shock to my system. I felt sick, but knew that in my heart I had really known the truth for some time. I guess I had just always felt that I was so much less a person than she was — that whatever she wanted, and whatever she said, must be "normal." I knew I had to get to the bottom of this thing before I could decide what to do next.

She often spent a great deal of time at the library, studying for some classes she was taking. So, I decided to surprise her one day and picked up her favorite Starbuck's coffee to take as an offering. When she saw me there she became enraged. She hissed, "What are you doing here? I come here to get away from everything at home. I can't believe you're interrupting me in *my* space!"

I apologized profusely and left immediately, yet I decided to hang around and see if I could learn anything from a distance. It wasn't long before I observed a man arrive and sit with her. They left together shortly after that. It became clear why she was so upset about my arrival – I almost caught her red-handed!

When she arrived home I confronted her with my knowledge. I said, "I know you're having an affair. Tell me about it."

She denied everything for about 20 minutes, at the same time she kept demanding, "How do you know?" At last, she told me everything: About the man at the library. About the boy from the Mexican resort (whom she had indeed spent the night with), and about the fact that she'd had a total of five affairs all together. I kept kicking myself for my blindness. She had wanted "male friends," which I never questioned. Yet she was having affairs with all of them.

She told me how sorry she was to have to tell me and that she'd never intended to hurt me. She had lots of excuses, but the underlying message was still that all had been my fault. She blamed me for her unhappiness. There was always something I did or didn't do, or that just wasn't good enough. I wasn't making enough money. I didn't think fast enough. I was forgetful. If only I'd had more material things. If only I was this way or that way, she would have been happy.

The ironic thing was that I believe it all. Yet, it seems so obvious now. The truth is I could never make her happy, no matter what I did.

We did go through counseling for a while, but that was short-lived. We divorced not long after. The hardest part now is that I still can't escape her, as we have four children between us. Fortunately they are not little ones, but she still uses them as weapons against me whenever possible. She tells me how much they don't like me and how they talk about me behind my back. Fortunately, I have a great relationship with my kids and that helps. I know the things she tells me are lies, just as she lied to me the whole time we were married.

Even more difficult is the financial position I ended up in. At the time of our divorce, a business partner owed me a huge sum of money. Of course, my wife was entitled to half and I was destined to pay her a lump sum once the transaction was complete. Unfortunately, the partner ended up in bankruptcy and I never received a dime of what he owed me. Yet, according to the divorce decree, I was still obligated to pay her. There was no way out of it. I ended up selling my business in order to pay some of what I owed her, yet I still owe her money and keep making payments to this day.

She's furious with me because I'm not making enough money now in my new, start-up business. She has burned through over $350,000 in about three years and keeps hounding me for more. She says I'm a bum and how I should get two jobs so I can pay her back faster. So she won't have to "struggle" so. She has her own career and is making money as well, but I guess there's just never enough in her eyes. She has since married again, only this guy doesn't have much money. I guess she thought she'd have a free ride on Easy Street and that I was a cash cow. Then suddenly it ended. So she's miserable and blames me once again.

At least now I understand that the problem is hers, not mine.

> *Yet, as I look back at all those years, I am most amazed about how I just kept taking it and taking it.*

I think about all the ongoing cuts to my psyche every day. I'm not even talking about the infidelities; just the slow, calculated brainwashing that tore me down, piece by piece. It was like getting a paper cut each and every day of my life with her. By themselves, each one smarted a little, but none of them screamed about the murder that was going on within my heart and soul.

I have to wonder how many other people suffer this silent, insidious torture. It's so easy to know that murder is putting a gun to someone's head and pulling the trigger, but this madness is equally as deadly – maybe more so. At least when you're murdered your brain stops. Whereas, in this living death, your brain just continues to torture you long after your torturer quits. It's absolutely insane.

Chapter 18
Liars, Users, and Manipulators

*N*arcissists are so good at lying, using, and manipulating people. From the tiniest exaggeration (he downplays the cost of an expensive item he bought), to the innocent white lie (he told you he had to work late when, in fact, he went out with the boys), to outright fabrications (he tells you that he's mentoring a young boy with his math studies when in fact he's having sex with him) – the deceptions can be endless.

So many of the victims and survivors shared their incredible stories of illusion and unbelievable falsehoods. These lies became ongoing weapons in the insidious games being played within the ever-manipulative world run by the narcissists in their lives.

The important thing to remember is that this type of manipulation is intended to keep the unsuspecting victim under the control of the narcissistic partner. It keeps her in the dark as to reality, as well as keeps her off balance. Oftentimes, it keeps her second-guessing herself.

Jennifer

I am a well educated, professional woman with an MBA from Stanford and two Bachelors of Arts degrees from UC Berkeley. I only open this story with these credentials as evidence that even the well-educated can be fooled and deceived by these predators. To this day, I will never know how he pulled the wool over my eyes so effectively and for so long.

As a single, forty-something mother, I'd been on my own for years and was tired of waking up alone every morning, having to be the one to remember to take out the garbage on Thursdays, cleaning the gutters all by myself each October, and having nobody beside me at dusk with whom to share a beautiful sunset. I ran an ad seeking a life-partner who shared my passions for skiing, hiking, camping, and backpacking in the Rockies. Over 30 men answered and I chose to connect with one who was a couple of years my senior, articulate, sensitive, not macho, an avid skier, had a good job as a computer programmer, loved to cook, shared my dream of building a cabin in the mountains, and claimed that no matter what adventure I proposed, he could "keep up."

After two months of dating, Charlie proposed ... sort of. Actually, he asked me when it would be seemly for him to ask me to marry him. I suggested he wait six months. We did. Meanwhile, I said we'd better try living together before we got married, so we set about fixing up his house so we could rent it out. About that time he said he'd prefer not to have sex until we were married. He felt that as a single mother, I should set an example for my children and show them that sex was a part of a loving marriage, not a more casual thing.

I said I would not dream of marrying a man unless I knew we were sexually compatible. To which Charlie said that I'd have to be patient with him because it had been five years since his long-term girlfriend, Kathy, had moved out and he was feeling pretty anxious about performing sexually again. He said everything would work out fine if I'd just be patient and understanding.

Charlie had a roommate named Tim who spent most of his time sequestered in a bedroom that had its windows boarded up. I thought this pretty weird, so I asked Charlie about him. Apparently Tim was a friend of Charlie's ex-girlfriend of 12 years, and had stayed on as a roommate after Charlie's relationship with Kathy had ended five years prior. Charlie said Tim was the victim of a hit-and-run hate crime for being gay, which was why Tim didn't work. I thought Charlie was a saint! How generous to keep Tim on as a roommate, giving him an inexpensive living situation, so he could get by on his monthly disability check.

After we'd spent a couple of months together, Charlie introduced me to Justin, an 18-year-old teenager who he had been mentoring for two years. As a State of Colorado employee, Charlie had responded when the Governor had asked for volunteers to be mentors for troubled youths. I met Justin, skied with him along with my own two children, and thought we would all have a wonderful life. Charlie built a little studio in my garage so that Justin could stay overnight when he visited and so Charlie could have a private place to keep his computer and some other personal things. I am a teacher and I worked with Justin once or twice on reading and math, finding that at age 18 he was functioning at only about a second or third grade level.

As time went on, Tim moved out of Charlie's house, we rented it out, and Charlie moved in with me. Yet it wasn't long before I grew uneasy about the situation with Justin. The weekend that Charlie moved in with me I discovered that Justin had dropped out of high school. I overheard Justin making plans on his cell phone (which Charlie had provided him), to hang out with friends on a school day. I asked Charlie if he knew Justin was no longer in school. While he was apparently unaware of the situation, he acted unconcerned and indicated if this was the case then he'd have to help Justin get through his High School Equivalency test, the GED. My inner voice questioned, "How can a man who is a mentor not know, or apparently care, when his charge drops out of high school?" Later, when Charlie announced that Justin had gotten his GED, the same inner voice queried, "How can someone with his skills in reading and math have succeeded in this?" I now suspect that Charlie took the test the same day Justin did and that they used each other's names on their tests so that Justin could pass a test he could have never have successfully completed on his own. Complicity in criminal behavior is one of the most binding of all ties.

Over time I discovered that their time together was either spent skiing or otherwise having fun, eating out, going to concerts, shopping for snowboards, skateboards, cool clothing, leather coats,

– everything at Charlie's expense. Yet he kept telling me that he had $20,000 in credit card debt. Justin had a good part-time job and was making close to a thousand dollars each month on his own, so I didn't understand the financial situation at all. In January after he moved in with me, Charlie began planning a trip to Europe with Justin for skiing and snowboarding; supposedly as a reward for successfully obtaining his GED. I was shocked when I learned Charlie was planning on footing the entire bill for the trip. This was too much. I began to feel as though the time they spent together was more like "dating" than mentoring. In fact one time I came home unexpectedly and found Charlie and Justin in the studio smoking marijuana

Throughout this time, Charlie kept assuring me that his interest in Justin was purely paternal. As he'd never been a father, he saw his relationship with Justin as the one and only chance in life he'd have to be a father-figure to someone. He accused me of being not the least bit generous, extremely shrewish, overly suspicious, and hateful toward a disadvantaged young man. I argued that since Justin was nearly 19 he should be responsible for at least some of his skiing, skateboarding, and other "fun" expenses. I said I thought it fine and admirable that Charlie was willing to pay the bill for Justin's education or job training. I also told him that he needed to give Justin his snowboarding equipment so that he could go boarding sometimes with his peers, rather than always going with his "mentor."

When Charlie left for Europe with Justin, I decided to look through the things he had stashed away in the studio. I found a poetry anthology inscribed by Charlie's brother, indicating that the gay poetry within the book reminded him of Charlie's own poetry. I then discovered a hand-written notebook in which Charlie admitted committing armed robbery for kicks many years before. He had never been caught. I continued to read page after page of Charlie's descriptions of his sexual obsession with teenage boys and of his abhorrence for women.

Ironically, he hated himself for his sexual orientation. He wrote about how men wanted him to be like a "prostitute" in adult gay sexual encounters. He wrote about seeking idealized love with a much younger man or a boy who was "slim and lithe, with a 28-inch waist, a gorgeous, sinewy, bronzed body, and small feet."

I was reeling after reading the things in that journal. I think I must have gone into a sort of self-protective denial. How could I have let such a man into my life? How could I have exposed my children to such danger and been such a bad mother? He had succeeded in imprisoning me in his dark closet of homosexuality. I was afraid and ashamed to tell anyone what I'd found and read. If I could not even admit its dire consequences to myself, how could I share it, and my feelings regarding the situation, with anyone else?

When I found out that Charlie had been paying Justin's legal fines for ten months, I confronted him. I told him there was nothing less mentor-like he could be doing for Justin. I told him to give me Justin's address so that I could mail the court's legal notices to Justin at his father's address. Charlie had been receiving these notices at a P.O. Box that he rented, which he claimed he had in order to keep his mail safe from my children, who sometimes misplaced it. It was becoming clear to me that Charlie used this P.O. Box to hide many of the things he did for Justin from Justin's father and me.

When I got an envelope and began to make motions to send Justin's court notices to his father, Charlie followed me and then attacked me. He toppled me over backwards with a swift, two-handed blow to my upper chest. He smashed me face-first against a wall as I tried to flee. He smothered me with his own torso as I vehemently berated him for his ill-disguised financial manipulations of the young man he was supposedly mentoring.

As I flailed to breathe and fought him off my face, he withdrew, grabbing me around the throat so I thought he was about to strangle me. Instead, he held my neck and jaw firmly so that I could not avert my face, hacked up a large quantity of sputum, and then spat directly into my eyes.

It has taken me a great deal of time and therapy to get past the post-traumatic shock of being assaulted by the man I had loved, wanted to marry, and spend my life with. Not only did I grieve for myself, but as a mother I was heartsick for Justin. For his lost future. For what he had been robbed of.

Somehow I was able to get the strength to get tested for the diseases to which Charlie had exposed me and admit to myself and my therapist how I was so cleverly duped and thus used as a cover for his illicit activities with an innocent teenager. My ability to relate the horror of what he did to me came months later than my ability to describe what I saw happening to someone else.

It took many attempts, but someone at the Center for Missing and Abused Children finally listened to my story and filed a report. Local law enforcement and child abuse agencies were uninterested because of Justin's age at the time I was reporting the suspected abuse. The Department of Justice's Sexual Predator Apprehension Team assigned an agent to investigate, after receiving the report from the Center for Missing and Abused Children, but as is often the case in child sexual abuse, the victim's father was in denial. He just kept repeating that he thought the relationship Charlie had with his son was above board because Charlie and I were engaged. Frequently in situations like this, the teenage victim is afraid or embarrassed to come forward. Further, he was probably filled with conflicting emotions for the man in a position of trust who gave him so much, yet abused his authority and became an abuser in the young man's troubled life. A straight boy who is sexually abused by a homosexual can very easily doubt his own sexual orientation and may actually blame himself, believing that he was chosen because he exhibited homosexual tendencies. His shame can be a result of this and from his incredulity that the person he had grown to trust and love, would do him such harm.

So what were the warning signs that Charlie was a narcissist?

It goes without saying that he was an accomplished liar. He once looked me in the eye and said that I should not feel bad about being lied to because he lied to everyone, and his entire life was a lie. He was obsessed with his physical appearance. For a man, he spent a great deal of time on facials, eyebrow plucking, and finding shoes that made his feet look small and "sexy." He was a risk-taker who drove fast, regularly getting speeding tickets, and who spent money recklessly, as if there were no tomorrow.

He did not believe society's laws applied to him and he made no effort to disguise his contempt for the lowly masses that he believed needed to conform to his standards. He was very skilled at using money as a tool to manipulate people. He dressed in rags when we first met and I bought him a whole new wardrobe, yet he would turn around and spend lavishly on others to attain their adoration. I guess that's why it seemed he never had anything left for himself. He was articulate and gifted in his ability to craft an argument, talking circles around the best communicators – this in spite of a severe speech impediment that tormented him throughout his school years and finally came under control with intensive speech therapy obtained in his 30s. If you mentioned his stuttering, however, he would look you in the eye and say, "What stuttering? I've been cured for years." In fact, anyone who listened to him for 30 seconds could readily hear the speech defect. He truly believed it was gone.

He surrounded himself with men who were his intellectual and financial inferiors, which gave him the upper hand at all times. He barked orders at these lackeys while expecting them to look up to him and admire him. When asked why he kept his roommate around when he could find someone more interesting, he replied, "He thinks I'm God."

His self-image was all-important to him. Criticism or public humiliation drew a rage response in which he would go off verbally, shouting hysterically for hours on end, or go off physically, becoming enraged. The rages began with a darkening of his eyes into a profound blackness that conveyed a look of hatred and evil that can only be described as deadly. He was masochistic, driving in his car without turning on the air conditioning when the outside air temperature was over 100 degrees Fahrenheit and any sane person would use the air conditioner.

I filed charges after the assault, but as we were living together at the time he was only convicted of "misdemeanor spousal battery not causing injury." He was sentenced to 20 days in jail, but that was commuted to community service in a park. It hardly seemed fair.

I spent a lot of time talking with the police and other child agencies after this, trying to understand it all better. As it turns out, Tim had originally reported Charlie to the police as a suspected child predator when the relationship with Justin had just begun. He later recanted his story, so no investigation or charges were ever pursued. I also found out that Tim had indeed been Charlie's "partner" for many years and there was substantial evidence of abuse there. Somehow all the boarded up windows on the house where I first met Tim had a whole new meaning in that light.

So much pain for so many people.

The healing has been slow but I'm improving every day. I am still appalled that he was able to drag me into the dark corners of his closet with him for so long. He enslaved me with fear of never being loved again by anyone because I was afraid I had contracted one or both of the diseases he carried. It took six months before I knew whether I was disease-free or destined to carry his sickness with me for the rest of my life. When faced with the truth initially, I went into denial, clinging to the fantasy love relationship I had hoped for, rather than cutting my losses, admitting defeat, and moving on.

I have since learned that he has an aversion to having rectal sex with men and hates men who demand this of him. He also hates boys who sell sexual favors to homosexual men. (Once again even the rules regarding homosexual behavior don't apply to him – he is obviously better than they are, yet still the same.) He has unprotected sex with them because he finds them so abhorrent and never bothers to tell them of the diseases he carries. As for Justin, I cannot prove whether or not they ever had sex or if perhaps Charlie may have simply used Justin as his "ideal love" he sought and captured for a non-sexual, love interest. I'm sure I'll never know. It was all so convoluted when I learned of his other sexual behaviors.

As for me, I've tried to date again, but I'm just not ready. I run away when someone gets too serious or else they run away when I tell them of my ordeal.

The worst part was running into him at a ski resort recently. When I saw him again I was overwhelmed with fear. I nearly peed my pants. He was in the role of ski instructor there and I immediately reported him to the company as a convicted perpetrator of assault and one accused of child sexual abuse. I don't know what happened after that, but I hoped that I might save some other young boy by reporting him.

The Post Traumatic Stress that I endured still comes back on occasion – especially if I see someone in a crowd who reminds me of Charlie. I realize that I just have to give myself time.

> "He was like Dr. Jekyll and Mr. Hyde.
> I just never knew who to expect when."
> Peggy – survivor

Chapter 19
I'm So Ugly, Stupid, Crazy, Incapable ...

*J*amie is 48 years old. At her friends' insistence, she called me after they read one of my columns on narcissism called, "When Mr. Right Is Really Mr. Wrong." Her friends had convinced her that I might be able to help her deal with her feelings concerning her abusive husband, who had left her self-esteem shredded to almost nothing. As we talked for over an hour, my heart ached for this woman's pain. She was definitely at the end of her rope. Hers was one of the worst stories of fear, manipulation, pain, torture, and brainwashing that I had heard throughout the course of gathering information for this book. While I am pleased to say that Jamie is healing, the road back from this much darkness can only be taken one step at a time.

Jamie

I was one of 12 children in my family. That alone is a setup for feeling lost and unimportant in the masses. Growing up, I certainly didn't feel special or valued in any way. In addition, I ended up with a stepfather who sexually abused me from the time I was 8 until I was 14. When I finally got up the nerve to tell my mother what was going on, she only reinforced my beliefs that I wasn't valuable to anyone – she simply told me that he wouldn't have abused me if I "hadn't asked for it." Talk about feeling devalued a second time!

The abuse went on until one day I'd had enough and I took a pool cue to the man and also to my parent's house. It's like I went berserk, ripping apart furniture and shattering glass. I guess I just snapped. Unfortunately, I ended up in jail for a while as a result. Just one more thing that taught me I was meaningless, that men were allowed to be controlling, and that I had to obey them at all costs. It was becoming clear that men were always right and I was always inferior.

I had been in a few relationships over the years but this last one with Bud has done the most damage, emotionally as well as physically. We have been married nearly 10 years and throughout that time I must have left him at least 20 times. Yet, each time I always returned with my tail between my legs, with Bud demanding that I beg *his* forgiveness. Even though I usually left because he had been physically abusing me, I still felt I was forced to come crawling back. I guess I did this because he had convinced me that I was so stupid, ugly, fat, and worthless that no one else could ever possibly want me. Being with him still seemed better than being alone.

He had so many little ways of manipulating and hurting me. I was not allowed to go to bed unless he told me I could. He never once gave me a Christmas card or present, or Valentines or birthday acknowledgement. I was certainly never allowed to have an opinion. In all the years we were together, he never even knew where I worked – that detail just wasn't important enough for him to bother with.

The abuse was so multifaceted that, as I look back, I am amazed. For years I begged him just to hold my hand or give me a hug, but he wouldn't allow such behavior. Yet if we went to the grocery store or out to a bar, and there were women he knew there, he would hug them openly in front of me. One time when I was hospitalized he even began flirting with a pretty nurse and disappeared with her for hours.

I would make elaborate meals for him and, just to spite me, he would take one look and then pick up his plate full of food and throw it in the trash. Then he would go make himself a baloney sandwich. To make matters worse, he would tell all our friends and neighbors that I never cooked for him. We'd have dinner at someone's home and he'd complain to them, "I wish I'd get stuff like this at my house."

One of his favorite daily rituals was telling me to be sure I realized that my entire value in life was only 29 cents – "the price of a bullet." He made me repeat this message each and every day of my life with him. He'd say, "Now don't give me the wrong answer, Jamie, or you'll pay. Tell me again, what you're worth," and I'd have to tell him "29 cents" or I'd be punished in some way. "And don't you ever forget it," he would remind me at the end of each ritual. Only now do I realize the constant brainwashing this daily message had on me. I spent years believing that I was absolutely worthless and I still struggle with that inner message every day.

He participated in everything from name-calling ("You're so stupid"), to physical beatings, to constant threats on my life. I was never allowed to come to breakfast with my pajamas or robe on. I was required to be fully dressed because I was "too ugly" to be seen any other way. Of course, it was quite acceptable for his daughter in her 30s to come to breakfast in her bra and panties. It didn't even occur to me until now that perhaps they were intimate and that's why she was allowed and encouraged to behave that way.

Making love with me was just one more avenue for finding fault. One time while we were in the middle of having intercourse, he stopped suddenly and said to me, "You know, I could get a $10 hooker and she'd do a better job than you." I was so hurt. I couldn't believe he'd said that. Then he wanted me to continue and was totally miffed when I no longer had the interest. Of course, I got punished for that too.

The sex game was played other ways. Sometimes he'd go for weeks at a time and withhold it from me. Then, he might walk in the house on any given night and simply say, "Do me." Of course he meant right now. I was supposed to drop and obey without question.

He also was a master of the "silent treatment." One time he refused to talk to me for two-and-a-half months. Imagine that. Coming home and serving your husband, your life partner, and having him totally ignore you for weeks at a time. That was yet another punishment for something I did wrong. I don't think he ever even told me what I'd done. Yet the silence was deafening and intensely powerful. He certainly showed me who was in control.

Sometimes he didn't even care who was around when he played the abuse game with me. One time we were having dinner with friends at a restaurant. I don't even remember what I said to him that set him off, but in front of our friends, in a fit of rage, he threw his drink on me and left the table. My friends were shocked and asked me why on earth he had done that. All I could say was, "Well, that's just Bud. He just gets like that sometimes." I never really understood, back then, that his behavior was out of the norm. That it was abusive. I just accepted it as my lot in life. After all, I was worthless – he told me so every day. Who was I to complain?

Once, on a motorcycle trip, he and I were riding double on our Harley. As we were approaching a cliff, he began to threaten me that he should just drive us both over the edge. At first I thought he was kidding, but as he kept driving I began to think that he was serious. In a sudden moment of fear I leaped off the bike, realizing that he just might carry out the threat. Within moments he jumped too. To my pure and utter amazement, he let the bike disappear over the cliff! It's moments like that when you wonder what the man really and truly is capable of.

Frequently he would tell me that if I ever thought about leaving him, he could bury me and my car so quickly that no one would ever find me. So despite how much I feared him, I was more afraid to leave than to stay. I got to the point where sometimes I wished that he would just get it over with and kill me. The threats and constant worry were exhausting. I was tired so much of the time I just didn't think I could take it anymore. I thought of suicide so many times, wondering if that would be my only reprieve to this life of torture. Yet he would always assure me that *he* would be the one to determine when I lived or died, so even suicide did not feel like an option.

He beat me often over the years. Rarely on my face, so no one could tell, but on less obvious areas of my body. He would take a tire iron to me, breaking my ribs and one time bruising my kidneys so I had to go to the hospital. He has shot at me with his shotgun so many times that one time he actually killed the cow that I had hid behind to avoid getting hit myself.

Even worse was the night that he got angry at me because he believed that I hadn't treated his grown daughter nicely. He made me sit on the floor of the closet for 10 hours and I had to hold his gun in my mouth the entire time. So there I sat for hours with that cold gun in my mouth and in utter terror to even breathe unless he gave me permission. At one point I told him that I needed to use the bathroom and he said, "Just piss on yourself." I dared not move until he allowed me to.

I can't even believe it now, looking back. All that seems like a scene from a horror movie. It seems surreal.

> *Could something that awful really have happened between a husband and wife? And worse, did I actually allow it? The ironic thing is that, despite everything, I continued to be more afraid to leave than to stay.*

He knew how to play the guilt manipulation game so well. He would always threaten to kill himself if I ever left. He'd taunt me with, "I should just relieve everyone's misery and go put a bullet in my brain right now. That would make everyone's life easier now, wouldn't it?" He'd actually sit in front of me and hold a gun to his chin. Then he'd even threatened to dig his own grave outside by the barn, so as not to bother anyone with the task. Oh, he was so clever with that game. He knew that I worried day and night that if he killed himself it would be my fault. He probably knew that would send me over the edge and I would be in the loony bin after that.

Somehow, I actually convinced him once that our marriage would be better if we'd see a marriage counselor. God knows how I did that. However, even that turned against me. The woman counselor blamed *me* for all of the problems in our marriage. She told me that my husband was the "man of the house" and that I had created all my own problems. That only gave him more ammunition to hurt me. I had hoped for someone to help me, but I guess this counselor had no clue about narcissism or else my husband had put on such a great act that she missed the clues completely. I can't tell you the devastating feeling I was left with.

Just a few months ago I finally summoned up enough courage to leave him. It was early November and despite the fact that the holidays were approaching, I just couldn't stay there with him one more day. Knowing I only had a few hours before he came home, I rented a U-Haul van, found a storage unit, and paid for it with a credit card I wasn't supposed to have. Then I went to stay with relatives. I was terrified to know what his reaction to my disappearance would be. When he finally located me by phone at my sister's house, he was livid and bellowed across the phone lines, "My housekeeper, my cook, my laundry person, my lackey, my sex toy, my punching bag — they've all moved out. Just what the hell am I supposed to do now?!" That left me frozen with fear and, at the same time, drowning in guilt for leaving him all alone.

I stood my ground and stayed at my sister's, but as each day went by I felt worse. The guilt of leaving him kept dragging me down. Instead of feeling free, I felt even more trapped by his omnipotent power. Then he made his grown kids call me all the time and tell me how cruel I was for leaving "poor Dad" during the holidays like that. They also used my grandbabies against me. If I ever wanted to see the babies again, they said, I needed to return right away. This from his kids who didn't even like me to begin with!

I admit to caving in at Christmas and I went back for a few days — but just with an overnight case. By this time I had learned about narcissism and I was more educated about the Red Flag behaviors. It was suddenly so much clearer to me than ever before. When I approached Bud with my new information on narcissism, he flew into a rage again and denied that he fit any of the profiles I described. In fact, he accused me of being the one who needed help. I left shortly after that, when it finally became clear to me that he was never going to change and that living with him would be the death of me.

I'm finally finding a new path and I'm slowly letting go. I keep catching myself wanting to ask his advice or to know who he is spending the night with, but I realize it's none of my business. I have bought my own house and a new car – all the while terrified of what he will say when he finds out. Isn't that odd? I'm working two jobs to keep my mind as well as my body busy – and to be able to pay for my own house without depending on anyone else. It's very freeing, but very frightening at the same time. I look for him whenever I get out of my car at night. I'm afraid he's stalking me, but I don't think he knows where I live. I am still overwhelmed with guilt about leaving him all the time. I only wish I understood that emotion better and could shake it, but it hangs over me like a shroud.

Of course, he has done his very best to get me back. His most amazing performance was when he went to some mutual friends of ours and sat there sobbing at their kitchen table – telling them how much he loved me and missed me. He even conned them into trying to convince me to call him and see if we couldn't work it out, but I just know it's not healthy for me to go back there ever again.

The sad thing is that these friends have no idea what went on behind closed doors. They only see the Bud he wants them to see – a successful businessman in the community.
A loving father. A great comedian.
They can't imagine the torture chamber I lived in for so many years.

Furthermore, they don't want to hear it.
No one wants to hear about the misery.

On the other hand, I now realize my contribution in destroying so many of my own relationships while I let Bud run my life. Of all my 12 brothers and sisters, only one sister remains faithful and helpful. I have alienated all the others. I think it's probably like having an alcoholic or drug addict in the family. Everyone tries and tries to help them get clean and sober, but they just keep going back and going back to their addiction – despite knowing what the drug or alcohol does to their health and their relationships. Bud had me so convinced that I didn't need anyone else but him, that I destroyed my relationships with my own siblings.

The hardest, but most important part, is recognizing the role I allowed myself to play in this vicious game. I never stood up for myself early in the relationship. I never set my boundaries and stuck to them. I let him mash me to bits and I just kept on staying. It's almost as though I was addicted to him. To his abuse. And felt justified in whining to everyone about my problems. I finally learned that people grow tired of hearing it and being unable to help. At some point they just give up.

I realize now that my life is up to me. I have to stand up for me and take care of me because it's not anyone else's job to do so. Part of the reason I bought a house is so that I would have a commitment to planting myself and not relying on someone else to take care of me.

I have to remind myself each and every day that I am a valuable person. A friend has helped me to change my daily mantra from: "I'm only worth 29 cents" to "I'm worth a million bucks!" It is so hard to change those deep-seated beliefs he brainwashed me with, but I'm going to do it. I still have a lot of good years left in me if I do things right from here on out. But I have to realize that it's up to me now.

Hopefully time will begin to heal old wounds with my family and I can reestablish those relationships again. I know in the beginning they won't believe I've changed, but I *will* prove this time that it's my turn. That I do *not* need Bud to define me anymore.

Of course, I worry for his next victim. Perhaps sharing this story will save some other unsuspecting woman from him, at least for a while.

It seems so ironic now. What games does the mind play that keeps us in such horrific situations?

I wish I knew.

> *"I have no doubt that*
> *had I not gotten out of my marriage,*
> *I would be dead by now."*
> *Jamie – survivor*

Part Three
Changing the Dance

"The best way to predict the future is to create it."
Jason Kaufmann

Chapter 20
The Deer in the Headlights

*I*f you've never seen the movie *American Beauty*, or even if you have, I highly suggest that you go out and rent it and watch it again. Why? Because now that you know what narcissism is, there is a very small character you might recognize this time; one you probably overlooked completely the first time. I bet if you did watch the movie already you won't even be able to picture her now, even after I describe her in depth. But armed with your new-found ammunition, she will clearly jump out at you as a fellow victim of narcissism.

You'll notice I said **victim** and not **survivor**.

The character I'm talking about is a woman played by Alison Janney, the actress made famous starring in television's *West Wing*. In the movie, Janney's character is the mother of a teenaged boy and is married to a retired military officer. As a result of years of living with her domineering husband, she has the "deer in the headlights" look throughout the movie. Looking into her eyes one gets the feeling that no one is home. She has been berated, held up for ridicule, and condemned for so long that she no longer fights her situation, believing that she is as unimportant as the furniture. That's why you barely noticed her the first time. It's as though she isn't there to begin with.

As I had just begun to explore and learn about narcissism at the time that movie came out, her character really left an impression on me, when she probably barely caught the eye of anyone else.

Whoever wrote that screenplay must have known narcissism inside out and backwards. This character's house is spotless, as her lifetime military husband will not tolerate anything less than perfectionism. She is invisible to others. They don't ask for her opinion or what she would like to do. It's like she's a maid in a hotel – totally unnoticed unless something is amiss.

As it turns out, we learn at the end of the movie that her "perfect" military husband – a retired career officer – is gay ... after he spends the entire movie condemning other gay men everywhere.

We've all heard the term a "broken spirit." In the old cowboy days, the way they broke a horse was to wear it down through exhaustion, demoralize it with physical abuse, withhold food and water, and literally hound it to death until it quit fighting and started "behaving." Fortunately even horse training these days has begun to utilize methods of gentling that are much more productive in working towards a partnership between horse and rider. I always find it ironic that animals seem to be more important to us in some ways. I remember reading as a kid that laws first came in to play to prevent cruelty to animals long before they did to prevent cruelty to humans. When I watched *American Beauty*, all I could think of was the "good old days" of horse breaking.

Another memorable movie depicting a woman in this captive mental position is *Sleeping With the Enemy*, which I mentioned earlier. (While you're expanding your understanding of narcissism, be sure to see this movie as well.) Julia Roberts' character is married to an incredible narcissistic abuser. One minute he's beating her and the next day he is bringing her sexy sleepwear from Victoria's Secret – a gift for her as an apology for his behavior the night before. He tells her that he "didn't really mean" to hit her, but if she hadn't said or done some perceived wrong he wouldn't have *had* to hit her to begin with. While he sees the negligee as a gift to her, it is in fact, just one more toy in his manipulation game. It's a tool to get her to "perform" in bed for him as one of her many duties as his wife, as he admires her black eye from his handiwork of the previous evening.

One of his other "quirks" is his anal retentive, perfectionistic behavior. He is compulsive about how he has the soup cans and other items lined up on the shelf, how the towels must be hung "just so" in the bathroom, and how spotless the house must be kept. She is punished regularly if she forgets to keep these details upheld. He holds a powerful position in his company and has money for all the greatest toys and cars and a fancy house. Life looked pretty perfect to all of Julia's friends who envied her wealthy, housewife life from a distance. Yet she had to lie to them about her recurrent bruises from all the beatings and explain them away as being sustained in gymnastics class.

What's incredibly wrong with this picture? Both these women see themselves as captives. They see no way out. They seemingly have given up every shred of their own lives for that of another. In Julia Roberts' case, she eventually escapes, but not without extreme risk. In Alison Janney's case we are left to believe that her spirit is already so broken that there is nothing left to salvage. That she is beyond help.

If you wonder about your relationship and your role in it, do yourself a favor and watch those movies very carefully. Can you see the "deer in the headlights" look? Can you relate to these women in any way? If you are in a narcissistic relationship, do you want to end up this way?

Certainly not every relationship is as bad as these two – yet some are worse. As you have been able to see from some of the stories contained in this book, narcissism is rampant. Many of these victims stayed in their torturous environments for years. Many are still there, feeling helpless to get out. Yet there are others who have chosen to take care of themselves. Not only have they moved on, but they have found environments so much safer, more loving, and more conducive to better emotional and physical health for themselves and their children.

But first they had to recognize the situation.

After that, they had to decide which steps to take
to change their situation.

The choice is yours.

> *"It's not that some people have willpower*
> *and some don't.*
> *It's that some people are ready to change*
> *and some are not."*
> *James Gordon, MD*

Chapter 21
Walking on Eggshells

*I*f I printed all the stories people have sent me, this book would be so big you couldn't carry it. Yet, one of the most interesting things about gathering real-life accounts was the commonality in language and feelings among respondents. I found it absolutely fascinating that these people, who came from all over the country and with completely different circumstances, could use exactly the same phrases and describe exactly the same feelings ...

❏ "I was always walking on eggshells around him."
❏ "It felt like I was on a never-ending roller coaster ride and I just couldn't figure out how to get off."
❏ "I felt like we lived inside a tornado."
❏ "The silent treatment was constant and deafening."
❏ "I never knew what I did wrong."
❏ "I always felt so stupid."
❏ "Everything was always my fault."
❏ "I carried such guilt every day of my life."

And, when victims first learn about narcissism and realize that they are not alone and they are not crazy to think or feel the way they do, they are all equally overwhelmed with relief. It's like they've awakened from a coma after years of sleep with continuous nightmares.

Then they start to examine their situations more closely for all the tell-tale tracks that narcissists leave in their wake. They start to see the Red Flags they ignored for so long. And only then do they begin to have hope and see the possibility of a future with sunshine and blue sky.

Susan

The warning signs of his narcissistic behavior appeared early on. He controlled every situation, without regard to my needs or feelings. In one instance, we were visiting his family in Europe and my period started a week early. He had some visits with friends scheduled that day and I told him that I needed to go to a drugstore. He insisted that we go to his friends' house immediately in order to stay on schedule. Needless to say, it was the most uncomfortable visit I have ever had! Just one more of those nagging Red Flags I chose to ignore. In hindsight, I wonder where my head was not to see the ridiculousness of it all.

Georgia

The fact is that life with one of these people is like living in a storm – always struggling to find the "eye of the hurricane" for a moment of peace. On the other hand, I believe that when we rely on seeking validation from others instead of ourselves, that's how we fall into their tempest to begin with. True validation is not something you can seek outside yourself. It is the fruit of an inner journey and discovery. To know oneself from the inside-out, rather than from the outside-in. Like love, we think it is outside ourselves so we try to grab it, hold it, and then control it ... then poof! It's gone, like an illusion or dream. Sometimes it takes falling apart to wake up and see what is real. That's when the inner work begins and passion becomes a product of grace, rather than greed or need.

Sam

Her verbal abuse was constant and mostly subtle. From an outsider's perspective, it might be seen as a form of friendly teasing. But the tone and frequency would indicate it was nothing but destructive. She maintained a sense of superiority by letting me know that I could not do anything as well as she could. She reminded me constantly that I was not as organized, knowledgeable, driven, ambitious, smart, or capable. She repeatedly told me that she had to do everything for me, because I was incapable of doing it right in her eyes.

Why did I believe her for so long?

Jackie

My birthday was always neglected. The first year it fell just before our wedding and was forgotten in the rush. The next year my husband was traveling and "didn't have time" to send a card or get me anything. When I pressed him on it, he brought out a present two weeks later. I was pleasantly surprised, until I saw that it was a windscreen for *his* car. The third year we actually had dinner together and he gave me a small gift. Then last year, he decided to throw me a birthday party. I was so pleased at first, but it turned out that the party was not actually for me. He invited his two groups of friends and a few of mine. Out of the 30 people who attended the party, I knew about 6. It was everything that *he* wanted; the music, the people, the alcohol. I put on a smiling face and thanked him for his effort. Then I went upstairs to take a phone call and was gone for about 25 minutes and no one even noticed my absence. He enjoyed himself and took pictures of his friends (I'm in two shots out of all of them). It was very clear that he threw himself a party and invited me along. This was one of the most insulting things I had experienced.

And yet I stayed.

Kris

He has now filed for divorce and has been pressing me to keep it out of court to minimize expenses. I decided that I am not going to go alone in this process without the support of legal counsel. He is threatening me that if I do not comply with his wishes, "We'll go bankrupt." It's obviously a ploy to make me feel insecure and question my own decision. Since I have been away from him, I feel much more confident and have begun to realize that almost everything he demands of me has an underlying motive for his self-interest. I feel that I am beginning the healing process through the physical and mental separation. I can now look objectively and see his manipulative ploys for what they are. I no longer get caught up in his emotionally charged tangents that used to make me feel confused and "less-than." This is the best thing that could have happened, given the circumstance. I now feel stronger and smarter and hope to develop a healthy relationship with an emotionally available man sometime in the future.

Cori

The marriage was definitely emotionally abusive. The remarks were always very subtle. He questioned every decision I made, from what type of mayonnaise I purchased to why I went to graduate school and incurred a student debt. He told me that I was using the wrong knife to cut vegetables. "Don't you know that?!" he would chastise me. Or, "I always have to do everything (correctly) for you" – implying I was incapable of doing anything right. He told me that my parents did not educate me properly – "Didn't they teach you how to 'open the bed' every morning to let the moisture out?!" He reminded me, "What would you do without me? Aren't you glad that you're with someone with a head on his shoulders?" Nothing I did could ever measure up to him.

It took me the longest time, but at last I learned to trust my gut and not what he said any longer.

Mitch

It's very subtle, the manipulation. You can't even see it happening. It creeps into your life. It's amazing and fascinating. It's not obvious abuse. You don't even have any scars to prove it. There was just something in her that was very sadistic and evil under his gorgeous exterior shell.

Jessica

My kids used to say I changed whenever I was around Tom. They knew the minute I would let him back into my life. "Where did you go? What happened to you? Is anybody home?" they would ask. And they weren't talking about my physical presence. They said I went to "Thomasville," whenever I was seeing him again. It wasn't a location – it was an emotional and behavioral place I lived in that was outside of the usual me. Like that old movie, *The Stepford Wives*. They said I was like a robot. Not even human.

I kept thinking if I just tried harder we could work it out, so despite my kids begging me I would pick up the phone and make up with him again and again. This last time was different though. I noticed some old and uncomfortable triggers that I knew I would not be strong enough to challenge. I immediately closed the door. However, the experience has helped me see how far I've come and how far I still have to go on the journey. I can't honestly say that I am completely over him, but I am getting there.

Keeping your head above the water when the waves are rough is exhausting, sometimes unbearable. If we don't drown, we become stronger swimmers and the joy and gratitude, when all is calm, magnifies everything.

If I don't believe this, I will drown.

Maybe that is having faith.

Suicidal Thoughts

Many victims and survivors frequently talk of entertaining suicidal thoughts. The never-ending mental exhaustion, depression, anxiety, sadness, chronic confusion, and fatigue leave them feeling that there is no other way to stop the noise. The fear they have of leaving their narcissist often outweighs the fear they have of staying. And so, they wonder if suicide is their only chance at peace.

Mary Beth

The last week he was living in the house I realized suicide was the only alternative to divorce. Thank God he left.

Jillian

For God's sake don't tell him you're thinking of killing yourself. You'll receive absolutely no empathy or compassion but plenty of criticism. I had suicidal thoughts all the time. Sometimes I fantasized that it would stop the pain. You start to think it's the only option. But here's the thing – you finally realize that if you kill yourself, your tormentor will still go on living and it just pisses you off when you think about it that way. I think that's what kept me alive through the worst of it. I refused to let him win.

Thank God I never went through with it.

My life is finally peaceful now. It was worth the wait.

Kathy

I used to wish I would die of natural causes. I was on antidepressants for years, but they never seemed to help. I even think I had some pretty risky behaviors from time to time. I flirted with death but never took pills or cut myself. I resorted to prayer and support groups to keep me alive until I figured a way to get out.

My own experience with suicide...

I was one of those who had to hit rock bottom before I could pull myself out of the darkness. My self-esteem torn to shreds. My personal belief in my value, non-existent. The depression so severe I slept half of every day away and yet remained exhausted. I felt as thought I was walking in a never-ending fog that wouldn't quit. Squinting to see daylight. Blinking my eyes in an attempt to clear them, but with no luck. And constantly hoping for some direction, some reprieve, some end to the emotional turmoil that ate me alive.

I actually wrote a suicide letter. Fortunately, the mere act of writing it scared me back into reality.

**The truth is I never really wanted to die.
I just wanted the pain to stop and couldn't figure out how.**

Yet, that terrible moment is probably what changed my life. It scared me so much that I knew I had to do something dramatically different or else I would just end up right back in that black abyss at a later date. Whether I took my own life or ran my car absentmindedly into traffic or just curled up in a corner and died of complete depression, it didn't matter. I knew it was only a matter of time if I didn't do something drastic. I made a conscious decision to live and to change.

I was especially lucky. I had some money stashed away and an empty nest that gave me the freedom to get "outside my boxx" and I moved to Cozumel, Mexico to live and work for six months. I escaped without car, phone, mail, or friend and I went so far away from my normal treadmill that change was bound to happen. It just couldn't help it.

My time in Mexico was the best gift I ever gave myself. It gave me space to breathe and heal and be mindless. It gave me the time to rebuild my self-esteem and become whole again. It gave me an environment and an opportunity to test my boundaries with new people. I know in my heart that had I not reached the point of seriously considering taking my own life, that I would still be a zombie walking in a fog. I guess the old adage is correct that God only gives you as much as you can handle. It has become my mantra.

I have a new respect for people who talk about suicide now. I know their pain. I find myself bristling when I hear those who don't understand, tell me that "suicide is the most selfish act anyone can ever do." What that tells me is that the voice behind that phrase has never been in such a dark place that the only way out appeared to be through death. They know not of what they speak.

However, what I also learned through this journey is that no matter how bad things may seem,

THERE IS ALWAYS AN ALTERNATIVE!

The greatest quote I discovered later is this:

SUICIDE IS A LONG-TERM ANSWER
TO A SHORT-TERM PROBLEM
(Iris Bolton, *The Phases of Grief*)

I only recently discovered the author of this quote and I want to thank her from the bottom of my heart for speaking these thoughts so perfectly. When looked at from that perspective, it is a lifeline for anyone on the edge of despair.

If ever you have suicidal thoughts, grab this quote and repeat it to yourself over and over and over until you believe it in your soul.

SUICIDE IS A LONG-TERM ANSWER
TO A SHORT-TERM PROBLEM

Let it be your mantra too. Let it remind you that no matter what you're dealing with in your life, there are answers. You may just need to find someone who knows how to help you find the switch to turn the light back on and bring you out of the darkness.

We are out there.

Find yourself someone you can count on for times like these and hold them in a special place in your heart. There are many of us who can help. Just reach out to us … we'll be glad to take your hand.

One more thing about suicide – narcissists rarely commit suicide. It is not generally in their makeup. I mean think about it for a minute – would God commit suicide? You see the ridiculousness of it? This is not to say that they are incapable, but is a gentle reminder that it is most commonly the victim who has suicidal feelings. So, if your narcissist threatens suicide if you leave, do not let that hold you. More than likely it is just another piece of his ammunition in his ongoing battle to keep you in your place.

Angelica

I feel like I have a future and hope again. I thought I was stuck on a horrific roller coaster and couldn't get off. I thought I had no control over my life and no hope for love, relationship, and family. Now I know that *I control my life.* I have a second chance. I am pursuing my dreams now and moving on to healthy relationships.

Life really is wonderful!

"Depression is merely anger without enthusiasm."
Steven Wright

Chapter 22
Now You Know

Knowledge is power. Congratulations! You have just earned your bachelor's degree in the School of Narcissism. (There are master's and doctoral level classes, if you're interested!) The best thing and the worst thing about having this new knowledge is this:

❏ You can never go back to being one of the uninformed.
❏ You can never go back to blaming someone else for your pain and suffering.
❏ You have come to the realization by now that you do have choices in all you do.
❏ How you live your life is up to you.
❏ From now on, you are not allowed to let anyone else choose your life for you.
❏ *You* are responsible for your actions.

While many of you may think you are trapped with your partner in your torturous Boxx of Narcissism, the fact is that you may have just forgotten what your options are. You gave up believing in yourself to begin with. And over time, you bought into the belief that you had no value of your own and …

- ❑ That you can't possibly live without your "perfect partner."
- ❑ That your survival depends upon them.
- ❑ That they love you like no one else can.
- ❑ That no one else might want you.
- ❑ That the world is a dangerous place and your safety and security depends upon your partner.
- ❑ That because you've invested so much time in your relationship, it is "a shame to throw it all away."
- ❑ That you can't support yourself financially on your own.
- ❑ That your partner won't "let you go."
- ❑ That he or she can't survive without you.
- ❑ That someone needs to "take care" of him or her.
- ❑ That your friends or family won't support your decision to leave.
- ❑ That all your relationship problems are your fault.
- ❑ That if you wait long enough, things will "get better."
- ❑ That your partner is "really a good person on the inside."
- ❑ That the bad times really "aren't that bad."

Think about these statements very carefully. They are very telling and can give you some great insight into your beliefs and your behaviors. Once you have clarity here it will help you determine the best course of action…

Whether or not you should "Love or Leave," the narcissist in your life.

Now that you have read the stories so many shared within the body of this book, it's time to reflect on how your own personal story is similar or different. Maybe you're fortunate and are in a healthy relationship with someone who cares for you and about you, as much as he or she cares about themselves. If you are, then congratulations are in order! You are one of the lucky ones who learned to set your boundaries early and often in your relationship and, by doing so, learned whether your partner was cooperative and caring, or not. If he was, you kept him. If not, you moved on.

However, if you see any similarities to your own life and the real-life stories within this book, then maybe it's time you ask yourself some serious questions about your relationships, whether they are with a significant other, co-worker, boss, friend, business partner, or parent:

❑ Why do I stay in this relationship?
❑ Why do I not feel I am entitled to fair treatment?
❑ Why do I keep taking the abuse dished out by my partner?
❑ Why don't I feel like an equal?
❑ Why aren't my needs important too?
❑ Why don't I set my boundaries and stick to them?
❑ Do I really want to spend the rest of my life this way?

These are questions only you can answer.
And perhaps it's high time you ask them.

It is not the intent of this book to tell anyone in a narcissistic relationship that they must leave those relationships. That's not realistic. Each of our situations is unique and where one person might be overwhelmed and engulfed in a narcissistic relationship, a stronger person might not feel the same level of frustration, anger, or any other emotion frequently experienced by a typical victim.

For example, think about what it must be like to be in a relationship with Donald Trump. He's probably one of the most powerful and wealthy men in the world. That alone would intimidate most of us. So what kind of woman can handle him? I suspect Oprah Winfrey wouldn't be the least bit intimidated by Donald Trump. She could probably go toe-to-toe with Donald and not feel one iota less than he. She is a tough, dynamo of a woman and probably knows how to set her boundaries quite clearly. Yet, you or I would probably feel pretty small in his presence. Pretty inferior. And that's without him even saying a word! If you're an Oprah-type person in a relationship with an extremely narcissistic person, you may do just fine. You may know how to set boundaries and stand up for yourself. Yet, if you are not that sure of yourself, you may easily be overwhelmed by your narcissistic partner and become engulfed. Only you know what role you play in your relationship.

Keep in mind that not every narcissist has full-blown Narcissistic Personality Disorder – or will necessarily get worse. Some may only show tendencies. The situation you are in may not be bad enough to dictate that you change your entire life around as a result – or maybe it does. It's all up to you. But it's important to remember that narcissism is on a scale. Think of it this way … on a scale of one to ten, consider one healthy narcissism and ten, Adolph Hitler. You might be in a relationship with someone anywhere in between. Yet even if your mate is only a three on that scale, his stuff combined with your stuff (leftover baggage from your past as well) can lead you to be over the top in emotional unhealthiness. Only you can weigh in on what each of you brings to the table; good, bad, or ugly.

Thus far, you have taken a good step toward understanding the inner workings of a narcissist and this can give you ammunition to better deal with their behaviors. If you are a strong person and are willing to adapt to best meet your partner's needs – to keep life as stable as possible – then that's what you might feel is your best option. If you've got four young kids, for example, and no way to earn a living on your own, you may feel that you cannot leave your relationship. (Yet, believe me … there are always alternative choices when your life depends on it.)

Or you may realize that your emotional health is deteriorating under the constant turmoil your partner creates on a daily basis. You may believe that something's going to "snap" somewhere pretty soon and you don't want your kids to suffer in this turbulent environment. If so, then you owe it to yourself to get out as soon as possible.

Some of the people who sent me their stories were survivors. They had escaped. For many, it was not easy – either emotionally or logistically. Most talk about their experiences like this:

❑ "I didn't know that the silent treatment was another form of abuse. I can't tell you how many years I must have lived like that. At one time he didn't speak to me for two-and-a-half months and we lived in the same house together all that time. I thought I was going to go crazy."

❑ "The eggshell-walking was the worst. I never knew what would set him off. Worse than that, I never knew what I did wrong for days until he decided to tell me."

❑ "A narcissist is really only married to himself. Never really to a spouse. It doesn't matter how long you're together or what you do for them, they just suck the life right out of you."

❑ "My mother raised three children in a strict, Catholic household. She instilled guilt and shame as a means of control. It almost killed me to leave her but it would certainly have killed my soul to have stayed any longer."

❑ "When we first met he presented me with a feast of life. Later, if he didn't like something, he would take something off the table. At the end, if I got anything I would be grateful. Like a bone on the table."

Only you can assess your emotional and physical health and well-being, for yourself as well as your children. Only you know why you stay. Only you can change your behaviors if you want to.

Realizing that you do have a choice is the first step.

My client Carolyn wrote this poem about her own recognition in learning to read between the lines. You may find it insightful and way too familiar.

Read Between the Lines

I love you.
You are stupid.
I love you.
You are not a very good cook.
I love you.
Your family is a bad influence on you.
I love you.
Your passion is a real turn off.
I love you.
I don't trust you.
I love you.
You are fat.
I love you.
You don't know what you are talking about.
I love you.
Your opinions don't matter.
I love you.
You are undesirable.
I love you.
The house isn't clean enough.
I love you.
You are not a very good mom.
I love you.
You really annoy me.
I love you.
You take too much effort.
I love you.
You are not worth my time.
I love you.
You don't have very good judgment.
I love you.
You are the problem.
I love you.
You say that you love me but I can read between the lines.

Chapter 23
But Is He Really a Narcissist?

*I*t's always encouraging to me to see my clients heal, as they put more and more distance between themselves and the unhealthy people who have caused much destruction, pain, and anguish in their lives. As they learn how to strengthen their boundaries for safety and love. And as they begin to truly believe they are valuable, worthy people ... people deserving to be treated well, loved unconditionally, and respected as equals in all their relationships. It's as though they have been living their lives in the dark and, for the first time, come out into the sunlight with healthy people. They can't believe the difference and most kick themselves for waiting so long to do something about their plight, once they begin to experience life in something other than a perpetual war zone.

And yet, when I first start working with these folks so desperate for help, I always smile because the most consistent question I always hear is, "Yes, but is he (she) *really* a narcissist?" It seems as though unless they get concrete proof of this diagnosis, many hesitate making any change to their situation, no matter what degree of DIS-ease is going on in their homes.

Labeling someone with a diagnosis of Narcissistic Personality Disorder is the job of a qualified psychological health professional. Of course there are psychological tests that can be done to diagnose this person, yet for the purposes of my clients I don't want to focus on that. (For unless the courts order a psych eval, most narcissists aren't too excited about taking one to begin with! As I mentioned earlier, these do hold up in court, however, and may be key in custody awarding, if nothing else.)

Yet I prefer to look at the overall picture differently than a therapist deciding whether or not someone suffers from a specific disorder. Certainly we all demonstrate some narcissistic behaviors from time to time, especially when we're having bad days or are under stress. While that doesn't mean we all have NPD, a consistent display of narcissistic traits can be destructive to those of us stuck interacting with the bad behaving ones, and that's where the problem lies.

So instead of asking the question, "But is he (or she) *really* a narcissist?" The questions I consistently ask them instead are ...

❏ Do you feel healthy in this relationship?

❏ Do you feel equal?

❏ Do you feel controlled and/or manipulated?

❏ Do you feel bad about yourself?

❏ Do you feel sorry for the way your children and other loved ones are treated in this environment?

❏ Are you struggling with constant depression?

❏ Do you feel like you're on an emotional roller coaster or are walking on eggshells around this person every time he's near?

These are truly the important questions; not the ones related to making a diagnosis. The partner driving this victim to these feelings may have any number of psychological ills going on. There may even be multiple diagnoses overlapping. Some may be treatable, some may not. (Remember that only a diagnosis by a psychological professional can determine this.)

However, what *is* important is that the victims do *something* about the situation! Remaining in a toxic environment, especially when children are being affected, is the unhealthiest part of the equation.

I also believe that each victim must understand that his or her own "baggage," combined with that of the victimizing partner, is what sets the dynamic up to begin with.

As I mentioned earlier, I look at narcissistic behaviors or traits on a sliding scale, with healthy narcissism being one (on a scale of one to ten), and Narcissistic Personality Disorder being a ten. My experience with my clients has led me to believe that a person doesn't have to be demonstrating behaviors in the eight or nine range to do some pretty extensive damage to those around them ... especially if those around them have issues in their past that leave them more vulnerable to abusive treatment to begin with.

Looked at from another angle, a very emotionally healthy and strong person might be able to work in an environment with someone with some severe narcissistic behaviors and still maintain her ongoing emotional health. She does this by setting strong emotional and physical boundaries, keeping her self-esteem intact, and understanding how not to play into the manipulative games of the narcissistic, or otherwise difficult person.

And yet, someone who may only demonstrate a low level of narcissistic traits on our scale can cause severe damage to someone much less protected. (For point of reference, let's say he's a three on our scale of one to ten.) Now throw him together with a weaker partner who comes from an abusive background, a childhood living with an alcoholic parent, or some other life-altering situation such as Post Traumatic Stress. This can just as easily become a setup for damage, and the manipulation and abuse that can occur within this relationship can be substantial. Each person brings his or her own emotional and behavioral "stuff" to every relationship and that's where the problem lies. Each one of us must heal from our own histories first, if any of our relationships are ever going to work in a healthy way.

Unfortunately, many narcissistic types refuse to seek help because they believe that all their problems are caused by others. They simply are incapable of recognizing their own role in the mess. They believe that if everyone else would just "get fixed" then all would be fine once again. Herein lies one of the key problems in being involved with these difficult people: for someone to change his behavior, he must first acknowledge that he actually has something to work on. So if your partner simply brushes off all the problems within your relationship as *yours* and is not willing to seek help for his role in the relationship, then this is one of your first clues that you are fighting an uphill battle.

> *And thus, I return to the question I ask of my new clients:*
> ***"Do you feel healthy (and safe) in this relationship?"***
> *If not ...*
> *whether or not he's a narcissist doesn't really matter.*

While your partner may or may not be narcissistic, there may be many other issues that he is dealing with: Borderline Personality Disorder, Bi-Polar, Schizophrenia, or others. (There may be more than one issue and/or diagnosis occurring at the same time.) While these may not be narcissistic issues, they can still leave an entire family struggling with pain, anguish, depression, confusion, fear, and life-long struggles with self-esteem. Thus another of my reasons for not getting hung up on whether or not narcissism is *the end-all* diagnosis.

And sadly enough, no matter what the cause, unhealthy patterns are generally destined to continue without intervention. Children raised in these unhealthy environments have much higher odds of repeating the cycle and ending up as grownups who create their own unhealthy environments as well, simply because they have no reference outside of their dysfunctional family, as to what really healthy relationships look like. Unless a conscious understanding of this situation occurs, and a conscious choice is made to take a different tack, a vast number of victims are destined to repeat their relationship patterns over and over again.

So if you find yourself in any kind of relationship where you are constantly feeling bad, unequal, controlled, manipulated, frightened, depressed, angry, unsafe, or like you're chronically walking on those proverbial eggshells around the one who is supposed to be your loving partner, business partner, parent, or best friend, then I once again return the question to you,

"Do you feel healthy in this relationship?"

Of course, then there is always the question:

> *"What are your issues that are allowing*
> *this relationship to continue?"*
> *After all, we are all the common denominator*
> *in all of our relationships.*

The bigger focus of my work in helping my clients heal is not spending so much time focusing on the behavior of the abuser, beyond simply clarifying and understanding how manipulation and abuse works. After all, by now you've learned that we cannot easily change anyone else, no matter what the root of his problem.

By better understanding what makes *us* tick, we can more easily see how we got into unhealthy relationships to begin with, what originally led us to believe we deserved such treatment from anyone, and most importantly, why we stayed. The next step is to learn how to get out, as well as how to break the unhealthy dynamic and move on to more emotionally healthy relationships with ourselves and others.

Difficult relationships can strip you of more than you know. Self-esteem. Enjoying life. Being passionate about something. Feeling safe in your own home.

> *And yet, I truly believe that*
> *the most difficult relationship that most people have*
> *is the one they have with themselves!*

Until you can get that most important relationship on a rock solid foundation, with a belief in your worth as a person on this planet, a strong self-esteem, and an ability to recognize inappropriate, abusive behavior (and not settle for it for yourself or your children), then dealing with difficult people will always be a constant in your life.

"But is he or she really a narcissist?"
It doesn't much matter.

What does matter is this question…

"Are my children and I living in an unhealthy relationship?"

Now that's a question that you can do something about. But no one can answer it honestly except you.

Chapter 24
But It's Not That Bad

Perhaps as you have been reading this you have decided that your partner is "not that bad." In many cases you will be right. We all have to give and take in any relationship. We all have bad days. Everyone has their own little quirks that play a part in any mix. Loving someone involves taking many of these situations in stride and persevering anyway.

If you are in a healthy relationship where you only have brief spells where you question things, then you're probably right – it isn't that bad.

Yet, there are many subtle games that any narcissist can play with us where we don't even realize we are being played with …

A Close Call

I fell prey to one of those relationships for a while, during my "running away from home" episode when I lived in Mexico. After leaving a 23-year marriage that left me feeling empty and lost, I felt pretty vulnerable, scared, and totally confused. For the longest time I was terrified to date, as my comfort level in men and confidence in myself was at an all-time low. As time passed and I slowly rebuilt my self-esteem in that wonderful, healing paradise, I fell madly in love with what I thought to be a truly wonderful man. He had been emotionally beaten up by his ex-wife and we both were able to commiserate with each other in our journeys towards healing. He was 10 years younger than I, so the fact that he was attracted to me was quite the ego-boost. He was handsome, polite, funny, and noticed so many of the small things that were important to me, that I was vastly impressed by his attentions. He was the most romantic man I had ever known and I was sure I would love him forever. The fact that he was Mexican was also fascinating to me – the differences in our cultures were intriguing, his passionate style inviting, and when he spoke to me in his native tongue I was like Jamie Lee Curtis in the movie *A Fish Called Wanda!* He was like a drug to me.

Unfortunately, when I returned to the States he remained in Cozumel and we attempted to keep our long distance relationship alive until such time that he could get his papers and would be able to join me. We were convinced that we would be together for the rest of our lives.

The logistics of communication at that distance was tough, but we were determined to succeed. We emailed daily and sometimes more often, which gave us our daily fix, yet it was just not the same as hearing each other's voices. As he didn't have his own phone where he lived (most people used cell phones, which were extraordinarily expensive), we devised a plan whereby I could call him late at night at a small hotel that belonged to a friend of mine. We would email during the day to set the plan for the phone call. Normally I would call him at 11p.m. and we would be able to talk without interruption from the usual daily noise and hustle and bustle of the hotel.

For quite some time this worked fairly well. We would call once a week or so and I would pick up the tab. Because I could buy cheap calling cards in the States it made sense for me to do the calling. It was literally cost-prohibitive for him to call me.

One night I called at the usual time and the hotel receptionist told me that Jose wasn't there. So I tried every 10 minutes for an hour and he never materialized. I was worried that something had happened to him and emailed him describing my feelings, hoping that everything was fine. For 24 hours I heard nothing from him and by that time I was really worried. I didn't really have any other way to reach him and just had to wait as patiently as I could to hear from him.

Two days later I received an email, just as if nothing out of the ordinary had ever happened. "Hi – how are you – what are you doing – are you fine?" The usual. I wrote back and asked what happened that he wasn't at the hotel to take my call. He gave me some excuse that seemed plausible at the time and I just blew it off as a night that had complications.

Not long after that, the same situation occurred. I was once again left wondering where he had disappeared to and when he finally surfaced it was as if nothing strange had happened. He muttered a quick, "I'm sorry but ..." and gave me another lame excuse and blew off the incident entirely.

By the time it happened for a third time I was getting angry. I spent a long time explaining to him that I felt he didn't respect my time or feelings and that I was hurt when he didn't do what he promised to do. He told me that I made too big an issue of the ordeal and dismissed it as me being too sensitive.

Not long after that I made a trip to Cozumel to see him. When he met me at the airport with a rose I knew all was wonderful and that we were going to have a wonderful week together. Yet, during dinner when I mentioned looking forward to visiting with a few of my other friends while I was in town, his expression grew irritable. While I fully intended to spend every possible minute with him during my visit, and had invited him to go with me while I said hello to my old friends, he strongly suggested that we really had no need to see these people to begin with.

I was a bit shocked. He knew these people as well as I did. One friend in particular was an American chiropractor named Joe who I had met when I had first moved to the island. He had helped me a lot during my transition of relocating there and he and his wife had remained great friends long after.

I suddenly realized that Jose was acting jealous over Joe and I mentioned my observation to him. At first he denied it and then at last conceded that he was a bit jealous, but that in his culture, jealousy was a valued behavior, because if you loved someone you showed them your love by being jealous.

We talked about jealousy for some time and while I tried to understand his position, I also tried to show him that in my culture jealousy is viewed as a sign of weakness. It always said to me that someone didn't trust me if they were jealous.

He reaffirmed again that he didn't want me to go see Joe and his family and I stood my ground. Then he told me that I'd have to go alone. I said fine. Then he tried to make me feel bad by telling me that I was shortchanging him from all the time he could possibly get with me. So I reminded him that he was welcome on my brief visit with my friend.

At last he accompanied me, but was irritated by the situation and I was irritated that it should even be an issue. Fortunately, I set my boundaries and stood by them. The rest of the vacation was wonderful and I soon forgot the little game he had tried to play with me. I was so caught up in the fact that he called me "Presiosa" (beautiful, precious one) as if it were my name, waited on me hand and foot, and put me on a pedestal of great importance unlike I had ever experienced before. I thought I was in heaven.

By the time I returned home I felt reaffirmed that our relationship was strong and wonderful. I was once again willing to be patient while his paperwork came through so he could come to the States. Yet much to my surprise, within days of returning home he began to play the phone game again. My Red Flags began waving frantically, yet I ignored them.

> *Although I was getting frustrated with the pattern that was developing, I kept justifying his actions and began to question myself instead of questioning him.*

I'd get angry with him and threaten over email to leave him and then he'd fall right back in line and call me out of the blue himself. We would discuss the issue and he would apologize for the hundredth time and we would be back on track until he fell into the old dance again.

Just as I was about to give up on the situation (What? Give up the most romantic man who made me feel more wonderful than in my entire life? How ridiculous!), he emailed that his papers had been cleared and he would be leaving for the States within days! I was overjoyed! After a long and convoluted year keeping this relationship alive, despite a multitude of odds against us, the reality that he would soon be joining me erased any questions in my mind. Now that we could be together, all those logistical problems would simply disappear. Or at least that's what I hoped and prayed.

He arrived in the States and emailed that he was officially on U.S. soil. I knew he was going to stop and spend a few days with his kids in Texas so I just bided my time trying to be patient until he arrived. He would email me every few days and tell me how wonderful it was to see his kids again and that he would be on his way soon. I gave him my calling card number so that he could reach me and I stayed as close to home as possible so that I wouldn't miss his call.

At the end of two weeks, he emailed and said he'd taken a temporary job to earn some money to pay for his trip to join me. While I was disappointed that there would again be a delay, I understood the situation and once again reminded him to call so we could talk. Yet the phone never rang.

By the end of the third week, I was growing anxious. He only emailed every few days, and very briefly at that. He had still never called. I couldn't understand why he wouldn't at least pick up the phone. How difficult could it be? It was even on my dime.

By the end of four weeks I had come to realize that it was never going to happen. In the entire time he'd been in this country he never picked up the phone to hear my voice, and yet his emails professed his undying love for me, "the love of his life."

I finally got the message ... he was never coming.

Looking back on this situation now I don't understand much of what transpired. What I do know is that I kept missing the caution signs that were trying to get my attention. While my conscious mind knew that people who love each other don't treat each other in ways they know will cause undue stress, anxiety, or pain, I kept listening to my love-struck heart that said Jose's excuses were valid. That he loved me more than anyone else possibly could. That I would certainly never find another love like this again and so I should hold onto it for dear life.

> *"It's really not that bad," I kept telling myself.*
> *But in reality, it was.*

He was in control. By regulating the phone situation he kept me off-balance. He kept me confused. And by the constant abundance of romantic words and actions in between the "cold shoulder" behavior, I kept hanging on believing in the "perfect partner." In the meantime I was filled with self-doubt. (Why isn't he calling? Why doesn't he love me enough to understand how much this hurts me? What's wrong with *me*?) The roller coaster ride my emotions took went from manic to depressive. My friends could see me stressing out, but didn't know how to help me or what to say.

It took me a while, but at last I figured out that in a healthy relationship people don't treat each other that way. I realized I deserved better.

And I finally moved on.

It seemed like I cried forever for a love lost. A love that had seemed like the last love I would ever have to search for. By ending the relationship I felt horrible. He kept emailing me over and over, begging me to take him back on one hand and then blaming me for the break up when I didn't give in. The pain felt overwhelming, but

I knew that my emotional health couldn't take it anymore. I kept begging God for an answer as to why things had not evolved as I hoped they would. He didn't answer me.

As it turns out, by ending that relationship – one that wasn't that bad – I found a more realistic relationship. I found a man who was compassionate, kind, caring, and honest. We developed trust in each other that didn't allow for jealousy. Each day we asked about important events in each other's lives. We followed-up on issues that may have left one or the other of us stressed, to see if the situation was improving or if we could offer help in any way. If we had a problem, we talked it through calmly and caringly, always being sure to end any discussion with a hug. We also knew how to offer each other a sincere apology when we made a mistake – one without strings attached. We simply admitted when we were wrong and took responsibility for our actions. Then we worked hard not to repeat our behaviors that may have left one of us feeling frustrated in any way.

Was our relationship perfect? Absolutely not. No relationship can be. However, with love, respect, and no need to control one another, it was amazing what were able to do and what were able to overcome.

"It's not that bad?"

It all depends on what "that bad" means to you. If you can live with certain not-so-great behaviors in a relationship that do not seem insurmountable, then that's great. If you can ignore behaviors that are less than optimal, then that works too. But if you are constantly chipping away at your self-esteem because you are allowing unhealthy behaviors to run rampant, then "not too bad" may indeed be "bad enough" to warrant changing them or changing your situation.

In addition, as long as you're staying with a partner who's "not that bad," you will be missing opportunities to find someone who might just be better. More kind. More loving. More caring. More compatible with you.

Linda

I hadn't been in a long-term relationship in three, long years when I met this pretty nice guy online. We met up and hit it off right off the bat. We loved the outdoors, hiking, biking, camping, our dogs, and spending long hours under the covers enjoying each other. I especially loved Larry's sense of humor and spontaneity, which were all pretty new to me after being involved with an unhappy perfectionist for so long.

I thought I had come to be a pretty good judge of people over the last few years, and Larry seemed to be a nice enough guy. He wasn't Mr. Charisma either, which I felt good about too. After all, my previous partners had swept me off my feet with their charm and good looks. While Larry wasn't bad to look at, he was just a simple guy but that suddenly felt so safe. No hype and no "me, me, me attitude" either. The relationship felt a little like that old friend you haven't seen in years who just steps back into place, as if no time had ever elapsed.

Yet, I ended the entire relationship after three and a half months, quite to Larry's surprise, for he never did anything that would suggest to most people that there was a thing wrong exactly.

What made me put the brakes on a relationship with a perfectly nice man? It was a lot of little things, actually. And in fact, I'm not sure I'd even qualify him as very narcissistic. He just wasn't in tune with others – and that included me and my feelings.

For example, he had a little dog – about 10 pounds – and mine was about 20. While he adored his pooch and she him, he did things that just felt uncomfortable to me. For example he would routinely pick her up by the collar. When he tried to do that to my bigger dog, I asked him please not to do that and asked why he thought it was OK to pick up any dog that way. He replied that he saw that's how it was done in the dog shows. (To me, that didn't make it right, since I certainly wouldn't want to be picked up by the collar! But I didn't choose to do battle over it. After all, it was his dog.)

Yet, when he did that to my dog a second time, I really put my foot down and repeated my wish that he not treat my dog that way. As a mom of grown-up kids myself, I suddenly had this vision of how boyfriends or step-dads can come into a family and put children at risk for abusive behavior if their mom doesn't have strong boundaries to stop any variety of improper behavior from the beginning. I thought my own boundaries were pretty strong, but I still felt uncomfortable standing up for my dog with him. He finally quit but switched to telling me how I babied my dog and just how spoiled he was.

Another little thing that just kept creeping up was how he loved to yell at drivers on the highway. It wasn't just occasionally when someone was really bad – it was on every single car trip. These outbursts certainly couldn't be heard by the guilty driver, but I had to listen to them instead, which simply isn't any fun for anyone.

One time he told me that he'd been exploring in my bedroom drawers and had found a little book (a quasi journal of mine I had specifically put away in a drawer so that it wasn't obviously lying out when he was over.) When I told him that his actions had left me feeling a bit vulnerable, he replied with, "Why, because you've only reached one of the five goals you have written there?"

> *My heart leapt to my throat. I wanted to scream.*
> *I couldn't believe that he had actually read my journal.*
> *No one I knew had ever been so bold or insensitive.*

I couldn't believe it. And he really didn't think it was a big deal.

While he was always polite, saying please and thank you to waiters and other service workers, I always felt a bit miffed when I would make a big fancy dinner for him and all I would get was a curt thank you. I could make king crab legs and he would barely notice. (Although he might notice some little thing that I forgot or left out and would be sure to bring it to my attention.)

Once again, his behavior certainly wasn't bad. He never yelled at me or called me names. And most of the time we generally had fun.

We laughed and teased a lot. And he was always open to my suggestions about what we should do and more. But something was just wrong. I just couldn't put my finger on any huge thing.

There were many other little things Larry did that just left me a bit uncertain, but of course they were mixed in with so many things that were great! Our summer camping in the mountains, our fabulous love making, even outings with the dogs. For the most part, things just weren't "that bad."

I think the final straw for me, though, was at a point where I had been feeling a growing sense of unrest with him but just couldn't put my finger on it. It had been so long since I'd been in a real relationship that the thought of being alone again was pretty depressing. I hadn't been feeling too well lately either ... stomach upset, headaches, and trouble sleeping had left me even more sensitive to anything that just felt off-kilter.

About that time we took a long drive one day into the mountains to view the fall colors. At one particular spot where several other folks were taking pictures, we got out and enjoyed the view ourselves. Larry asked me to take some pictures of him and he posed in a variety of positions as I snapped away. About that time a passer-by asked us if we'd like him to take our picture together, to which Larry simply said, "No thanks."

I think it was that moment that I realized that after three and a half months we didn't have a single photo of us together and yet when an opportunity struck, Larry had no interest in even taking one, but had certainly wanted plenty of himself.

I felt very small that day. Lonely, yet not physically alone. In a relationship with someone, but without hope for love. I knew then that it really "was that bad" for me.

I'm sure one might wonder why I was willing to give up a not-so-bad relationship and be alone again. Even my family all questioned my sanity about giving up on the relationship, and were sure to remind me just how lonely I'd been (for so long) before Larry had arrived on the scene. All I can tell you is that within days of breaking up with Larry my headaches, stomach upset, and insomnia cleared up and haven't come back. My dog seems less stressed and we both enjoy our solitude because we know we're healthier this way.

"Not that bad?" It was hard to see for a while. But I've learned that a relationship has got to be pretty darn great for me from here out. I'm simply not willing to settle for less than that ever again. My health demands it. And my dog deserves it.

He Who Cares the Least Holds the Power

Having been a victim of several tough relationships myself over the years, I know first-hand just how turbulent, painful, and anguish-laden they can be. And what I can clearly state as cold, hard truth is this: The victim is always left second-guessing herself – often straining her brain as to just what she might do to keep her love alive or make her partner love her. Yet she tends to forget that no one can make someone else feel anything they don't want to. And in fact that …

> *Whoever cares the least in a relationship*
> *is the one who literally holds the power:*
> *Power over where the relationship will go,*
> *how much love or attention is handed out,*
> *or whether or not the relationship will end and when.*

What happens for many of us is that we *think* the situation we're in is a loving relationship (or at least we may tell ourselves it is), yet instead, it is truly *dependency on another*. And it is exactly the root of how people get themselves stuck in so many unfulfilling and dead-end relationships and don't move forward to find themselves truly healthy and loving ones.

Of course some of the problem is simply laziness. It's certainly a lot harder to take the time and energy to find someone new with the hopes that it might be a better relationship, than it is to stick it out in a relationship where you know what to expect, whether you like the situation or not.

I'll say it once and I'll say it again: the biggest underlying issue with these victims is their persistent fear (either consciously or subconsciously) that if they let this partner go, another one might not come down the road!

> *The bottom line is this:*
> *They would rather be in a relationship that leaves them in constant pain and second-guessing themselves, than risk being alone.*
>
> *And their fear keeps them in unhealthy and unequal relationships, sometimes for years, or even for life.*

Chapter 25
They Just Can't Change

"*I*t's like he's an untamed lion and wants so badly to be a lamb, but he doesn't know how." Jodi – survivor

Jodi sums it all up perfectly. As you weigh whether to stay or leave your relationship, the most important piece of information you must understand is that most narcissistic people do not change. To get people to agree to change, they must first acknowledge they have a behavior that needs to change. In the case of a narcissist, he simply doesn't see where he is doing anything wrong in the first place. As a matter of fact, he will more likely suggest that *you* are the one with the problem – not him. Furthermore, he'll do a great job of convincing any therapist that he is right. Of course, by the time you actually see a counselor with the hopes of saving your relationship, the emotional war zone you have lived in for so long has left you looking like the crazy one, while he looks completely healthy.

Getting your partner to go to therapy can be a challenge – unless he thinks that the therapist will tell you how screwed up *you* are – thus validating his beliefs that he's perfect and you're not.

However, you might actually get compliance out of your narcissist if he or she feels threatened that you might actually leave them – thus cutting off their narcissistic supply – their "fix" – namely you. So let's say you get them to agree to go to counseling or some other form of therapy. Here's the next sad truth:

**There is no medication they can take
to change their behavior.**

**Psychotherapy has shown very
little effect on this problem.**

So now you have the honest truth. There is very little, if any hope for change in someone with this personality disorder.

The Lion

Let's go back to an earlier chapter where I asked you to think about your narcissist as if he were a male lion. By expanding on that analogy a bit further, it may help you understand the concept of talking change to your narcissist, and how unrealistic that expectation is and why ...

The male lion is the king of the jungle. He has no natural enemies. He reigns supreme, instilling fear of his prowess and might throughout his kingdom. While a female lion hunts not only for herself, but to feed her young, a male lion does not hunt for anyone else. He does not think in terms of anyone else. He has no concern for anyone else. There is only him. He is the Master of his Universe.

When he's hungry, he simply hunts. He doesn't sit up all night plotting where's he's going to lie in wait for some unsuspecting, vulnerable target. He doesn't give a thought to the fact that anyone he kills is a victim, but is simply a source of food to satisfy his need. In much the same way that you or I go to the grocery store and grab a package of hamburger out of the cooler, he sees his target as just an item in his food pantry.

As he crouches near a herd of antelope, he studies the scene. He decides which animal will offer him the least amount of work in his attempt to find lunch. Whichever one happens to be closest and easiest is the one he chooses. At last he leaps out of hiding, chases his prey, and makes his kill. After he dines, he gives absolutely no further thought to the antelope. He certainly has no guilt, feelings of remorse or shame, or sympathy for the creature. Why should he?

After all, it was in his environment for him to take. And take he did. The next time he is hungry, he will simply repeat the process.

Now imagine that we could have a conversation with this lion to try to show him how brutal he is, how uncaring, how hurtful and fear-provoking to those in his environment. How everyone would love him so much more if he showed a little compassion. How if he only killed the old and the weak, all in his world would be so much happier with him. How it would be ideal if he left the newborns alone, because they haven't had a chance at life yet. That if he would just hang around the herd long enough, surely someone would die of natural causes periodically and then he could eat without the guilt of needing to take a life. And if he did all those things, wouldn't he feel like a better lion for his efforts?

If that lion could honestly converse with you I suspect he would look at you in total confusion. His first response might be, "What is this thing you call guilt?" You might spend hours explaining the concept to him yet he still wouldn't understand. It's just not part of his makeup.

He would probably object to all the extra patience he would have to summon up just to sit around and wait for someone to die off, while he could be hungry for days or weeks in anticipation of a death by natural causes. It would not take him long to realize that there was nothing he would gain by these new behaviors, and in fact, his life would grow more difficult if he took your advice about his hunting methods.

This is the insight of a narcissist.

He is not necessarily hateful, spiteful, or vindictive (although some are). He does not understand your pain as you do. He does not feel guilt, as he doesn't even understand the concept or the feelings to begin with. He is simply behaving in a manner that has worked for him for so long he sees no reason to change.

In the case of an extremely narcissistic lion, he might even turn the conversation this way: "You know, since I am so noble, so omnipotent, so wonderful, why don't you suggest to the antelope

-270-

herd that they should feel honored to be my lunch and that each day they should draw straws to see who gets to appease my hunger. Then, whoever wins the honor can just walk over to me and lie down, with their throats bared, sacrificing themselves for me, knowing they are giving their lives for one who reins supreme. They shouldn't see it as a sacrifice, rather as their duty in life – to honor me."

While this analogy may seem extreme, after reading some of the stories in this book you can see where a select group of narcissists could fit this category completely.

And yet, if the lion suddenly awoke one day and all the herds had disappeared, he would have a rude awakening. When his stomach growled with hunger and he had no food supply in sight, he would have the first realization that something had definitely gotten out of his control. He might roar with anger, demanding that his universe return to normal. When it didn't, he might suddenly sense a moment of panic, not knowing where his next supply might come from. And he would have to change his hunting patterns to find another herd to chase.

He may become frustrated searching for the traces of the herd, but he will persist until he finds them. Once he finds them again, he will breathe a sign of relief, study the new victims for his next choice dinner guest, and then kill as before. His universe once again sane and under his control, he continues as normal. Yet, for the short time he had lost his herd, he was vulnerable. He was in terror. He was just as weak as the rest of the animal kingdom, for without anyone to rule, without anyone to honor him as king, without anyone to dominate – he is just a lion and nothing more. Just like a bully on the playground who has no kids to intimidate, he's a bully in a void and his power holds no meaning.

While this is a pretty extreme analogy, it is the perfect picture of behavior dictated only by supply and demand. Until there is reason to change, change is avoided at all costs. And once a crisis is over and control is once again regained, the old instincts and behavior patterns return.

There is no treatment to stop narcissistic behaviors.

You will not change this person you love.

He will not bring back "Mr. Perfect" once he has you, unless he fears that his herd (you) might disappear, and then he will reel you in with just enough of those old charms to mesmerize you back under his control.

Joan

He would scream and holler and carry on – throw things, call me names, and so much more. Yet, whenever I left and was gone for hours and he suspected that I was serious about leaving permanently, I would find a totally different Craig when I returned home. When I'd walk in the door I would find him lying by our fireplace with a bottle of wine and two glasses, waiting for me, and with that look that said, "Oh, honey – come on. You know I didn't mean it. Come here and let's have a drink and make up."

I didn't recognize the pattern for the longest time, but when I did, it all made perfect sense. When Craig thought his supply was about to disappear, he was motivated to change his tactics. Yet once the storm had passed and I was "back in line," he would always return to his earlier ways.

To his dismay I finally reached a point where I didn't return ever again.

Randi

His emotional state is that of a three-year-old who can pull your hair one minute and kiss you the next. He doesn't realize he's doing anything wrong unless someone tells him after the fact. He is truly emotionally empty. I guess I kept thinking I could fix him.

While the narcissist will probably show little ability to change, that doesn't mean that therapy is useless for *you*. Having an outside person to talk to about your relationship is certainly a great place to start. Not all relationships are necessarily narcissistic and you may have other relationship issues that lend themselves better to treatment in therapy than narcissistic issues do. In addition, as the partner who may feel pretty beat up in an overly controlling situation, you may feel the need to talk to someone about your own feelings. Individual therapy may be a breath of fresh air as you sort through your issues, questions, and options.

However, Narcissistic Personality Disorder is still rather misunderstood by many professionals. While most have probably been exposed to the diagnostic criteria and may have an overall understanding of the concept, there are probably many who have no clue of the insidious game played behind closed doors. One therapist I know shared with me that while she had dealt with several couples in therapy where one partner was a narcissist, she truly had no idea of the depths of pain and covert abuse that took place until she found herself in her own narcissistic relationship:

"I had no idea the emotional exhaustion my patients had described to me until I found myself caught in the same web of confusion. No amount of education I gleaned from text books, lectures, or couples' therapy could have prepared me for the devastating experiences I lived with. The self-doubt, the second guessing of my own behaviors and beliefs, the demeaning treatment I took and didn't even recognize – you can't even begin to understand it unless you live it. I will certainly have a much better insight to what my clients are describing now and will be much more understanding of their situations and their needs."

I find so many therapists who tell me these exact same thoughts. Why I even have a psychiatrist as a client. As he explained to me, the diagnosis of NPD was not a valid label until 1980. How many therapists were trained before this date? That alone explains why many never received proper training about the disorder.

Yet even today, unless one focuses specifically on this topic in psychotherapy training, they may miss much. In fact, a gal friend of mine spent years becoming a psychotherapist, including earning her PhD and spending hour upon hour in couples counseling, and yet she had virtually no knowledge of narcissism until I shared my work with her. This serious gap in knowledge is not only frightening, but may leave many clients desperate for someone who understands their plight.

It may take a visit to a few therapists until you find one who understands this disorder well enough to help you and not blame you.

> *Remember, by the time many couples finally seek help, the victim is so worn down that she may look like the crazy one. Of course that's just what the narcissist is hoping for.*

With this in mind, you may want to chat individually with a counselor or therapist before going as a couple, just to assess his or her knowledge, understanding, and experiences in dealing with Narcissistic Personality Disorder.

Good therapists are worth their weight in gold, so don't give up if the first one or two don't provide what you're looking for. Just as you'd shop for the safest baby products to protect your child, take your time and shop for the best professional to help you on your journey. There are some great ones out there but you may have to do your research.

If you can't find a qualified therapist in your area, you might consider finding a support group or even contacting those of us survivors who now consult with clients via phone. With the vast array of technology at our fingertips, geography shouldn't be a barrier to working with someone who might have the answers you need. (I have clients from as far away as Canada and London.) So do not feel restricted by the two therapists who are within your 10-mile radius. Help is out there. You just have to decide what works best for you.

It's also important to remember that it does "take two to tango." We each bring our behaviors to the table. I realize now that in more than one of the relationships I was in, some of my own behaviors added to the problem. For example, whenever I felt that no matter what I did wasn't good enough, I would just quit doing anything. I guess I felt that if I was going to get yelled at anyway, I may as well not put the work into the project to begin with. Of course, by doing so, I only agitated my partner even more, who then felt that I was intentionally trying to make him mad.

Sadly enough, by that point, maybe I was.

Remember that two people in any relationship take part in a dance. As a general rule, it's a pattern that repeats itself. There is a great quote: "Insanity is doing the same thing over and over, expecting different results."

As long as you and your partner continue on in the same dance, nothing will change. While changing the dance, or pattern may be hard, it is your *only* chance at changing the outcome.

> *"Unless you live with someone with this disorder, you could never possibly understand the craziness of it all. The amount of effort that goes into attempting to create normalcy, on the part of the sane half of the partnership, is purely amazing."*
> *Max – survivor*

Chapter 26
Seeing Where This Relationship Will Go

I can't tell you how many times I hear this expression from my clients – so much so that I've decided it's time to seriously talk about it here.

So let me set the stage: The gal (or guy) I'm working with contacts me because she is unhappy in their relationship. It could be for a variety of reasons (not all of them narcissism-related) but usually their main complaints sound something like:

My partner …

- ❏ doesn't treat me well.
- ❏ is emotionally or physically unavailable.
- ❏ has different interests than I do.
- ❏ isn't trustworthy.
- ❏ has different values and/or beliefs than I do.
- ❏ has different sexual needs or interests than I do.
- ❏ lies.
- ❏ doesn't have time for me.
- ❏ wants more (or less) from this relationship than I do.
- ❏ is a workaholic.
- ❏ would rather be with his (or her) friends than with me.
- ❏ doesn't appreciate me.
- ❏ doesn't respect my time or space.

- ❏ is always late.
- ❏ is a huge slob.
- ❏ is very controlling.
- ❏ is very anally retentive and hates the fact that I'm a slob.
- ❏ is not meeting my needs or I'm not meeting his
- ❏ is always jealous of anyone I talk to.
- ❏ takes advantage of me.

The list goes on and on, but you get the idea.

Anyway, most of these folks are seriously frustrated about whatever their situation is, and yet when I ask them why they choose to stay in this relationship that is obviously bothering them the usual answer is, "Well, I just want to see where this relationship is going to go."

Hmmm … I guess I want to know where they *think* it will go? Since most of us don't change unless dire circumstances dictate it, why would our behaviors change in a relationship?

Oh yes – there is that "potential" thing. That little belief that goes on in the back of our minds where our magical thinking leads us to believe that once we get engaged, married, move in with someone, or take some other next step that the person we're involved with will somehow simply change! Or else we believe in our own heart of hearts that we can change our misguided mate or can heal him somehow.

"But he (or she) has such great *potential*," I hear clients say. Or, "This could be the relationship of my dreams, if he (or she) will only do such-and-such."

Can you hear the ridiculousness of this? Let's use me as an example. I have great potential to become the shy, demure type. Yep. I can picture me now doing the wallflower thing. Eyes lowered. Never getting animated and outgoing about some topic that interests me. Absolutely, the *potential's* there. Yet what is the reality of this actually happening?

Those of you who know me personally know just how absurd that is! Even if I wanted to change myself into that wallflower, the work it would take would be huge! And what would be in it for me to do so?

So let's go back to the statement, "I'm just seeing where this relationship will go," and then apply this *potential* concept to the scheme of things and it starts to become clear that where the relationship is going is no different than where it is right now.

> *Put one more way:*
> *If you want to know how someone will behave tomorrow,*
> *then simply study how they have behaved yesterday*
> *as well as today.*
> *Odds are, it will pretty much be the same.*

Now I'm not saying that all relationships with tough moments should be thrown out the window! We all have some difficult times and life challenges that can be overcome when *both partners are willing* to put in the time and energy to work through them. In addition, some tough situations are temporary and, once survived, the couple will more than likely find themselves more settled once again. Thus the need to not make hasty decisions regarding your relationship status while you are under stress.

However, when people get into or stay in relationships that are not what they are truly seeking, from the get-go (with the misguided assumption of the great *potential* for where the relationship *can* go, versus the reality of where the relationship *is* going), then it's a relationship set up for frustration and failure.

I would suspect that you may have fallen into this trap in your early days of dating this person you are now totally frustrated with. Some of us were simply desperate daters who were terrified that no one else might come along. Some were totally engulfed in the charade that took place between the amazing Dr. Jekyll and the alter-ego Mr. Hyde, who showed up only after the wedding day. (So many have even told me it was their wedding night when everything suddenly changed!)

I think what happens to so many of us who end up stuck is that, for so long, it seemed like no one understood us. We felt awkward somehow, perhaps with an abusive history that left us feeling like damaged goods, and we believed that if anyone ever found out, they'd leave us for sure.

And then, out of the blue came the first person who really "got us." They listened. They cared. They noticed the little things that let us know they really paid attention to us. And as such, our selective blindness set us up for missing the Red Flags that are usually there in some fashion all along.

Can you look back on your dating history now and see some of those warning signs? Most of my clients tell me absolutely yes. Hindsight is certainly 20/20, but there's no use blaming yourself for your lack of knowledge at the time. That's part of the joy of getting older … we're simply smarter. (As is evidenced by the fact that most of my clients are mid-thirties on up to their seventies. The younger crowd is still walking in the dark about the reality of difficult relationships, and for many of them, the pain just hasn't grown aggravating enough yet.)

By the time most of my clients realize that they are truly in a dead-end relationship and mourn the ideal but unrealistic relationship they thought they had, their next reaction is to berate themselves for wasting so much of their lives when they could have had something so much better.

Well, if you feel similarly, quit chastising yourself and remember that you're much smarter now, based on all you've learned about this subject. Consider yourself having earned a degree in Relationship Smarts instead of seeing yourself as a dropout of Relationship U, where you were simply the under-achiever. While some folks spent tons of money to earn diplomas and certificates that entitle them to practice law or medicine, you paid tuition with your emotions, feelings, and time, which entitled you to earn a valuable degree in human relations. And with that power behind you, you're certain to make much smarter decisions in the future – *if* that's how you choose to reflect on and appreciate the experiences.

Often, when my clients finally realize that they've been doing themselves no favors by remaining in a bad relationship, they give themselves a hefty thump on the head and groan, "I can't believe I wasted twenty years of my life like this!" I simply smile and remind them that they've earned their PhD in Relationships. Nothing is ever in vain. The lessons learned were priceless, even if for some it took years for those lessons to become crystal clear.

And just think – now your kids can benefit from your wisdom!

When There Are Children Involved

Many of us get married with the intent of having children, and coincidentally the majority of my clients finally begin to take proactive steps out of some pretty destructive and unhealthy relationships when they finally start to question the effect that the narcissistic parent is having upon the kids. Either they see their children become withdrawn, terrified, anxious, depressed and a variety of other behaviors based upon the abusive atmosphere they are constantly subjected to, or else they start seeing tell-tale signs of new narcissists developing right under their noses. For children who spend years watching the variety of skills in the arsenal of an abuser, they can learn these exact same skills as well.

Unfortunately, the damage that our children can sustain can occur in a very short time. It doesn't take years for kids to learn to emulate their parents – good or bad. And regrettably, by the time the victimized parent starts truly recognizing the fact that her children are being horribly indoctrinated into the world of abusive narcissism, much damage could already have taken place.

There is no time to waste. Children learn what they live, so if you can be the one parent who becomes healthy and breaks out of your emotional prison, then they at least have a couple of role modeling behaviors to choose from.

Yet, if you continue to stay in an abusive relationship where they watch as your codependent behaviors enable your abuser, then you are teaching them that this is *normal behavior*. How on earth would they learn to believe anything else?

And odds are, you yourself grew up with some similar beliefs and situations in your own background as well, or you wouldn't likely be in this difficult relationship you are in today.

Just as children of alcoholics have a great tendency to grow up and marry alcoholics (despite the fact they may have hated the alcoholic lifestyle), this behavior looked normal to their childhood eyes. It is a similar situation for those who grew up with abusers. Odds are, they will marry abusers themselves, only perpetuating the pattern.

Children look to us as parents to keep them safe. If one parent can't provide that environment, then it's the other parent's place to do what they can to do so.

What are you doing to help your kids be safe?

What happens when you just keep waiting to see where your relationship will go? Well, sometimes people wait too long and as a result, things go terribly, horribly wrong. Living in a pressure cooker can sometimes lead to an explosion that few see coming and yet that leave broken hearts, broken bodies, and broken families.

In the case of Mary Winkler, I wasn't at all surprised...

Mary Winkler, Corena Bobbitt, and How Many Others?

When Mary Winkler was arrested and accused of shooting her minister husband to death in 2006, people were shocked. This seemed to be the perfect American family; 2.5 kids, picket fence, dog in the yard. How could this God-fearing, good Christian family have ended up in murder and mayhem? Certainly neither members of the congregation nor friends or family ever saw this coming.

And yet, months later the story began to unfold, and frankly, I wasn't the least bit surprised. What actually does surprise me is that we don't hear of this kind of thing more often.

While I'm sure there are those who may think that Mary Winkler was grasping at a defense, claiming an abusive relationship at the hands of her husband, I suspected that abuse was at the root of the situation the moment I heard the breaking news story the day she shot her husband in the back as he lay sleeping in bed.

Then of course there was the evidence which came out at her trial regarding the ongoing sexual humiliation, emotional abuse, and more. Imagine a small town minister's wife struggling constantly with maintaining her image as a religious mentor within her congregation, at the same time that she balanced wearing 4-inch platform shoes and other sexually suggestive clothing for her husband, whose external minister behaviors didn't exactly mesh with his behind-closed-doors roles.

My take on it is that she absolutely snapped after one too many episodes of her husband's abusive behaviors led her into her own unhealthy mental crisis. Sadly, this left the children in the confusing state of wondering what in heaven's name happened to their family.

Of course, years ago Lorena Bobbitt had her own sanity-escaping moment, slicing off her husband's penis in a moment of one-too-many abusive moments in the bedroom. I believe a jury acquitted her with a similar defense. One wonders just what torture she must have lived under to take such extreme measures.

And now Mary Winkler has seemingly fallen into the same trap; the one that says marriage is sanctimonious in all circumstances. The trap that our culture has taught women where men are more important than *they* are and that being loved by someone – even irregularly and with abusive layers – is better than not having anyone love you at all. That being alone is unacceptable, abnormal, and frightening. That the stigma of divorce for some is just too much to bear in the eyes of friends, family, or the church and that "Till death do us part" can literally be the case when things get out of hand.

Unfortunately, many of us will never begin to realize just how many toxic situations go on behind closed doors until it is too late; until yet another Mary Winkler snaps and does the unthinkable.

And for those who simply ask, "Why didn't she just leave him?" let me say this: It's not as easy as it seems. Throw children and financial dependence in the pot and extricating oneself from an unhealthy relationship grows more complicated by the moment.

For one of my clients, the divorce process itself is now in its fourth year as her husband continues to fight her, demoralize her, play the children as pawns, and manipulate the court system in ways that leave her nearly penniless (while he hides the family money and continues to threaten her life and safety on a daily basis). She's trapped. The police won't even respond anymore to her ongoing pleas to enforce the restraining order she has in place against him, despite video footage she has of him nearly running her down with his car more than once.

Until women learn to believe themselves to be equal to men, until two people within a relationship believe that they are both worthy of respect and love (even despite their differences or during an argument), and until women are not so "desperate for love," these unhealthy relationships will continue.

But I bet the media will be glad to run the story the day that the next woman snaps and someone else ends up dead. And just like with Mary Winkler, they will probably question how such a good woman could possibly have led two lives – the one where she stayed quiet for years at the hands of her husband whose abusive ways remained hidden behind closed doors, and the one where she stood up to get away and no one would listen until her nightmare life became public when it made the front page.

Regrettably, situations similar to this abound throughout our country and the world, yet most occur on a smaller scale and because they take place behind closed doors, most will never be recognized. As I consult with folks in difficult relationships, I am constantly shocked about the stories they tell me...

Ellen

I spent 12 years in a turbulent marriage, filled with physical abuse. What did I know? I believed my wedding vows and we had a son who I didn't want to traumatize by subjecting him to the instability and uncertainty of divorce. Time after time my husband would mercilessly beat me, yet was always sure to remind me that if I told anyone of his behavior, or tried to involve the police, that he would be glad to kill me instead. And I had no doubts he would do it.

Yet one day, after years of not fighting back, something snapped in me. Call it self-preservation or simply the last shreds of self-esteem fighting their way to the surface, but that day when Daniel was getting ready to strike me yet again, I reached for the butcher knife on the table and said to him, in my strongest voice, "Go ahead," as I held the knife pointed directly at him. That's all I did was point it at him.

Unfortunately, because I had never filed a police report during those 12 horrific years, the sad turn of events of this story is that it was Daniel who called the police and filed a complaint against me for assault and battery and I was the one who ended up in jail!

To add insult to injury I watched my teenaged son adopt his father's behaviors. By the time I came home from doing my time in prison, he was a teenager who had spent enough time with his father that he simply mimicked Daniel's behavior towards me in his own way. He would scream obscenities at me and threaten me with bodily harm, without even batting an eye.

It about killed me but I simply had to walk away from both of them. They are both evil. And the only way I can get healthy is to start my life over elsewhere.

I miss my son, but the boy he is now barely resembles the son I remember. I wish that I would have left sooner, back when it wasn't so bad. I really just didn't feel strong enough to get by on my own. Yet here I am now anyway, and my son is a stranger to me.

My advice to anyone in this horrible situation? Run away. Take your kids and get all of you to a healthy environment as soon as you can. You can't change the past, but you can change the future for all of you.

And remember not to let it get as bad as mine did. There were so many stages early-on in my marriage where I knew things weren't healthy, even before the physical abuse became the regular activity of choice by my husband. I certainly never expected any of this. Of course I always envisioned physical abusers came from low socio-economic families as well, and we were both bringing in huge incomes. That was one of the bigger shocks to me as I look at the big picture. I was fooled by all of it.

And the worst part is that I realize I have to take responsibility for my role in allowing things to get so out of hand. I could have left at any time, but I didn't.

> *Don't wait until it's too late to escape an environment that is toxic to both you and your children.*
> *Your kids are counting on you*
> *to keep them safe.*

Escaping From the Cult-like World

You may know someone in one of these destructive relationships and wish you could help them escape their emotional hell. You might be a friend, parent, grandparent, or other family member. And you may be pulling your hair out trying to figure out how to help them and get them to safety.

One woman wrote me about her daughter who was married to a very wealthy and prominent attorney. The marriage had grown extremely unhealthy and the wife filed for divorce. Of course there were children involved, so that complicated things. And the fact that he was a high-powered attorney meant that he held all the cards.

While the woman wanted to take the children and flee for all of their safety and well being, had she done so she would have been accused of kidnapping. Yet if she left the children with her husband while she tried to get out herself, he was within his rights to accuse her of abandoning the children. She was damned if she did and damned if she didn't.

Her only recourse was to lock herself in her bedroom 24/7, and live like a prisoner in her own home for the many months that he made sure the divorce proceedings dragged out ad infinitum.

Living in the world of certain narcissists is like living in one of the cults that had such a bad name back in the 60's and 70's.

❑   There is one supreme ruler. All others are underlings.

❑   Everyone must comply with the supreme ruler's expectations or punishment will be handed out.

❑   No one can leave once they join the group.

❑   The members of the group will be ostracized from any former ties as these are now unnecessary.

❑   Emotional brainwashing takes place almost methodically.

❑   After a while, the victims become almost robotic in their interactions with the world.

❑   They retain no individuality, no sense of direction, no goals of their own.

❑   They become numb and blindly follow the supreme leader wherever they are directed to go.

❑   They are generally unaware of their personality changes.

Of course, if we remember Reverend Jim Jones who took his entire cult to Guyana back in the 70's, we will also remember that he led over 900 people to their deaths, following his direction of mass suicide.

There is no doubt that brainwashing and mind control are powerful forces for controlling and manipulating others. This is the difficulty one faces in any attempt to help a victim of narcissism escape their world.

While most are certainly not to the degree of the Jamestown massacre led by Jim Jones, the numbers of victims of torture and manipulation throughout this world are hard to imagine, as exhibited by even these few stories you've already read throughout this book.

Torture is torture. Abuse is abuse. It doesn't matter if it's one-on-one or in the large numbers of the cults of old.

But the hard role to be in is that of someone who wishes to help a victim of narcissism, when that same victim may either not wish for your help (because they can't truly see what is actually happening in their lives), or they do want your help, but do not know how to access it. Certainly the victim may fear retaliation from their abuser should they reach out to you.

On the other hand, so many of my clients tell me how they realize they have alienated their friends and family through their unhealthy behavior, and that they fear no one is left to help them should they find a window of escape. (Of course that is the point of isolating to begin with; it keeps the narcissist center stage in his victim's life, and all others at too great a distance to interfere.)

How You Can Help

First and foremost, ambient abuse is so stealthy a process that the biggest problem for many victims is that no one can possibly believe it's going on. Of course the narcissist seems to keep outsiders charmed with his own talents, keeping all other eyes off his mate and onto himself to the degree that best friends and family members may need serious convincing to even suspect this wonderful soul could abuse their loved one.

With this in mind, my first directive to you is *listen carefully* for signs, symptoms, and dropped hints that things aren't so great at home. Many times the victims themselves may not even realize what is going on, thus their confusion doesn't make it easy to convey their fears to you. You may need to become a great observer of body language to even get a glimpse that something is amiss.

You might notice things like your friend or family member growing quieter than normal. She may start wearing long-sleeved clothes even during warm months (to hide bruising). She may not be able to maintain eye contact with others. She may not call as often. She may seem distant. You may notice that when the couple is together, she seems to spend more time playing with her food during dinner than interacting with others. She may seem unable to concentrate or stay on top of the conversation. When walking as a couple, it may seem that he is several steps ahead of her, and she is not even aware of where she is. She may lose or gain a great deal of weight or experience various illnesses or physical symptoms. And she may have quit caring about her appearance.

Certainly kids show the stress and worry in very similar ways, although other signs to watch for with the children may include dropping grades in school, avoiding playtime with friends (or conversely – begging to stay with friends more and more), inability to concentrate, shutting themselves in their rooms, and acting out.

As concerned friends and family members, the best thing you can do is let your victimized loved ones know that you are there for them. Be cautious of being judgmental, yet be a listening ear. Understand that if they don't call you, it may not be because they don't want to. Rather, it may be because they aren't *allowed* to call you.

If you can gently introduce them to knowledge about narcissism, you might just light a spark for change, for oftentimes these folks are absolutely convinced that all that is wrong is their fault, or they may feel that they are the only person in this situation. Once they discover how they are not alone, it is an open door for them to begin to understand the vicious cycle they are in.

Do be cautious that neither you nor they give this book or any other information regarding narcissism to the narcissist in their life. For one of two things will happen … true narcissists will either blow it off as having nothing to do with them, or worse, they will fly into a rage, only making life even worse for their victims. Believe me, it will surely backfire. Since we can't change the narcissist, the emphasis needs to be on getting help to the victims and their kids.

Certainly suggesting counseling for the victim is a great idea, provided that the therapist is thoroughly familiar with this particular disorder, otherwise more damage can be done than good. For those who fear therapy, can't afford it, or wouldn't be "allowed" by their controlling mate to participate in it, what has proven helpful is resources such as this book where your victim friend can read other people's true stories. The realization that she is not alone is usually the best eye-opener you can help your friend discover.

But remember, if she denies that there is a problem, you may simply have to wait until she is more ready to hear what you have to say. If you recall the earlier story of Marti and Erica, who were both in love with Gus, I was the friend who eventually introduced Marti to the narcissism explanation. While I recognized all the Red Flags early on, I also realized that Marti was too swept off her feet in the early stages to even hear anything I might want to tell her. She simply had to experience some of it first-hand before she could ever believe that what I said was true. And you may find yourself in this exact spot.

It can be a hard job being a friend of a codependent. It takes a lot of energy, because sometimes they're so emotionally exhausting to be around that they simply drain you.

They certainly don't have any extra energy to be an equal friend who wants to help you as well. And this is why so many victims actually lose friends and family – especially when some victims keep leaving and returning over and over to their abusive mates, when their friends can clearly see the destruction going on. It's simply too painful to watch.

Yet if you do reach through the veil of darkness that your co-dependent friend is living under, you have a good chance of turning her life around once and for all. But you truly have to recognize that just as with any addictive person (whether alcoholic, drug addict, or whatever), breaking an addiction is a tough road.

> *Believe it or not, the codependent has oftentimes become*
> ***addicted to abuse***
> *and will need to go through withdrawal, emotional rehab,*
> *and care just as any other addict does.*

And it's a long and uphill road for all involved. Yet your friend will thank you with all her heart once she sees how wonderful life is on the other side, *if* you have the patience, empathy, and compassion to help get her there.

Chapter 27
Loving or Leaving?

Perhaps the hardest part about being in a relationship with a narcissist is that, despite their behaviors that may leave us totally devastated, most of us still love our partners deeply. We may have spent years with them, believe in our marriage vows, or have young children with them and do not wish to upset the family dynamics, no matter how emotionally unhealthy we may feel.

The ironic thing is that while being abandoned is what a narcissist fears most, he or she never understands the role they take in pushing their loved ones out of their lives to begin with. And it does no good to explain this phenomenon to them.

This is a difficult spot to be in. Deciding to stay with or leave someone who treats you in a manner that isn't healthy is much more obvious when his or her behavior is clearly abusive. If your husband has been arrested for beating you, there is concrete evidence that things are definitely wrong. (Yet how many battered wives still refuse to leave their batterers?) Harder still is trying to sort through the confusion and self-doubt that accompanies the subtle behaviors you can't quantify – the silent treatment, controlling issues, constant criticisms – none of which seem to be big issues by themselves. Yet, when appreciated for the overwhelming negative brainwashing and emotional abuse they really are, these behaviors are hard to refute.

One idea that may help you make your decision is to picture someone else in your situation. For example, if you have a grown daughter, think of how you might feel if you knew she might be suffering in a similar relationship. Would you want her to stay or go? Would you want her to continue to receive the abuse, the silent treatment, or suffer the emotional roller coaster you have been living with? What would you advise her to do? Would you want her to do everything possible to salvage her emotional and possibly her physical health, or that of your grandchildren? Or would you want her to stay in a relationship for all the wrong reasons? Because of the time she's invested. Because he's "really not that bad." Because what would the neighbors say if she left?

When you are the one in the position of having to decide to stay or leave a relationship such as this, no one can make the decision for you. However, it may be helpful to know that depending on whether or not you stay with the one you love or leave him or her behind, there are some important things you can do to help you in either situation.

Loving and Staying

For whatever reason you are staying in your relationship, the bottom line is that you are getting something out of it. Financial security, a roof over your head, dependency on someone else, a commitment to your marriage vows, or believing that no one else could ever love you are frequently mentioned as reasons to stay. Yet consider these frequently cited comments: "I love my house and would hate to leave it," or "I've earned the most money over the course of our marriage, why should I let him take half?" These are not reasons that take into account the value of your emotional and/or physical well-being in the equation. Your health is priceless compared to any material possession you might risk leaving behind.

If you have decided to stay, making the best of your situation is crucial for your optimum survival.

You already know that a positive change in your partner's behavior is nearly impossible, and that the only person you can control is yourself. You control your feelings, your responses, your behaviors, and your attitude. Remember, unless they literally have a gun to your head, no one can "make" you do, think, or feel something without your permission.

With that in mind, here is a list of strategies to help you in your ongoing goal of making life as comfortable as possible with your narcissist:

Staying Behaviors

- ❑ Recognize your partner as the Master of the Universe at all times.
- ❑ Understand that, in his eyes, your role is to be his constant source of Narcissistic Supply. He is an addict – you are the drug.
- ❑ Know that at some point, when you no longer fill that need, he may dump you suddenly and without warning.
- ❑ Accept that you must be the one to accommodate to him, and that he is virtually incapable of change of any kind.
- ❑ Recognize that he is unable to experience or understand your emotions. Empathy is something he will *never* be capable of.
- ❑ Appreciate that while you may love him, he is truly incapable of loving you in the same way.
- ❑ Set your boundaries for things you will and will not do, and stick with them. Do not tolerate inappropriate behavior or abuse of any kind.
- ❑ Realize that your personality may change as a result of remaining in this emotionally empty and unpredictable environment.
- ❑ Believe in your heart that no matter what you do to try to "fix" your partner, you will not succeed at this honorable mission.
- ❑ Understand that your partner is a great actor, pretender, and exaggerator of the truth; therefore you can never completely trust him.
- ❑ Look for anything you do that seems to encourage his good behavior and repeat this often.
- ❑ Let him think he is in control at all times. Assure him of this with phrases like, "Whatever you think, dear," or "You're so much better at this than I am." Never tell him he's wrong or question his "expertise" in anything.

- ❏ Never show him fear – he only sees it as a sign of weakness and will use it against you.
- ❏ Do not let him think you are happy – this may insight a rage. Since he's not able to experience happiness, why should you?
- ❏ Ignore his childish behavior. As much as possible, act as if it didn't happen and it certainly didn't upset you.
- ❏ Do not show your emotions. He sees all emotions as a sign of weakness and will punish you for them. Certainly do not expect him to show you his emotions, other than the negative emotional behaviors, like rage, anger, hostility, silent treatment, and others.
- ❏ Do not expect him to ever grace you with gifts or adoration unless you threaten to leave him. When he feels that his supply, his badly needed fix (you) is about to disappear, he may suddenly change into Mr. Perfect once again. Do not expect this to last.
- ❏ If possible, develop a "second you." The you that is cold, unfeeling, non-emotional, and stoic. Use this personality when you are with your partner, but keep the real you healthy by bringing it out when you are with others outside of your narcissistic environment.
- ❏ Live your own life, but do not expect to share your life experiences with him and get any supportive comments in return. He does not care about your life, unless it causes an interruption to his Narcissistic Supply.
- ❏ If at all possible, maintain your own financial accounts. Do not hand over all your money to him or give up your own ability to maintain an income. If the day comes when he discards you, it is imperative to have a plan for self-sufficiency.
- ❏ Do not keep his behavior secret from your family and friends. Keep them aware of your whereabouts. Do not sever your relationships with them, no matter what he tells you.
- ❏ Praise him often. Tell him how wonderful he is, how great he is at his job, how everyone loves him. Thank him profusely for the least little thing he does. Do not criticize his behaviors. This will only cause you grief. There is no rationalizing with him.

- Do not expect him to admit to being a narcissist, no matter what information you provide him to the contrary. He will probably accuse you of being the one who needs help.
- When all else fails, treat him to a dose of his own medicine: reflect his behaviors back to him. Scream, holler, threaten, or leave him. This will bring him to his knees in fear of losing you.
- Above all, remember this is not your fault. You are not to blame for his frustrations in life. You do not make him angry. He is angry all by himself. You are merely a pawn in his life, just something he uses like his car or bicycle. He sees you no differently than that.

A Word About Religion Here

If you have strong religious beliefs and affiliations, you may be struggling with balancing those and your wedding vows (till death do us part) against leaving the abusive environment you and your kids may be living in. I have many clients who struggle with this and while I can't make the decision for them, what I can do is recount what my friend and colleague, Tom Joseph, recently shared with me. Tom is a Licensed Clinical Pastoral Counselor, as well as an ordained minister and Biblical historian. He also has a Christian radio show in the Denver area. His unique background and education were why I chose him to address this issue; for it is a tough one for those whose faith is a cornerstone in their lives. They certainly want to make the right decision, and yet it is a difficult emotional battle for most of them.

The way Tom explains it is like this: While there are certainly numerous Biblical passages about turning the other cheek (many which are taken out of context or have been horribly misinterpreted) there are also an equal number that support Christians in keeping themselves and their children safe from those who might do them harm.

And absolutely nowhere in the Bible does God or Jesus encourage people to stay in abusive situations.

Tom goes on to explain that people who are worried about leaving an abusive relationship based upon their religious values about marriage and divorce should understand that, according to the Bible, even God divorced Israel for all of Israel's abuse against him.

In addition, narcissists were certainly alive and well in the time of Christ, however most of us would recognize them in the Scriptures as Scribes and Pharisees. And you can bet that Christ did not stand for their abuse either. According to Tom's historical study of the Bible, Christ was actually somewhat of a rabble-rouser against them.

Furthermore, when God directed Christians to "Separate yourself from evil," he did not discriminate who might be excluded from that dictate; whether that be husband, wife, parent, or friend. And in fact, he described the blessings to come instead of pain, when you separate yourself from those who would do you harm, according to Tom.

So if you are struggling with this issue, reach out with your faith and talk to God about it. Don't get hung up on the guilt that frequently gets us befuddled. Being a victim was not your fault, so forgive yourself for your role in the events. For, in fact, if God can forgive us our sins, then who are we not to? That rather implies we are better than God now, doesn't it?

I hope this brief account gives those of you seeking validation that leaving your relationship is not an ungodly behavior when so much is at stake for you and your children. For more information you may want to learn more about Tom and his work at www.AtTheWell.net. In fact, in his audio archives you will find us doing a show on narcissism, which you can download for free.

Leaving

Deciding to leave your partner is never an easy decision, even when he is not a narcissist. Whether a business partner, friend, family member, or significant other, you'll have issues that overlap into every part of your lives together and can lead to a variety of feelings as a result. When the one you're leaving is indeed a narcissist, everything seems exceedingly more painful and complicated. The emotional instability they have created can leave you filled with overwhelming guilt, fear, anxiety, shame, and self-doubt to the point where you go running back to him at first chance. Or, if he is the one who left you, the constant fantasies of his return can keep you in his Victim Boxx for a lifetime if you don't recognize what is happening.

If you are the one leaving, it's helpful to have a plan. (Although if at any time you risk injury, leave immediately! Get yourself out of harm's way and figure out the details later.) If possible, leave when he is not home, as you will best avoid his raging behavior that way. (He will suddenly be vulnerable to losing his Narcissistic Supply and will be overwhelmed with fear and any variety of reactions.) Developing a plan may take you days or weeks. Finding a place to live, moving money to new accounts, lining up friends and family to help, and finding a knowledgeable lawyer, are all good planning strategies before you just walk out the door.

Once you have removed yourself from the situation, here are some strategies to use on your journey to freedom. (Keep in mind to always obey issues that pertain to the law, such as court-mandated visitation with children, etc.)

There are two very important things to keep in mind in this process: 1) Leaving him physically is one thing – the emotional separation takes substantially longer; 2) As long as he thinks there is a chance at re-establishing his supply (you), he will do so.

These behaviors can help you cope with the struggle:

Leaving Behaviors

❑ Understand that, while it will not be easy to let go, your physical and emotional health depend upon it.
❑ Do not give in to requests by mutual friends who beg you to give him just one more chance.
❑ If possible, (and when there are no children involved) sever absolutely all contact with him. Do not answer or return his calls. Change your number if possible. Return any mail

unopened. Block him on your email. Do not accept any gifts from him. Do not call him or meet him, even for a special occasion. He must see you as a dead end or he will continue to haunt you.

❑ Understand that you may be seen and described as the "crazy one." He will blame you for everything. All will be your fault. Ignore it and go on.

❑ Never show fear. Learn to develop a great poker face. Ignore him whenever possible.

❑ Do not believe him when he says he promises to change – remember that he is practically incapable of doing so.

❑ Never trust him.

❑ Do not ask him for anything, if at all possible. Doing so will admit you need him, and that gives him another direction to control you.

❑ If you must talk to or meet with him (when you have children involved you may still have visitation issues, etc.), never give him any personal information about yourself, especially as it pertains to someone new in your life. This is only asking for him to rage.

❑ If you must communicate, do it in writing, which provides potentially vital documentation. Email is perfect, as it tracks dates and more. If you don't have your own email account, get one. There are several free services out there.

❑ Keep your boundaries up and strong. Do not accept unacceptable behavior or abuse of any kind.

❑ Be fully prepared for things to get ugly in court. Hiring a good lawyer can be very helpful. Your narcissist will not let you go without a fight and will use all avenues possible to hurt you, whether they be financial, custody issues, or others.

❑ Let law enforcement know if he threatens you. Get a restraining order to protect yourself if necessary.

❑ Do not use words or phrases that let him think you believe he is, in any way, superior. As a matter of fact, as often as possible, refer to him as "average" or "normal." A narcissist's greatest fear is not to be seen as God-like.

❑ Seek the advice of a therapist or an experienced, emotionally healthy survivor. You may be suffering from depression, anxiety, and even Post Traumatic Stress. Finding an understanding counselor who can help you work through your own grief and adjustments on your road back into a healthier world can be a lifeline to healing. This may also be crucial for your children who may have had their own issues throughout your relationship.

❑ Be cautious about spending much time on Internet chat sites with others who are victimized. While it sounds like a good idea, many have not yet healed and as such, can suck you into emotional cesspools of depression, anger, and more.

❑ Get on top of all your financial records and accounts. You may need to set up a separate account for yourself in case your narcissist decides to lock you out of accounts.

❑ Be kind to yourself. Believe in yourself. Know that you were not the crazy one here – despite frequent feelings to the contrary. Know that there is light at the end of the tunnel.

Even Tighter Boundaries

If you do decide to leave, it's important that you strengthen your boundaries as much as possible. For example, one male client of mine was divorced by his very narcissistic wife. Although she chose to divorce him, she delighted in continuing to drive him crazy, and with a child between them, there was still that need to communicate.

> *Her way of testing his boundaries was to call and absolutely fill his answering machine with 27 voice mails.*
> *She would scream, carry on, lecture – you name it – all just to fill up the machine and irritate the hell out of him.*

I assured him that the best way to take control of that situation was to tell her that she could leave all the messages that she wanted, but he would only listen to the first one. By being true to this boundary, she quit playing telephone games when she realized he was no longer playing either.

Yet another client shared with me how whenever her ex would drop the kids back off with her after his designated weekend with them, he would leave all their dirty clothes for her to wash as well. Her solution? She simply left the suitcase of dirty clothes in the hall closet until he picked up the kids again and she sent them right back with the kids for her ex to wash. It didn't take him long to figure out she wouldn't play the game either.

Another client simply did not want her ex to know exactly where her new apartment was. Despite his asking, she refused to tell him, even though he had trained their two year old to beg Mommy to let Daddy see the child's new room. It was tough, because of course the two year old was caught in the middle, yet my client valued her privacy and stuck to her guns.

These are just a few ideas that you'll need to consider regarding your boundaries and the juggling that goes with establishing a new life. Keep your radar up for other boundary crashings that your ex may attempt to employ. He may remember how your boundaries really didn't mean anything before, so it may take some convincing on your part before he believes that they mean something new now. Remember, consistency is the key.

Courtroom Strategies

For those of you deciding to leave, many will end up in court and I want to give you some idea of what you are in store for. Mostly I want to warn you that you may be shocked by the convoluted journey that may ensue. There may be custody battles, property wars, psychological evaluations, social workers or child advocates, lies that will defy belief, restraining orders, and expenses you never dreamed of. Worse than that, you may be thrust in the middle of judges and lawyers who haven't a clue about narcissism, and if you're not careful in how you manage yourself and your case, you will end up looking like the crazy one by the time you finally get to court, which can go against you badly in settlements, custody, and more.

Of course that's how your narcissist plans it, for it makes him look like the saint and you like the difficult, emotionally disturbed one. After all, remember how charming you thought he was when you first met? That's the image that the court will generally see too, thus, the most important thing you can do is to interview several lawyers to determine who has dealt specifically with narcissistic issues and knows what the heck you're talking about when you describe the crazy-making world you have lived in.

I have several tricks up my sleeve that you and your lawyer may want to employ, but I don't want to get into them here for fear that many narcissists and their lawyers will learn these strategies and use them against their victims.

For more on these specifics, please consult with me directly and we can set up a strategy.

What I will tell you is this: The most important thing you can do during this entire fiasco will be to get yourself as emotionally and physically healthy as possible. Your ideal persona in the courtroom and in the various interviews ahead with child advocates (and even psychologists if psych evals are mandated) must be one of an emotionally healthy, kind, caring, but *unflappable* parent or spouse. If you have a good poker face you'll need to use it, for your narcissist will pull any variety of dirty tricks out of his hat and may shock you to pieces with the lies, demands, and accusations you simply won't see coming. Of course he is just waiting to see you melt into a heap on the floor, which as we know is a huge turn-on for him. So, if you can keep your composure, it may lead to him losing his. And if he loses composure in front of a judge, the odds will be shifted in your favor instead.

I can't tell you the number of victims I know who have gone to court in horrible shape from the months of emotional game playing.

They look haggard, exhausted, depressed, anxious, on edge, agitated, and sometimes even paranoid. Of course you can imagine how the narcissist will come across. Now picture both of these people in your mind and it's easy to see how the victim can easily get mowed over by the courts.

So, do whatever you can to get help to keep yourself strong. Find a good therapist. Join a support group. Attend a workshop. Go to the gym. Enlist help from your family. Eat, sleep, and exercise in a healthy manner. Take time off to get out of the melee whenever possible. Go on a trip somewhere – even if it's just a weekend with your gal friends – just get out of the line of fire as much as possible.

Many of these horrific court battles last a year or more, so this is definitely a marathon, not a sprint. And it will become easy for your kids to get caught in the mess as well. Here again, if they have at least one healthy parent to be their role model, their own emotional health will benefit as well.

While the process of leaving may be a long, difficult path, just remember that once you make it to the other side of this nightmare, you won't believe the peace, safety, and unbelievable life that is yours without the narcissistic ruler you have been used to. Most of my clients can't believe they waited so long once they find out how wonderful life is on the other side. And the healthy differences they report in their kids (once the storm has blown over) is priceless.

When They Won't Leave You Alone

Joseph M. Carver, PhD, has a great analogy that may make sense to those of you who can't seem to get your narcissist to let go. He points out that if you are playing the slot machines in Las Vegas, there is a certain feedback loop that helps you determine which machines you will play and which you will leave. If you put your money in a given machine and after several attempts receive no payout, you may put in one last coin before moving on. Yet, when that last quarter suddenly lights the machine up and quarters begin falling like mad, it becomes much more difficult to abandon that which has just produced a jackpot. If it's been a winner once, maybe it will be again. And thus you keep playing your favorite machine, with the hopes that it will give you the payout you dream of.

Thus it is with the narcissist. Dr. Carver believes that the narcissist who has been abandoned looks at his former partner as a slot machine.[11] For each positive response it gives out (however small) he is convinced that it will certainly give him more. In other words, if you say no 10 times to his request to "just meet for lunch," but you finally get sick of his nagging and hope that if you say yes just one time he will leave you alone, guess again. The one time you say yes is the equivalent to the jackpot going off! Why should he give up on you now?

On the other hand, if he feels that his odds of reuniting with you are completely and utterly futile, he may reject you altogether. It is important to remember that he sees you as no more than an extension of himself, much like his hands. I remember a Stephen King or *Twilight Zone* story from several years ago where a man's hands revolted against him. Not only did they not obey him, they joined forces and tried to kill him. The crazed man eventually cut off his hands to save his own life.

The narcissist may see you as rebellious as those revolting hands. With any luck, and your consistent position of offering nothing but a tightly closed door in his face, he may sever his relationship with you completely and move on.

Lucky for you.

Not so lucky for his next, unsuspecting victim.

*If I could only have known how wonderful my life
would turn out once I got on the other side of this
veil of darkness, pain, and distress,
I would have left years ago.*

*To live in an emotionally healthy environment
and to see the safe haven my kids have now
that they never had in our former emotionally toxic home,
I kick myself over and over that I waited so long.
Mary Beth – survivor*

Chapter 28
The Myth About Closure

*F*or so many victims, the last thing they really hope for before they feel they can move on with their lives is *closure*. I'm not sure where we learned that closure exists in all things, but if you're awaiting closure from a narcissist, believe me, you'll be waiting till hell freezes over!

As sad as that is, the sooner you realize that concept and quit waiting for that magic wand that either helps you understand how what was once magic has turned so incredibly bad, or helps you better accept your future without your unhappy mate, the sooner you will heal.

> *Why can't you get closure?*
> *Some completion? Some resolution to your feelings?*
> *Because closure must come from within*
> *YOU*
> *and not from another person.*

One of the things that helps my clients move on is to get a better understanding of what makes a narcissist tick. While they may have learned the psychological explanation I evolved earlier, it's often hard to translate that understanding to really "getting" this behavior. With that in mind, I have found these two analogies to be the most helpful in giving them a clearer picture of why the closure they want is a nebulous concept at best...

Emotionally Retarded

Most of us are familiar with mental retardation. There are many individuals who are mentally limited, yet who function adequately in life, hold jobs, go to school, participate in sports, and marry and have families.

And yet, what are the odds that a mentally retarded person, even with extra tutoring, training, or other variety of education, could ever reach a level of functioning to be able to run for the job of President of the United States?

Odds are between slim and none, right? Why? Because there is simply a limitation on their ability to function intelligently. To be the leader of the free world requires not only intelligence, but the ability to handle stress, to multitask well, and to conceptualize about a huge variety of "what if's" that go along with the job. Few people of average intelligence could handle the job, much less someone who is mentally challenged.

Now, if you modify that angle to look at narcissistic people as *emotionally retarded or limited*, it may become a bit easier to truly see why it is that they just don't "get" things like empathy, compassion, understanding, kindness, and sensitivity to others.

They simply aren't capable!
It's almost as if the gene for those traits
does not exist in these individuals.

So try as you might to explain yourself during your relationship or after, your justifications, pleading, and emotional request for their acknowledgements will only fall on deaf ears. They simply don't understand. Nor will they ever. It is truly beyond their intelligence quotient for their emotional capacity. Just as the mentally retarded are never going to understand advanced calculus, the emotionally retarded aren't going to understand you or your emotions. Period.

And thus, picturing them as emotionally retarded may help you begin to see why closure is the last thing on their minds.

Thanking Your Car

The other analogy that seems to help folks better understand the callousness, hurtfulness, and ignoring behaviors of a narcissist can best be explained using my car story...

So, let me ask you, when you drive your car from home to work every day, do you get out of your car and turn back to it, lovingly caressing it, and say, "Thank you, car! You are amazing. You take such good care of me and I'm so happy with you that I'm going to bring you something special when I come back after work today. Have a good day. You're the best. I love you."

Of course not! It's a car. An inanimate object. It's supposed to be there at your beck and call. It's supposed to turn on when you tell it to. It's supposed to keep you safe. It's supposed to carry out your wishes without question. And it's not supposed to give you any grief. In fact we rarely give our cars a second thought and almost take them for granted, unless of course they suddenly refuse to perform in the way we expect them to. (Like when the battery's dead and our plans to go somewhere are in peril.)

Am I right?

Well, sadly, that's how many narcissists view everyone else around them – even their loved ones. The same way as we view a car or a robot or any other inanimate object that's here to serve us.

In their minds we are put here on earth specifically to serve them. We are supposed to jump when they say jump. We are supposed to perform to their liking when and how they dictate. And God forbid if we ever go against their direction, break down, or not function in a manner consistent with their expectations or there will be hell to pay. And above all, they absolutely don't recognize that we have feelings of any kind, for certainly a car has no feelings now, does it?

With this new insight in mind, can you see how closure is simply a dream that will never be met? Emotional feelings and responses in the way that you envision them are simply not in these people. Yet oddly enough it appears as though they are hypersensitive to any emotional slight they perceive from *you*. Thus if you forget to thank them for something, or perhaps you roll your eyes when you are in fact frustrated at yourself, they may interpret this as a huge slight or insult. Their receiving radar (as it pertains to emotional touchiness) seems to be so much higher than ours, but their radar about anyone else's just seems to be broken or non-existent. And there's nothing we can do to change it.

So closure?
It simply doesn't make sense to them.
For why would they ever apologize to their car?!

A Word About Projection

Lastly, narcissists are particularly good at projection, and this is vital to help you better understand your role in this convoluted dance.

> *The dictionary defines projection as:*
> *"The attribution of one's own ideas, feelings, or attitudes to other people; especially the externalization of blame, guilt, or responsibility as a defense against anxiety."*

Narcissists love to project their own dysfunctional feelings, behaviors, and beliefs onto you, leaving you feeling like the badly behaving one in the relationship. For example, they might tell you that you are paranoid, bad with money, emotionally unstable, hypercritical, unhappy with life, a terrible parent, selfish, ugly, or any other variety of not-so-nice claims, when in fact these issues are frequently their own.

Does any of this ring true to what you've been experiencing? I have had clients struggle for years with messages they've been given about themselves, which they can't seem to make sense of until they begin to understand the manipulative behavior of projection.

So if the messages your narcissist has been giving you about yourself just don't add up, it may be because he or she has used projection to keep you off balance for a very long time. And usually, it works very effectively.

Again, it may be helpful to understand that narcissists don't do this consciously, it is simply part of their makeup. But it works most effectively in keeping their victims totally lost and confused, with a constantly eroding self-esteem.

So in that elusive conversation that you keep wishing you could have that would give all your experiences closure, keep in mind that understanding years of narcissistic projection is truly where your healing will begin, as opposed to any conversation that you might ever have with the narcissist who planted those feelings in your head for you.

So you see, getting closure from a narcissistic relationship is not about meeting with someone else to get your stuff off your chest, for the reality is that your unhappy mate will never speak those words you want to hear. And if it's an apology you're waiting for so that you can go on to heal, let it go. That will never happen either.

> *The true road to closure is to create your own,*
> *and the best way to achieve that is to heal fully*
> *and move on to healthy relationships.*
> *That truly is the sweetest revenge.*

Chapter 29
Victim Versus Survivor —
It's Your Choice

"*I* returned to him once and then he wouldn't let me go again for years. I just wanted to not be enemies, but he wanted to be 'best friends.' It's bad enough that we're still in the same town, but we have a dog we both love. The dog is old and I don't want to traumatize him and so I stay here in this town for his sake, rather than move back to my home across the country. He uses my relationship with my pet to manipulate me." – Voice of a victim.

There is a distinct difference between being a victim and a being a survivor:

- A survivor has already lived through the trauma and has chosen to move on.

- A victim is still living there – even if he or she has been out of the traumatic environment for some time.

- Survivors heal.

- Victims fester and do not move forward.

- Survivors take responsibility for their actions and their consequences.

- Victims find it easier to blame others for their situation because then they do not have to take responsibility for their role in the relationship.

Being either a victim or a survivor is a conscious choice.

Some of the letters I received were full of hate, anger, pain, and so much more: anguish for lost years, for the realization of the abuse that occurred, and even for shame at not recognizing sooner that the ability to end the tyranny was always in the hands of the victim.

What they experienced are the completely normal feelings and behaviors of going through (and healing from) various types of grief: Denial, Anger, Bargaining, Depression, and Acceptance.[12]

We all start out as victims. Understanding and believing that we are safely out of the situation where we felt we were held captive, doesn't happen overnight. The time involved will vary for everyone. While some people are so invigorated by their new-found freedom they shed their cocoon of victim-hood almost immediately, others need time to validate and rebuild themselves into someone they recognize as new, or even to find their old selves again.

It's natural. You need to vent for a while. Scream, holler, cry, pound your fists, run away from home, journal – do whatever you have to do to get your feelings out so that you can look at them, recognize them, and then put them to bed. In my own case I had to deal with my victim anger from events that had taken place 30 years ago. The repressed memories of being sexually abused came back as fresh as yesterday. While some people were amazed that events from so long ago kept me locked up in my Boxx of Fear, for me it seemed like it was all new again. Try as I might, I couldn't just wish the memories to go away – and I wanted to be angry for as long as I could. I desperately clung to the victim role for a long time.

Yet, reaching the stage of Acceptance is what allows you to move past being a victim and on towards becoming a survivor. Stopping at any stage before you work your way all the way through to Acceptance will only short-change your healing and hold you back from experiencing the best that life has to offer.

Remaining a victim is a conscious choice. By rehashing your story over and over, you reach a point where it is no longer helpful and, instead, you remain in your Victim Boxx, hoping to justify your angry feelings. Choosing to learn from your past and forgive yourself are the first steps in refusing to keep living with the pain.

The distinction between the victims and the survivors in the letters I received was crystal clear. Survivors had learned from their pain. They had quit looking back. They were looking forward to the future. Many had already jumped back into the deep end of the pool and were actively participating in life. Mind you, they had new knowledge that was taking them on a different path from their last one. They knew the Red Flags to watch for. They knew how to set their boundaries and take care of themselves first. They had hope for a bright future. In many cases, they had even forgiven their former partner for his or her transgressions.

Yet, the most important thing they had done was to quit hoping for their partner's return and they totally and completely understood that their former "perfect partner" was not ever real to begin with. That nobody is perfect. That it was all just a myth.

And they chose to be survivors.

Here's what they had to say:

Tammy

There is absolutely nothing I would change in my life, despite everything. The insights I've gained throughout my journey are priceless. I wouldn't necessarily do it the same way again, but I do appreciate the understanding and wisdom I've gained.

Rick

Now that I understand and recognize the game she's playing I've simply stopped playing and have moved on.

Jenny

I've learned that sticking up to a bulldozer just doesn't work. The only thing that works is to disengage and leave, never to return. I love and adore my life now. I am at peace with myself and with everything that has happened to me. I have done a lot of healing.

Jane

I am not choosing to be in another relationship right now. I don't trust myself and I don't trust another man yet. I am instead focusing on my boys and my life and getting to know myself better. I have spent my whole life trying to get away from abusers. My mother, my father, my first husband, and my second husband. I am now living in harmony with myself.

Teri

I'm 44 years old now and would still love to have another family. I finally love myself, my daughter, and my life, so I know that things are as they are supposed to be. I have even enrolled in a master's program in counseling so that I can help others who are going through the same pain I went through. I'm convinced God gave me this experience for a reason and looking at it that way gives it all a new light.

Graham

I feel great! Not every day, not all the time, but for the most part I have come to accept that there was nothing I could do to change the situation. The marriage was destined to end this way. It lasted so long because of my ability to put up with all the shit, which wasn't the least bit healthy for any of us. I have hopefully read enough, thought enough, and had enough therapy to move on to a healthier and happier relationship. My ex-wife has been calling me (very drunk) late at night, trying to dump her anger somewhere and telling me she needs to find someone so she can feel better. I feel sorry for the next, unsuspecting man! My prayer and goal now is to have my children understand that they are responsible for their own happiness, actions, and life!

Julie

I am dating again and enjoying the experience of having a relationship with someone who can truly be intimate. Anything would be an improvement over a narcissist. So I'm like a kid in a candy store – exploring my wants and needs in a relationship and not settling. I've had one relationship with a suspected narcissist and I was aware enough to get out of the relationship early. I still worry that maybe I will fall prey again, but I'm a different person now because of this experience. I'm stronger, more confident and no one is going to suck the life out of me for their own existence again. That is what my ex did to me. I lived for him and for making him feel good about himself. It's the dysfunctional dance that two people share when they are unhealthy. I'm healthy now so I think my chances of this happening again are very small. I'm OK with being alone and on my own, so a relationship will need to add value to my life, not take from it. That is the biggest difference now.

Jodi

It's taken me three long years of therapy, introspection, forgiveness, and self-awareness to move on with my life. I feel nothing for him anymore. I'm much happier and at peace with myself now than I ever was married to him. I thought I was happy with him and I was not. I lived a lie. I lived in denial. I lived a dream. I lived on the surface and not in real intimacy. I do now! Real intimacy is glorious! Real connection is possible now, so there is great hope for the future. Now my focus is my daughter and being aware of her pains and the ramifications of this mess. I don't want her to marry someone like her father. She is doing great with the help of therapy as well.

Jordan

I recall while going through my divorce I had a strong need to challenge myself in many areas. Maybe it was to avoid the pain of the loss, or to find something greater outside the process of divorce. I searched to feel something through the numbness. That's when I took up scuba diving; went parasailing, rock climbing, mastered a high ropes course, confronted roller coasters, traveled alone with young children, volunteered to speak in front of an audience, opened a business, moved to a hobby ranch and raised horses, and more incredible things than I ever dreamed of. I learned to challenge myself so the bumps in the road did not feel like mountains to climb. Whew, and what a ride it was! Now I simply approach new challenges as opportunities with a "What the hell, it can't be harder than surviving a marriage and a divorce from a narcissist!" And, it's a good thing as I find myself back into the throws of raising a 15-year-old passionate, bright, and strong-willed female daughter who needs a healthy mom!

Alexis

It's taken me a while, but I'm finally finding the positive in all this, and I have discovered my soul in the process. If another man comes into my life it will be because of growth ... an unfortunate, but necessary growth channel that led me to where I am now. I believe everything has a purpose and there are no coincidences. There just must have been something I needed to learn through this painful and traumatic relationship to be able to get to where I am right now.

My best lessons learned have been to give new relationships time and to let my friends and family act as extra eyes and ears in watching and listening to the way a man treats me. I understand now that I can be blinded by love. And that it can cost me. This time I go in with my eyes wide open.

NOW COMPARE THE PRIOR STATEMENTS OF SURVIVORS
WITH THEIR COUNTERPARTS, THE VICTIMS:

Amy

I have decided not to have any more relationships. I am ruined in every way.

Rita

I am an adult child of a recovered alcoholic – with little self-esteem left – and a huge, giving heart. I tried to heal my alcoholic father but never could, so I guess I've been seeking to help others all my life. Always doing for others – I was a prime target for a narcissist. Even though I have a clinical understanding of what happened to me, I still can't believe it.

He is living with another woman now. He has only known her for a year and has given her everything he promised me! I took care of his dying mother for ages and as soon as she died he threw me out. He hides behind his doctor (God) complex.

If he called me right now and asked me to come back I'd be elated, but deep inside I know I could never trust him again. In my mind I know I should say, "Get the f___ out of my life," but in my heart I'm saying the opposite. I still have fantasies that he'll call, begging me to come back. It's my fantasy versus reality. I know it won't happen.

Steve

There was a time (about a year) when things looked very bleak. I'm getting back on track, but it is a slow process. I've returned to the work I love and am enjoying it. Yet the loneliness burns like a fire in my heart and mind, and remembrances of her haunt me every day.

I've gone on a few dates. They've been disappointing. The danger now is that I can't trust and have faith like I once did. I guess I believe love is hopeless

The worst part is that I feel like I've wasted my best years and no one attractive will love me or be available now.

Eleanor

After yet again one more demeaning, devaluing fight, I declared defeat and left. (Maybe I finally decided I deserved better.) There has been no contact since then. It has been very hard and very painful. I know that I must move on. I miss him and still love him a lot and wish that we could have been together for a lifetime. I feel a lot of frustration where he is concerned and think that he must be treating his new woman a lot better than he treated me.

Elissa

I've recently been dating a wonderful man. Kind, caring, funny, giving, honest … you name it, he's got it. The problem is I just don't feel any chemistry with him. All my friends love him and I know I should too. But he'll just never be as wonderful as John. No one will.

Laurie

By the time I finally got out of the relationship I was experiencing chronic migraines and often passed out from the ongoing anxiety. I basically had a nervous breakdown. I was sent to a therapist who diagnosed me with a major depression and Post Traumatic Stress Disorder as a direct result of living with this man. The constant brainwashing just ate me away, piece by piece. Even now, months later, I still suffer from headaches, allergies, and constant anxiety. I am on disability with multiple chemical sensitivities and chronic fatigue syndrome.

Because of being ill now, life is hard to take.

It's Your Choice

The biggest problem about remaining a victim is that it prohibits you from moving on and healing. It keeps you from owning your own decisions and behaviors. It lets you blame all your issues on someone else and not take responsibility for the role you allowed yourself to play in the troubled relationship to begin with. It lets you off the hook and puts all the blame on other circumstances. This only leads to you devaluing yourself further and can keep you from doing what you want.

It may seem like those who remain victims don't really want to get better. They may unconsciously prefer the pain. They won't accept help. It's almost as if they are masochistic. Of course, they may not be able to see this from the inside, but those of us on the outside can, and we don't know how to help them.

It's important to ask yourself what you accomplish by remaining a victim. What do you get by staying where you are? Or, from a different approach, what is it worth to you to stay there? Certainly you can take antidepressants to feel better, but as long as you allow the old wound to fester, you will only be masking the symptoms. You will only be kidding yourself that you are unable to heal.

Another problem with remaining a victim is that sometimes you can lose your closest friends. They can grow weary of your ongoing victim stories. Most will want to help you heal, but the longer you remain a victim, the less able they are to reach you and pull you out of the tidal wave that's engulfing you. After a while, some will tire of the effort and will simply give up.

Continuing to live in the past doesn't let you create a future. As long as you carry those old photographs around with you, with the smallest hope that the perfect life will return, you will not help yourself move forward.

On the other hand, as long as you keep holding out for a "perfect partner" just like your last one first appeared to be, you will never find happiness. For after all, just how perfect did he really turn out to be?

Chapter 30
Learning to Love Yourself – Finally!

*M*any of us wish for a great relationship with someone, yet the crucial piece we often don't recognize is that we must first find a great relationship with ourselves before any healthy relationships can even exist, no matter who we're with. (Your mate, kids, parents, best friends, boss, and so on.)

Learning to believe in ourselves and love ourselves first is the most important component in having great relationships with all others in our lives. And when we don't or can't love ourselves first and foremost, it's frequently the first dangerous step to accepting just any old relationship that comes along. And that's where the problem begins.

Looking back on the relationship mess you're in now, can you see how that might have been the case?

> *You simply cannot love someone else in a healthy way unless you love yourself first.*

While this concept has been around for ages, many folks never understand how to take the steps to fulfill the task. While it's easy to simply say, "Love yourself," it's anything but easy to change patterns of behavior we have had for a lifetime. God knows, if we knew how to do it all this time, most of us would have done something about it long before now!

We all come into this world with a clean slate. None of us are born thinking there is something wrong with us or that we are unlovable. We learn from others what *they* believe our value to be, even though their beliefs about us may not necessarily be accurate. Whether it was your parents, teachers, siblings, minister, coach, or someone else who may have taught you that you weren't smart enough, cute enough, loveable, kind, deserving, or whatever, in fact *they were basing those judgments on their opinions.* And who is to say that they were right? In fact, more than likely, they weren't.

Yet, way too often those same erroneous beliefs of others lead us to participate in sad and self-destructive behaviors to prove to ourselves just how bad or unlovable we are! It almost becomes a self-fulfilling prophecy.

> *Is it any wonder then*
> *that the most difficult relationship most of us have*
> *is the one we have with ourselves?*

Of course there is also the fear that in loving yourself you are being selfish and most of us learned when we were little kids that being selfish was not OK. Well, let me tell you something …

♥ **Selfish** is when you only care for yourself, to the exclusion of others.

♥ **Self-care** is about loving yourself enough that you take care of yourself first, so that you are able to care for and about others.

This is one of the most difficult concepts that so many of my clients struggle with. Yet when they can approach the idea of the necessity of self-love from this view, it makes it much easier to see the difference between being narcissistic or selfish, and loving themselves in a way that is not only much healthier for them but for everyone else in their lives as well.

One of the best analogies I use to provide more clarity is this: When you're on a plane and listening to the flight attendant discuss the routine safety drill, he or she always describes what to do in the event that oxygen is needed during the flight. The attendant is especially careful to explain to parents traveling with small children who should get the oxygen first.

Is it the parents or the children? Do you remember?

When I ask this of my clients, the majority of loving and caring people – especially parents – always insist that the children get the oxygen first. However, they are absolutely wrong!

Why so? Don't we always care for the weak or vulnerable first? Especially knowing that we are the strong, more fully capable ones?

Well, while at first thought it would seem reasonable to get oxygen to the children first, the opposite actually makes the most sense. Why? Because should you expend all your energy (and what little oxygen might be in the cabin) getting your kids' oxygen on their faces, you might pass out and end up collapsed in a heap on the floor. Then exactly who would care for the kids?

This example seems to help many people (especially the caretaker types) get the first glimpse at just how important it is to care for and about yourself first. Most have just never thought of it that way because so many times we have been told that we're selfish, or worse, when we put ourselves first.

It is this backward, "selfish" thinking (usually based on years of guilt handed down from some authority figure or another) that gets us into so much trouble. The codependent frequently begins and ends by putting her mate's needs first. Not occasionally. Not in a way that takes turns or compromises. But in a way that denies her own value, worth, importance, or equality. And that's one of the first and most common ways that relationships become unbalanced and unhealthy to begin with.

If you've been involved in a narcissistic relationship for any length of time, you may have actually lost who you are along the way. Did you use to have a passion for singing, music, art, dancing, running, or some other activity but it simply no longer exists in your life? Did you use to have a reasonable self-esteem but now it seems in shreds? Did you use to feel comfortable within your own skin, but now you keep looking for others to tell you your worth?

> *Attempting to be everything*
> *that everyone else wants you to be*
> *(and not who you want to be)*
> *can lead you to losing your sense of self completely.*

With this in mind, it's time you learn to love yourself and rediscover yourself once again. Fletcher's story may shed some light on what happens when you do ...

Fletcher

When we trust and believe in ourselves, we do not have to look for our worth or identity anywhere else. However, when we are looking outside ourselves then we are *using* others to validate our self-worth. And the scary part is this: What if they don't?

It's taken me quite a while – too many years, actually – to get to this realization but what is most refreshing is that I now recognize that my life is about *me* deciding what is right and best for *me*. After some serious work studying my behaviors and beliefs, and making some significant readjustments, I started believing in myself and trusting myself again. Once that became more solid, I also began setting healthier boundaries for myself and for the people in my life. Funny, I used to do that pretty well when I was younger, but somehow I think I lost my faith in myself along the way.

> *I think I just listened to what everyone else's beliefs and expectations of me were, and my needs and wants just kept getting moved further and further down the list until I guess I felt as though I didn't even exist anymore. It was like I was simply an extension of my family. My needs and interests were always less important than theirs.*
> *Fletcher – victim*

De-Programming the Brainwashing

It's imperative to your healing that you first recognize that all those negative messages we've played in our heads for years usually started with someone else planting them there! Your parents, coach, priest, neighbor, teacher, or someone else who you gave more power to than yourself may have convinced you that you are imperfect in some way that has left you believing it.

Well, not to worry! For if they can program you, then you can be de-programmed as well! It's all within the power of the words and messages that you choose to feed yourself!

The Revealing Questions!

I have three deeply revealing questions I ask all my clients who are muddied about their relationships and/or struggling with issues of self-esteem. Each helps me gain some pretty clear insight about them as it pertains to 1.) How they really see themselves and 2.) What they are passionate about. I suggest you answer them for yourself here...

1. List all the things you like about yourself. (Your hair, body, sense of style, or the fact that you multitask better than anyone! You're a good mother, cook, or organizer. You are great at your job, a compassionate and caring friend, an empathetic listener, etc.) Be specific and as extensive as possible. Shoot for 10 to 20 things.

2. Now make a list of all the things you don't like about yourself and/or that others have told you are your weaknesses. (You're too fat, tall, skinny, disorganized, lazy, bad with finances, too sensitive, take things too personally, etc.)

Now, compare these two lists. Is there anything in the Bad List that, when you compare it to the Good List, simply doesn't mesh?

For example, I have had clients tell me that in the Good List they say they are a kind and loving friend and mother.

Yet, in the Bad List they mention how they are "too sensitive and care too much for other people." Hmmm … somehow it seems to me that if they were sensitive and cared for other people it was probably a big part of how they got to be a loving friend and mother to begin with! See what I mean?

Or else they might say they're great at their job on their Good List (which could even be something as tough as being an accountant) and yet their Bad List points out their belief that they are a stupid failure. Do you see the incongruity here? How can one possibly be good at being an accountant – a pretty detailed, intense job – and yet be a stupid failure? It just doesn't add up.

Believe it or not, the original problem may have been with the person who told you that you were "too sensitive"! Perhaps he or she wasn't sensitive enough! So, of course, you would appear too sensitive to them. And yet it has been that person's opinion that has molded your beliefs about yourself all these years.

And of course now that you understand how projection works, can you see how the "stupid failure" could have easily been the problem of the person who delivered the message, not you? Remember, narcissists tend to project their own issues onto everyone else in the path. So perhaps your mentor should have looked in the mirror to see who the "stupid failure" really was. Of course, it was much easier for him to give you the title. Are you beginning to see how that works?

It's always amazing to hear the recognition in my clients' voices as they become aware that the brainwashing that had left them with these very mixed messages was indeed that; purely brainwashing. For some of them, this simple exercise lets them see things with a new view for the first time in years.

We all have the complete ability to accept those old tapes or throw them out! For starters, consider the source of those folks who planted those great brainwashed lies into your head to begin with. Do any of these sound familiar?

❑ Your alcoholic father, who, in his drunken stupor had no concept of the torture he was handing out to those around him, including you.

❑ Your narcissistic mother who had never learned to love herself since her parents didn't know how to show her unconditional love either.

❑ Your fire-and-brimstone minister who did his best to shovel out guilt to all who were game to claim it – including you.

❑ Your kindergarten teacher who (unknown to you) was going through her own divorce and was stressed out to the max when she yelled at her class all the time, leaving them all frightened and confused.

❑ Your Little League coach who thought coaching meant being condescending, critical, and constantly threatening in order to produce winners.

❑ The person (or persons) who verbally, physically, emotionally and/or sexually abused you by taking advantage of your youth and their power, then added insult to injury by convincing you that if you told anyone you'd be punished again.

These people may have taught others around them (including *you!*) to fear, blame, and hate themselves, and that they should constantly second guess their value in life.

> *But you can unlearn those behaviors*
> *the same way you learned them!*

Of course, if you can see that most of those people listed above were also probably unhealthy and struggling with their own issues of low self-esteem, it may help you make peace with their behavior towards you. Remember, if they didn't love themselves first (which they didn't), then they couldn't love anyone else either – including you. And thus you see how easily the cycle perpetuates itself.

Although you probably didn't recognize the brainwashing you were receiving all those years ago, you are now old enough and conscious enough as an adult to take your life back – to dissect those old beliefs and build new ones, and to choose how you interact with your world, the people in it, and yourself. On your journey to valuing yourself and seeking out healthy and more rewarding relationships, this basic awareness is one of the most powerful tools you can have in your arsenal. Keep it in front of you constantly and it may keep you out of a bunch of bad relationships.

So What?

In addition to considering the original source of all your bad emotional tapes and beliefs, sometimes one can simply say, "So what?" to some of those Bad List things. So what if you're disorganized? So what if you're 20 pounds overweight? So what if you're a not a detail person? Just because you're not good at keeping a spotless house doesn't mean you're not loveable or a good person! And yet that's what so many get hung up on!

On the other hand, you may have been brainwashed with these "beliefs" years ago and they may not even be true today. Remember when we were all gawky teenagers? I remember the super skinny girls who got called "Bean Pole." They hated being so skinny. Well, how many of us would die for such a body in today's size two super-model world? And yet our skinny friend from high school still probably hears Bean Pole in her head anytime someone tells her how thin she is.

Isn't this just mixed up? These are great insights to study when you really examine that Bad List as it compares to your Good List.

So take the time to go through them with a fine-tooth comb, asking yourself not only who first "gave" you that item on your Bad List, but what his or her issues were when they gave it to you. So many of those nagging items can lose much of their power over you when you look at them through newly educated eyes!

The Island

This is a question I have found uniquely helpful to determine what you're passionate about...

You are being sent to a deserted island for six months. You will have all your needs for safety, shelter, and supplies met so you don't have to worry about anything. You will be going alone. You can take one thing with you to occupy your time but it cannot communicate with the outside world, thus, no phone, TV, or Internet. (You can take a computer if that's your thing; just no Internet.) One idea might be paper and paints so you can create beauty on canvas. Or perhaps a sewing machine and fabric to design new fashions. Or just something as simple as your hiking boots. Think about this question carefully and write your answer here. By the way, no pets either. Sorry.

If you are an emotionally healthy person you probably came up with an answer pretty easily. Your camera, musical instrument, Bible, running shoes, scrap booking supplies, gardening tools, etc. For me, of course, it is my laptop so I could work on tons of writing projects. Yep, writing is still my passion!

If, on the other hand, you haven't a clue what you might take, odds are that you are living your life in the shadow of another and you have morphed yourself into that person's life in a way that you may have lost yours! If so, think back to what you might have taken twenty years ago before you lost yourself and your consciousness of what you truly enjoy doing.

No matter what one item you choose to take, it should give you a glimpse of what you're truly passionate about. The next question is, are you following your passion right now? Are you squeezing something related to what you'd take to the island with you in your everyday life? And if not, why not?

Life is short. We only get one go-round, so it's extremely important that we participate in it with the things and activities we love. It's one key component to staying healthy.

In addition, when you bring your passion for life into any relationship you show your partner that you have a life of your own as well. It validates that you're not dependent upon him or her for you to be somebody.

Getting Rid of the Self in Self-Esteem

So many people struggle with issues of low self-esteem that it seems almost an epidemic. While their pasts may have set them up for the low self-esteem struggle, there are many who still sadly carry this label as their excuse for why they cannot do things – apply for a certain job, give a speech in front of an audience, try something new – or certainly leave an abusive mate and create a much healthier life for themselves and their children.

Well, I heard a new take on low self-esteem lately and it struck me as interesting. Again I refer to my friend and colleague Tom Joseph, the counselor. He recently wrote a fabulous book called *Why We Stay Stuck: When Love Is Not Enough to Fix Our Relationships.*

While Tom discusses a wide variety of psychological reasons we oftentimes stay stuck, one thing he mentions is the issue of low self-esteem as it pertains to relationship issues. He approaches low self-esteem from a completely different angle than most. Basically, he says that pampering someone does nothing to help rebuild their self-esteem. Rather, we have to get rid of the "self" in self-esteem to turn someone's belief system about themselves around.

What does this mean? That folks with low self-esteem issues are oftentimes so all-consumed with their terrible, unhappy feelings about themselves, that they become paralyzed by their own self-consumption. Let me explain.

In his book he says the following:

"Low self-esteem is mostly demonstrated when our unrealistic expectations for perfection are not met, causing us to become angrier and angrier. Then, we expect others to feel sorry for us and feed into our 'poor me' attitude. Then, when we still don't get the attention we're looking for, we can become, depressed, angry, or even suicidal."

He continues, "I have a saying that goes like this: 'Get rid of self and there will be no esteem to worry about.' As ironic as this may sound, those with low self-esteem are too focused on themselves. In an attempt to stop pains of the past or as a reward for existing in this world, they crave constant proof of their significance. They have an unquenchable appetite for others who will feed their sense of worth, and they devour attention."

"In fact, they're so focused on self that it can make them easy prey. Abusers tend to look for those who need attention and lots of encouragement. Then they swoop down and give this person all they're asking for, and in doing so, make for themselves a new victim."

Is your low self-esteem setting you up to keep attracting abusers to your life? Or perhaps it's keeping you from reaching the great things in life that you desire. Want to turn it around? Here are a few ideas Tom feels can make a difference:

❑ Accept yourself as imperfect – after all, who is perfect anyway?

❑ Be willing to make mistakes, for isn't that how we all learn?

❑ Extricate yourself from negative friendships. You surely don't need those kind of folks in your life.

❑ Disregard (or remove yourself from) overly critical family members. What makes them and their opinions better anyway?

❑ Learn to take risks. Each time you're successful with something new, you build your self-esteem.

Then start taking your focus off of you and your problems and start looking around at the world around you. Who can you help? Who is worse off than you? By putting yourself out there you put some of your energy into contributing to the world around you and begin to build your own increasingly healthy sense of self, one step at a time.

And of course, remember that we all teach our kids by our example. If for no other reason than sending them on a much healthier course than you spent much of your life on, isn't it time you attack your self-esteem issues head-on?

Other Self-Esteem Builders

You can find tons of other tools to help you build healthy self-esteem and love yourself again. Sometimes just stepping "out of your boxx" and trying something new will open up doors you never imagined. These next techniques may seem odd, but believe it or not they can really make you happier about yourself, and it's that inner happiness that is so important throughout all aspects of our lives. See if any of these speak to you:

- ❑ Go back to school. Broadening your horizons can give you new passions. (By the way, you're never too old to go back to school!)

- ❑ Take up belly dancing. (Not only is it great exercise, just think what it can do for your figure!)

- ❑ Join a gym and get your body into a level of fitness that helps you feel better about yourself.

- ❑ Inhale all the books you can get your hands on that can help you to find new ideas about yourself, love, relationships, self-esteem, and of course, getting "out of your boxx."

- ❑ Hire a life coach who can help you look at goal setting in your professional and/or personal life. This will help give you direction and confidence that will spill over to your general feeling about yourself.

- ❑ Take up a new hobby or rekindle an old one. Perhaps you're an artist or musician and don't even know it yet.

- ❑ Set up a weekly girls' night out with your friends. It's amazing what a night of laughter can do for you.

None of these tools have to cost an arm and a leg. The library is full of books, tapes, and other resources to help folks be the best they can be. Dust off your library card and start digging.

Learning is a life-long process. The most important key is to find out what works best for you. With the Internet at your fingertips, information is in abundance. Seek your answers and don't quit until you find them.

So spend some serious time learning about who you are and developing who you want to be. Then promise me you'll do the next two things:

CHOOSE TO BE A SURVIVOR.

LET THE "VICTIM-HOOD" GO.

You have all the power you need to go forward. Burn the old photographs at a special ceremony to set yourself free. Quit looking for narcissists everywhere and pick yourself up like that toddler learning to walk, knowing that you might just fall again, yet you forge ahead despite your fears so that you can play with the other kids.

Remember, as long as you remain a victim,
your narcissist has won.
He still has you under his control.
He is still abusing you from afar.
And all because you are allowing him to do so.

Chapter 31
Voices From the Other Side

You have heard so many stories of victims throughout this book that I thought it would be helpful at this point to share with you the voices of so many who have won the battle and made it to the other side; to a healthy life! Their words speak more than I ever can.

Christine

It's been just over three years since I've been free of the hurt, pain, and abuse of my ex. I've been in therapy and have been working with a church recovery group and some great, supportive friends during this time. They've been there with me as I spent time taking care of me and actually figuring out who I am and what I want and need from a relationship.

I'd have to say that I have gone from believing that I was a powerless victim to becoming an empowered, giving person. I learned that God made me to be beautiful and deserving of love and respect. I had to learn how to believe it and communicate to others that I expect them to treat me well from day one. It is from this position of strength that I can give of myself willingly and not because demands are placed upon me, or because I'm desperate.

This transformation absolutely affected my dating world. I did the online dating adventure and met a variety of men – mostly good guys and a few who left me feeling awkward and uncomfortable, disrespecting my boundaries, not treating me nicely. Years ago I would never have tuned into those feelings. I hate to admit that in my earlier days I was terrified of being alone and feeling unwanted and unloved and as a result I was a desperate dater, being satisfied with just any guy who wanted to date me, no matter what his behavior.

But that's not me anymore. The new, improved me has learned to graciously and sometimes forcibly tell certain men, "No, this is just not working for me," even as they would press me for more.

The best part of this journey is that last summer I met a wonderful man named Mike. He said that he was attracted to me because I was focused. I knew what I wanted in a relationship and simply would not accept less. He said he also valued my empathy and compassion – all things he was seeking in a partner as well. I guess I evolved these qualities through the experiences from my past relationships that were not particularly successful, especially my unhealthy marriage.

This new relationship with Mike has been unlike anything I have ever experienced before. He's been respectful of me. It's amazing. He is, by far, the most conscientious man I have ever met. He's always looking out for my welfare; he is kind, caring, and he never presses any issue when I say no to anything I don't feel comfortable with. It is this type of response that makes me feel very safe and secure. The best part is that he really listens to what I have to say and enjoys being with me. He makes me a priority and always follows through with his promises. And I do the same for him. It is so refreshing to be in a relationship with someone of integrity. His actions actually follow his words ... something I now put as a high priority and am very aware of, especially early in any new relationship.

> *I've seen for myself how, by being healthier,*
> *I'm actually attracting healthier people into my life.*

Mike and I are now engaged to be married this fall. I feel great knowing that this decision is made from strength – I don't *need* to find myself a man to be happy, much less a perfect man. I am content with my life now as a healthy, single person and I have the opportunity to share it with someone who also truly enjoys his life and wants to share his in return. I'm not listening to any external voices that tell me what I should or shouldn't do or what is logically or politically correct. However, I am listening to my God-given intuition, which has also been confirmed by family and friends who have walked the many peaks and valleys with me.

Looking back, I see that my marriage to the wrong partner was all part of the lessons I was meant to learn in this life. I realize that it was a bad choice that I made, which brought me much pain and frustration. However, it was my choice to be with the wrong partner to begin with. I am a much stronger person now – more able to love and relate to others in ways that I could have never imagined.

I have a much stronger relationship with my immediate family and have more intimate friendships as well. If you would have asked me three years ago if I could go back and change the course of events in my life so that I would have avoided my unhealthy relationship, I would have said absolutely! Today, however, I realize that I would not change a thing. I now see that the pain and suffering I survived was only the catalyst for changing my life into many years of love, hope, and grace. As the saying goes, "What doesn't kill you will make you stronger."

The biggest lesson I learned here is this – I will not try to earn love from anybody ever again. If it is not there to begin with, it probably never will be. So, why try to earn it? On the other hand, people have to earn their way into my life. And that takes time, trust, and consistency.

In addition, I no longer fear the withdrawal of love. That is *huge* for me! The freedom I have through understanding that piece alone makes so much difference. If I'm in a relationship with no one other than myself, then that's OK too because I like myself enough to take care of myself. Being alone is not the same as being lonely. I know the difference now.

Al has a similar story from the man's side of things...

Al

I can't believe the way my relationship is now. After so many lousy relationships I spent a lot of time trying to figure *me* out. I realized that my relationships had all ended in disaster and as such it was high time I figured out why, especially when I realized that I was a common denominator in them all! I found a great therapist and she and I worked on a lot of my baggage and I really started to realize that much of the trouble I had with women were my old issues I kept getting hung up on: Was I loveable? Would they leave me? Would they hurt me? All those things and more. Plus, I realized that I somehow kept attracting unhealthy people to me. It's no wonder things never seemed to work out.

Becoming healthier has helped me to choose more healthy mates, and the difference is like night and day. Of course, it's also helped me to better recognize unhealthy partners earlier and give them a wide berth. I'm also learning to pick people for who they are, not what their potential is and how I think I can change them.

What a difference! Not only is my intimate relationship so much better, but all my relationships are better in general – my friends, co-workers, and even my family. Trying to change other people? It just doesn't work.

It's so amazing to me now, having a wonderful partner who's kind, caring, considerate, sensitive; all those things you wonder if it's really possible to have in a relationship, or if it's only real on TV and in movies. Believe me it is possible.

However, had I continued languishing in my last relationship as I did for some time – continually trying to keep patching it together, forever hoping that things would get better, going to huge lengths to change me to make my partner happy – I would have never found this absolutely wonderful gal. She's my best friend, my greatest support system, and my lover all rolled into one. I feel so blessed to have her in my life.

It's absolutely true that you first have to let go of the old to make room for the new. It took me a long time to believe in that theory and regrettably, I have to admit that I was terrified of leaving even the tiniest hope behind that my past unhealthy relationship might still have a chance to work. That was probably the hardest thing to come to grips with. You might even say that I was addicted to the pain. I just seemed to keep going back for crappy treatment over and over, somehow believing that there really wasn't anyone out there who would treat me any better.

I was so wrong on that one!

Now I advise anyone who is in a relationship that leaves them questioning themselves or the relationship that if these questions are plaguing them at all, it's just not the right relationship to be in. Because when it's right it's simply great, it's easy, it's rewarding, and there are no questions to be asked. You just know.

Healing From Your Family

When you are in a romantic relationship with a narcissist you can decide to leave that person behind, go on, and never look back. Yet it's quite another story when it's your blood relatives surrounding you and making you crazy! They can seem impossible to deal with! My client Kristi has an older sister, a (mostly distant) father, and a extremely manipulative grandmother, who are all narcissists and want to run her life. Kristi's sister has claimed the role of controller (and mother) since their real mother died years ago. She also hides behind the church as her center of power and beliefs about how life should be lived.

Here's how Kristi handled the holidays and how she's handling her life, by choosing to take it back. Despite being surrounded by a family of narcissists, Kristi's words show us how it can be done. She hasn't closed them out of her life completely – she's just set firm boundaries in dealing with them. And feels better about herself and her life as a result

Kristi

Our holidays were "narcissist-free" this year! It was so nice to decide what *I* wanted to do and for once I did what made *me* happy. *(Without all the guilt!)*

I cannot tell you how much healthier I feel now that I am taking care of me first. (Not to the exclusion of others, but before others.) I made some serious changes over last summer – regarding my boundaries, beliefs, and actions and because of that I can't believe how *everything else* has changed for the better as well – my emotions, feelings, mental stability, self-esteem, self-worth = my life.

What changes, you ask? What results?

1. I have only talked to my grandmother a couple of times in the past three months or so. I have not seen her since September. I no longer feel that *hot, anxiety, horrible panic feeling* that I always got after being around her.

2. I talk to my sister only about once a week. I keep it short and always remember that she is full of crap.

3. I talk to my dad only a couple times a month. Same as above.

4. I do not feel guilty about living my life the way that I believe is best for me. I do not feel guilty about not sacrificing my life for their never-ending voids.

5. I feel stronger every minute that I take this stand for myself.

6. Everyday that goes by I need less and less outside validation.

7. I am making wiser choices about who I spend time with and it makes a huge difference in the way I see things.

8. I guess I could say that I am more in control of things (my life!) and see a great, bright future for me, now and ahead.

I cannot explain it exactly but all of a sudden I woke up and did not have the same bad tapes replaying in my head and was just living and *enjoying* life. The funny thing is, I love and respect myself so much now that my main priority is whether I am OK – not the narcissistic vultures in my family and the rest of the world. And that's OK, for they are not crumbling and their lives are not caving in because my life does not center around them and their needs anymore.

I guess you could say that I finally re-discovered the real me. My likes and dislikes. Who I want to be around and who I don't. My career path is getting clearer every day. My priorities are mine and only mine. My hobbies are becoming more and more interesting to me. I really do not care what anybody thinks about all of this and if they don't like it then they need to find somebody else to spend time with because I am not changing for one single person ever again.

Saying that, I am now able to give unconditionally and with real love. But I do not feel like I have to give myself away to be loved because I am already loved by the most important person for me to be loved by – me.

Billie

Had I not discovered your writings about narcissism early on, I might still be in my Narcissistic Hell. I have not only jumped out of my boxx, I am making a new one with picture windows! I've lived through a lot besides the abuse. Add cancer to the list as well. But I am a lot stronger now, the effects of the chemo are all but gone and I am feeling pretty powerful as a woman! What a change!

I plan to begin my flying lessons next spring. Flying! It is the metaphor for my life now. I have wanted to fly since my childhood and I always succumbed to the beliefs of others that I should *not* follow my passion and learn. Now it is my turn. I was simply meant to fly. The cool thing is that I will turn it into a business venture when I am certified (and a really good pilot). I plan to offer photo excursions. I will first concentrate on fixed wing and then go to helicopters.

And I am working diligently on my five-year plan for financial security. I am doing this for *me!* Not with someone, just me! I do see the effects of becoming strong and taking care of myself. Also, I have weeded out any negative thinkers in my life. I surround myself with only the strong, wonderful people who encourage me to be everything I can be.

I know all too well that we codependents oftentimes roll around in a quagmire with moments of self-discovery, but then we often get stuck there rather than forge further ahead. And sometimes even our personal epiphanies do not take us too far past acknowledging our condition. With that possibility in mind, I recognized that I had to jump in fully and if I hadn't, I certainly wouldn't be where I am today.

When I face my soon-to-be-ex, I will be dressed to the nines, looking like a million bucks, and exuding all the grace and dignity I have. My attorney understands and wants me to make sure to show that man just how badly he screwed up. If I feel any fear at all, he will never see it on me!

And the best thing is that win lose or draw, I am free of the nightmare, and that is worth more than any amount of money.

At least I know there is life after 20 years as a cowgirl in Narcissism Hell. And if I can get it, anyone can.

Taking Their Lives Back

Can you just feel the amazing passion for life these people are experiencing while being on the other side of the darkness? This freedom can be there for any of you who choose to step out of your boxx and take your life back! They are absolute proof and they are only a handful of the letters I get every week! Come out into the light and join those of us who have found ourselves and our lives again. You won't believe how much fun it is out here ... and what our kids are learning about being healthy as well!

Chapter 32
Letter to Myself

*E*scaping the clutches of the narcissist in your life will be one of the most difficult things you ever do. Congratulations are in order for those of you who have taken that step. Yet let's say you've already crossed that bridge and you're ready to move on from a role of victim to one of survivor. Now what?

Well, now comes the time of transition. The time where you may have second thoughts. The time where your friends and family are breathing a sigh of relief, hoping that you will now be safe and can find happiness. Yet you may still feel empty, lonely, and numb. Endlessly struggling with the disbelief of the entire situation. So many respondents commented that even years later they were still wishing that their narcissist would simply come back to them. Of course, they also wished that none of the bad times would ever return and that their person would have changed back to the original perfect partner. That life would be like it was at the beginning. Yet, consciously they know that it was all a lie from the start. They know it can never be the way they wish. And they continue to mourn for those lost memories and dreams.

Some said they are beginning to take steps out of their boxx and have begun to date again, but many of them related that they continue attracting narcissistic people and repeating the pattern. Or … they go to the other extreme. They see narcissists everywhere! They live in fear of taking the risk of finding themselves in a living hell again. As a result, they intentionally stay alone. Although they hate the loneliness, they fear the captivity of narcissism far more.

Because of this I thought it might be helpful if I wrote a letter that you can read to yourself to remind you of a few things when you are in this very confusing place. It may speak to you … it may not. It is my hope that for some of you, it will be a resource to come back to, time and again, as you progress through the stages of narcissism survival. It is filled with many of my own experiences and those of others.

Most of all, it is filled with love and respect to give to yourself.

Letter to Myself

I am a survivor, but sometimes it helps me to remember where I have come from and where I am going, especially when I have a tendency to look back at all the good times in the relationship I left behind and tend to block the times that were not healthy for me. Because of that, this is my reminder to myself so that I never forget. I will read this list out loud to myself whenever I am struggling with my emotions or my intentions. Because I know how strong I really am when I want to be, this list will be my armor to keep me safe when I face the difficult moments in my life's journey:

✓ Today is the first day of the *best* of my life!

✓ I will remember this statement every moment of the day. I will remind myself throughout the day that I am already a survivor. That I have already lived through the darkness and am now on a path towards the light at the end of the tunnel.

✓ I remember that I am free of the confining, humiliating, painful relationship I was in for so long. The relationship where I always felt if only I tried harder or was a better person, that everything would be fine.

✓ I will continue to remember that it was a relationship without real love. Rather, it was a relationship with someone I only *thought* was perfect. A relationship where I was always left wondering what was wrong with me. Where I was not treated as an equal. It was a relationship that was actually abusive, despite all my memories of good times. Where I thought I was deeply loved, but now I understand that this is *not* what love looks like.

✓ I remember it took courage for me to leave that situation. I was strong and stood up for myself because I know that I am a valuable person. I am as good as anyone else. No matter what, I deserve to be treated well. I deserve real love. I deserve empathy and compassion in all aspects of my life. And I deserve to be cared for the same way I would care for someone I deeply love.

✓ I will always remember that I do not deserve to be talked down to, treated as a child, humiliated, abused, ignored or given the "silent treatment," called names, mistreated in any way, or told that I am anything less than a wonderful person, because I am a wonderful person. I understand that abuse can be physical, sexual, or emotional and while they are all different, they can all hurt and leave lasting scars that I will no longer tolerate in any fashion.

✓ I understand that in a real loving relationship people treat each other as equals. They respect each other's feelings. They compromise. They listen with compassion and empathy, and they *never* demand something of their partner that will lead to humiliation, discomfort or pain. Never.

✓ I will also remember that I am entitled to having and enjoying my own friends and family in my life and that no one who truly loves me in a healthy way will ever expect me to completely give up these important people because I "only need my partner now." While I need to balance time with friends, family, and my significant other, I also recognize that sometimes I need some time out with others to bring balance to my life. Forcing me to sever all relations with friends and family is something I would expect from a cult – not from someone I love.

✓ I will always remember that in all areas of my life, but especially in the bedroom, I will never compromise myself or my body in any way. I will clearly set my boundaries and let my partner know what I am comfortable with and what I am not, and I will not let him or her pressure me into doing anything where I feel uneasy, tense, or uncomfortable. While I recognize that each person in any relationship (sexual or otherwise) has needs and desires, I also understand that compromise often needs to come from both partners in order to leave each person feeling safe, loved, and valued. I promise that I will never again settle for behavior that leaves me feeling uncomfortable in any way with a partner who is not understanding, compassionate, caring, and loving. I will remember that love and sex should never be about power, humiliation, or domination and I will *run* from any relationship that becomes that way.

✓ On the other hand, I will always remember that when babies learn to walk they fall down a lot, and since they keep picking themselves up after each skinned elbow or each bruised chin, I can do the same on this new path I am on. I am strong. I have learned well from my experiences. I know that one or two falls doesn't mean there will be falls every single day or week. I will also remember that obstacles that are overcome and lessons that are learned, all lead to me becoming a stronger, better person. Just think of the new journey I am on and all the wonderful experiences and people that await me! I have incredible hope for wonderment each and every day that comes my way!

✓ I still believe in the good of humanity and knowing there are kind, caring people out there. I do not have to believe everyone in the world is a narcissist. However, I now recognize Red Flag narcissistic behaviors and I will not fall prey to the wiles of these people again. While I do understand that this personality disorder is not their fault, it does not mean I have to live with it. I must take care of myself first.

✓ With this in mind, I will remember to take "baby steps" in any new relationships. Baby steps will allow me to take lots of time to get to know any new person in my life. This may mean months of dating without giving away my body, my money, or my personal time or space to another person until I have truly investigated the integrity of the one I am getting involved with.

✓ I understand that integrity, compassion, and empathy are visible in so many little things that people do. The signs are so obvious in how others treat the insignificant people in their lives – the waiters, the grocery store clerks, the taxi cab drivers, or small children they are not related to. Do they offer them respect, a smile, a kind word, especially in times of difficulty? Or do they simply ignore them, unless needed? Do they refer to them all as "idiots"? Do they give them a hard time, no matter what the situation? Do they talk down to them or throw their weight around? These are Red Flag behaviors of narcissists that will catch my attention and make me pay very careful attention.

✓ In addition, I will be careful to observe how they treat their loved ones. Do they make time for them? Do they show warmth and understanding – especially when things go wrong? Do they offer a hug when someone feels bad? Do they offer to help when needed? Do they share equally in work around the house or do they expect others to do everything for them? Do they give gifts and cards to family members on special occasions or do they find these things unnecessary? Do they ignore, criticize, chastise, name call, or tease their loved ones (even under the guise of "friendly teasing")? I will readily recognize these are Red Flags as well.

✓ I will also notice how they treat their pets. Do they tell me they love them and then act in ways that prove otherwise? Do they pull their pets by the ears or grab their head between their hands and hold them in positions they choose not to be in? Do they beat them, even on occasion, and then tell me that they needed to "teach them a lesson"? Do they curse at them, yell at them, or ignore them completely? Or do they teach them to be aggressive with others? These are Red Flag behaviors.

✓ I will watch what happens when things are out of their control, such as when they are detained in traffic or made to wait in long lines at the airport. I will notice if they fuss and fume or act as if they shouldn't have to suffer such injustices. Or feel that while others might have to put up with these life difficulties, *they* should not have to be bothered with these irritations – because, of course, they are better than anyone else. I will notice that these are Red Flags that are crying out to me.

✓ I will ask myself if they feel that traffic laws (and other general rules) don't apply to them. Do they bully their way into traffic or never give way to others? Do they attempt to buy their way out of traffic tickets? Do they tell me that while two drinks might be the limit for most people before they need to worry about drinking and driving, they can handle much more without any problem? And if they find themselves detained for drinking and driving situations, do they blame the police officer and not themselves? These are dangerous warning signs as well.

✓ I will also observe whether they feel they deserve special treatment for reasons not obvious to anyone else but themselves. And ask myself whether they feel they are an expert in everything, even though they are not educated in all fields. Do they imply that they know everything and I couldn't possibly know as much as they do? These are Red Flags that can cost me dearly as a relationship develops.

✓ I promise myself I will watch for all these Red Flags and any other situations that don't feel comfortable to me. Each day I will judge the degree to which I feel safe in this relationship. I will watch my own feelings to determine if I look forward to being together with this person ... or instead, if I find myself worrying about what might occur when we get together.

✓ I will watch for inconsistencies in behavior – inconsistencies in how he treats me, how I feel about him, or what our expectations are of each other. I will also remember that in good, loving relationships people sometimes disagree or fight, but in these relationships both parties should be comfortable offering an apology when appropriate. I also recognize that apologies are not real or sincere if they sound like this: "Honey, I'm sorry I got mad at you, but if you hadn't done (whatever behavior) I wouldn't have gotten mad in the first place." This is not an apology – it is still passing blame! I will beware of this covert behavior. I also understand that in healthy relationships both parties may have bad days, angry moments, or times of feeling frustrated. While this is natural, it is unnatural when only one member in a relationship feels this way 100% of the time. In healthy relationships people still offer love and understanding for each other because they want to.

✓ I will recognize that sometimes I accept less-than-loving behavior from others. I am learning to identify this pattern in myself and will stop it as soon as I recognize it so that I will take care of myself first in any relationship. Because of old beliefs I have had pounded into me over the years, I might sometimes worry that I may never again find a good relationship and no one might ever want me or love me again. I now recognize that what I once thought was love to begin with, was never really love at all. It was a lie. And now I only have room in my life for truth and honesty because I deserve this, just as all good people deserve this. I now have the skills to judge real love and I will not settle for less.

✓ I have also come to realize that while I may not like being alone, many times it is safer and healthier for me to be alone than to be in any relationship that is unhealthy and unloving. I also recognize that if I believe I am a victim and act like a victim and continue to live my life from painful memories that hold me captive (the Boxx of my Past) that I will continue to attract people to me who seek victims. I will not attract the type of people I really want. I will not attract loving people to me.

✓ And so, I hereby resolve to put my past behind me. To see whatever has happened to me as a life lesson given to me for some reason I may simply not understand. I realize that I took an active or passive role in my past and that some things were indeed my responsibility. I will remember that the past is not the present or the future, and that I am in charge of my life and my future.

✓ I resolve that every choice I make is *my* choice and that I will never allow anyone to be in charge of my life or make me do anything ever again.

✓ I resolve that no one can really *make* me do anything, nor have they ever been able to, and the sooner I believe that in my heart, the sooner I can move on. That while I cannot control anyone else in their thoughts or actions, I can control my attitude each and every day and I know that my attitude will affect how I react to everyone else in my life.

✓ I promise myself that I will always take care of *me* first because if I don't take care of myself, how can I take care of those I love? If I don't take care of myself first, why should anyone else take care of me as part of a loving relationship? If I don't take care of myself first, why should anyone respect me? If I don't take care of myself first, it's a reflection of a time when I believed I wasn't worth taking care of and I have moved beyond that belief today and for every day of the rest of my life.

✓ I now understand that good people who take care of themselves and respect themselves and others, who have good attitudes, and who are empathetic and compassionate, put out messages that attract similar people to them. From now on I am, and always will be, one of those people. Knowing that, I will seek only kind, empathetic, compassionate, self-respecting people in my life.

✓ I will not settle for less.

✓ I will not be a victim.

✓ I will only be a survivor.

✓ Because survivors are strong.

✓ They have already endured.

✓ They have become better people because of their experiences. And at some point, when I am ready, I will help others learn to be strong as well.

✓ I deserve greatness. I deserve love. I deserve kindness.

✓ And I will get it.

✓ I will never forget that.

✓ I *will* forget the pain.

✓ I *will* let go of the past.

And most importantly,
I look towards a bright future now.
I am so glad that there is light at the end of the tunnel
and I will never live in the darkness again ...
Ever!

Chapter 33
A Word About Healing

The first question most of my readers and clients ask me after they decide to extricate themselves from a difficult relationship is, "How long will it take until I don't feel this horrible anymore?"

Of course there are many factors that go into that answer, but they are usually shocked when I ask them in return, "Well, how long do you want it to take? Get out your calendar and let's pick a goal for when you want to be healed."

> *For some reason they all have in their minds that healing must take a very, very long time. And to that I say, "Bah, humbug!"*

One thing we all have control over is our attitudes. Just as you saw the difference between the victims and the survivors, you could clearly see that it was their attitudes that directed their healing.

We all may feel like victims after a breakup. And while healing doesn't happen overnight, the time involved will vary for everyone. It's natural and usually means going through various stages of grief described by psychiatrist Elizabeth Kubler-Ross in her famous book, *On Death and Dying*: Denial, Anger, Bargaining, Depression, and Acceptance are all a part of moving from grief into healing. You've simply got to go through all the steps before you can move on. But there's nothing that says it has to take forever. It truly depends on how you make peace with it in your own mind. For if you cling to the notion that you'll never find love again and fear the possible aloneness more than the pain of your past, then it will indeed take you a *very* long time to heal.

Yet, if you will embrace the fact that you have a new chance for a clean slate and a healthy relationship for yourself and your kids, then you will be amazed at just how fast you will grow, change, and become healthier than you may have been for a long time.

Feelings of Loss

No matter what type of relationship you've been in (intimate, family, friendship, or workplace) when a breakup occurs you may certainly experience a great sense of loss. Yet when the relationship has been narcissistic, there may be even more confusion, frustration, depression, guilt, and pain due to the additional emotional and possibly physical trauma you lived through.

Survivors must mourn the ending of the relationship and go through the same phases of loss that they would if their partner had literally passed away – perhaps not exactly the same as a death, but as equally emotionally charged.

This is an exhausting, emotional roller coaster ride for anyone. The guilt, the blame, the years of living through brainwashing that led to feelings of being inferior can all make the healing journey more complicated than it might normally be.

Although you may consciously be aware that you'll be healthier once out of this relationship, the splitting process is certainly never easy. On top of that, the victim not only mourns the person she was involved with, she mourns the *image and dream of* that original perfect partner as well.

**However, reaching the level of Acceptance is possible.
Do not accept anything less.**

If you are a survivor of a narcissistic relationship, it is important to give yourself permission to heal. Finding supportive people who can help you piece your world back together when it feels like it's shattered, is just one step towards recovery. Getting help from a compassionate and understanding therapist, and/or survivor who understands Narcissistic Personality Disorder in depth, is another. When you connect with a support group or an individual with similar experiences who can prove that you are not alone, it can make all the difference in the world. Realizing that you are not crazy or stupid or useless is so important, especially after you have spent months or years with someone who continued to hope that you would believe otherwise.

> *The shattered self-esteem experienced at the hands of these manipulative and cunning people*
> *may take a while to rebuild, but it is possible.*
> *Believe it. There are many of us here today to prove it.*

It is also important that you remember that *your past is not your future* and that each day is a new opportunity for growth, recovery, and happiness. Yes, true happiness can be found *if you choose it*. The first step is deciding to let the past stay in the past. To learn from it and not make the same mistakes again. To go forward just like a toddler learning to walk … falling down and tripping occasionally. Maybe even getting a bump or a bruise from landing face-first on the sidewalk, but always going forward.

❏ Always choosing a future that speaks to you.

❏ Never settling for someone or something that doesn't fit or doesn't feel right.

❏ And always believing that you deserve to be treated with respect, kindness, compassion, and true love.

Everyone has his or her own unique pathway to healing. You may need to vent for a while. Scream, cry, pound your fists, run away from home, journal – do whatever you have to do to get your feelings out so that you can look at them, recognize them, and then put them to bed.

Some people simply want to be angry for as long as possible and desperately cling to the victim role for a long time. Yet, reaching the Stage of Acceptance is what allows us to move past the pain and on towards healing. Stopping at any stage before you work your way through to Acceptance will only short-change the healing and hold you back from experiencing healthy love – including loving yourself.

> *I will caution you that one consistent and unfortunate pattern I have discovered about codependents is this:*
> *They do not feel comfortable spending money on themselves.*
> *(After all, they've been told they were worthless for so long, they don't deserve to have great things, right?)*
> *With this phenomenon in mind, what they don't realize is that, in effect, they delay their healing because of it.*

They have put themselves last for so long that they almost don't know how to put themselves first for once. While they may work two jobs just to pay for their teenager's car and music lessons, they won't spend thirty dollars on a book, a hundred on a workshop, or a few hundred on some serious counseling that might in fact change their lives and the lives of their children. Essentially, their ongoing "I can't" mantra keeps them perpetually stuck. If they could only see what investing in themselves could do to change everything. Sure, many may not have the money in their pocket at the moment, but most have resources in family and friends who would be thrilled to help – especially if they knew their friend had hope for a new life. You would be amazed at the calls and emails I get from those very friends asking how they can help. Yet, sometimes, pure pride gets in the way of accepting help. I hope you don't let that be the case for you.

So many victims think they can heal alone, and while many can, the extra time involved when you do it yourself can end up hurting you more in the long-run. It's a bit like an alcoholic who thinks he can not only detox, but can give up alcohol all by himself. Many have tried but few have succeeded. And many keep living a terrible life while they live in denial.

Yet those alcoholics who put serious work into healing, joining Alcoholics Anonymous, and following the 12 Steps can find that the light at the end of the tunnel is attainable. And the rewards are priceless. Most kick themselves for the years they wasted dragging their feet. The same can be true for the victims of narcissists.

Remaining a victim is truly a conscious choice, although it may not feel like it. By rehashing your story over and over (to yourselves and your friends who eventually grow exhausted listening to it) you reach a point where it is no longer helpful and, instead, it actually holds you back. And sometimes it even seems to justify your angry feelings. (That's why I caution my clients about the online chat rooms that can sometimes be a giant bitch-and-moan session. Unless there is a healthy voice among them, the victims can literally keep each other sick.)

Most importantly, until you can recognize the role you played in the whole ugly relationship, you will simply stay stuck, like Brenda who wrote to me asking for help …

Brenda

I was in a relationship lasting three years that left me drained, depressed, and even now, two years after it ended and despite having moved from one country to the other to escape the ghosts, I still can't feel joy or any sense of achievement. I just keep trying to put one foot in front of the other. The mornings start in tears and I stuff it all in to face the day and to keep my kids from having the burden of an unhappy mother. I had 18 months of counseling and have read everything I can get my hands on, but the pain is there still and I find myself just wanting the next 40 years to pass so I don't have to endure life anymore. I know I am fortunate; I have amazing kids, a good job, caring friends, health, and a loving family but I still can't feel joy no matter how I try. I fill my days with work or other things just so I don't have to think and feel the pain so much. Can you help?

The Power of Your Words

When I work with clients like Brenda, the first thing we work on is their words, for our words are literally the compass we set for ourselves to follow. What we say consciously goes directly to our subconscious mind, which is then absolutely glad to set the course for our actions to match our beliefs.

At one of my victim support groups one night I tried something new. I decided to get the group off the whining, victim angle and aimed them on an even stronger survivor path instead. The goal was to make everyone much more aware of how their words were holding them back from healing.

So I instituted some new ground rules for the night. We were supposed to stick to "I" statements and anytime someone strayed back to the "he said, he did" statements, the group was to say, "Ahhhhhhhhhhh," as a reminder to the one speaking that she had gotten off track of taking her own responsibility.

Secondly, if anyone said, "I can't" or, "I'm trying," then the group would have to say "Ooooohhhhhhh." This response was to remind the speaker that whenever we say, "I can't" we imply that someone else has power over us and that we are not in charge of our lives. Substituting the words "I choose not" instead of "I can't" allows us each to take responsibility for our actions and choices, and has a different meaning entirely. (I *choose not* to get him out of my mind, versus I *can't* get him out of my mind … see the difference?) Plus, being the one who is responsible for all the choices that are made is a clear reminder of the power you really do have in life.

> As for the word "trying" – here's my take on that:
> "Tryin's lyin'!"

Even Yoda in *Star Wars* taught Luke Skywalker, "There is no *try* ... only *do* or *don't do!*" (Ever *try* to lose weight? Did you succeed?)

The task was tough that night! One new woman to the group told us three times in her first minute of introducing herself that she'd been "trying" to break up with her abusive boyfriend for two years.

At that point I set a pen in front of her on the table and said, "Please try to pick up this pen." She looked at me quizzically, and then promptly picked up the pen.

Then I said, "I didn't say *pick* up the pen! ... I said *try* to pick up the pen." Then I demonstrated with my hand hovering over the pen that *trying* did not mean *doing*, and as such, my hand could only hover over the pen as though it had a force field protecting it. And thus, since no action would ever take place, the pen was sure to remain untouched, much less unmoved.

"Now," I said ... "see why you haven't broken up with him yet? You've only been *trying*, you haven't been *doing!*"

The look on her face was priceless! A light bulb went off in her head as she suddenly realized that she hadn't ever taken concrete steps to *make* a serious break with her partner! For whatever reason, she had only been *trying* to break up with him. She was not taking full responsibility for her situation and had simply been hoping or praying that things would get better or someone else would "fix" it for her.

Pretty strong visual, isn't it?

So become intensely aware of your words. Are you using "I" statements about your situation, or are you blaming someone else, the universe, or your narcissist for whatever you're unhappy with?

If so, you can be waiting a long, long time for change and healing to take place! If you *just can't* get him out of your mind, then you *just can't* heal either. And that's the cold, hard truth.

Now go back and re-read Brenda's letter and see where she's limiting herself from her own healing.

Bad-mouthing Doesn't Help

The other thing I need to caution you about is bad-mouthing your narcissist – *especially to your kids*. This does nothing to help the situation, and can actually do damage. I'm talking about a mother who might say something like, "Your father is such a loser. I can't believe I ever married such an idiot." While it may feel good to say this, it will definitely add to the confusion, anguish, anxiety, and frustration that your kids already deal with being in the middle of the struggle, because, like it or not, this person will always be their parent. And ironically, what usually happens instead is that the child who constantly hears his or her parent being verbally attacked by the other (whether the narcissist is physically present or the victim is just complaining about how bad the narcissist is), that child is likely to either attach himself more deeply to the narcissist (who isn't there to defend himself), or learn to be a critical grownup too.

Remember, the goal here is to teach your children what a healthy person (and relationship) looks like so that they can develop their own. To do this it's imperative that they have an emotionally healthy role model to follow … especially as they compare that to the otherwise unhealthy narcissistic parent. So, as I've said, it is imperative that you become healthy as quickly as possible! And bad-mouthing your ex has got to stop.

Instead, show your children how healthy you are by using non-judgmental questions and statements. For example, when they come home from their time with Dad, you might say, "How's Dad today? Did you all have fun?" Or, "I'm sure you guys had a great time. I know how much your Dad enjoys playing miniature golf with you."

Do you see how this type of statement takes all accusations and judgment out of the equation? It encourages your kids to still enjoy what they can with their at-risk, narcissistic parent and it keeps you from looking like the bad guy. It also helps you keep working towards your own positive outlook on life and not continue to live in the negative cesspool of the victim.

Furthermore, if your ex is constantly bad-mouthing you when the kids are with him, they'll soon see which parent they are more comfortable and trusting with. They'll likely feel safer with you, if your overall attitude about life and the world is predominantly positive and not filled with hate, fear, and loathing.

Pick Your Date for Healing

So tune in carefully to your words and set the stage verbally for the future you want to create. Then pull out your calendar and pick a date ... say two weeks, a month, two months (NO more than that!) for however long you want to take to heal. Then draw a big red circle around that day and write "I'm healed" in big red letters. Then keep your sights and your attitudes aimed for that very day to be the day you start living your life as a healthy person, knowing that all the days between now and then you are immersed in the healing process.

Celebrate that date because you get a second chance – a redo, so to speak! And you can create any kind of life you dream of. And as with any goal, once it's written down, it's much more real. And this is one goal you're going to want to keep for yourself. You might even plan a "Freedom Party" with your friends for that day. Let them all know your plans so that they can help you. Maybe even burn some old photos in celebration. And just as those who have learned that they truly beat cancer, you will celebrate a fresh new start after paying your dues to belong to the network of Narcissism Survivors everywhere! Welcome to the club!

> *Oh yes, and by the way, take a photograph of yourself now and tuck it away somewhere. Then, be sure to take more photos of yourself up to your healing day and beyond. Then compare the photos...*

You won't believe the change in your appearance once you remove the ongoing stress and fatigue you were living under before. My friends love to give me a hard time over my passport photo, for I had it taken during the middle of my divorce. They can't believe I'm the same person and actually tease me that the passport photo must be my evil twin sister for I look angry, exhausted, and absolutely wrung through the wringer. The stress of divorce alone had taken its toll on me. I had no idea just how much strain I carried in my face in those dark days. Thank God it's not permanent! It's amazing the photographs I take now! I look years younger than I did so many years ago! And you can too!

Faith Can Help

Are you a religious or spiritual person? If so, your faith can be a great lifeline to your healing. And it doesn't matter if you believe in God, Jesus, Buddha, Spirit, or any other power greater than you. As I mentioned earlier, looking at any variety of terrible things that may happen in your life as "life lessons" can help them all make so much more sense than simply believing that God abandoned you or was punishing you, or even that you were simply the most unlucky person on earth.

For example, in my own healing from childhood sexual abuse, I discovered a true faith for the first time, and that very faith was what helped me change from being a life-long victim, to a blessed survivor. How so? Well, for the longest time after I recognized my abusive past I experienced fear, shame, anguish, guilt, and so much more. And I hung onto my pain as if it were my lot in life. Someone had harmed me and I had every right to be a victim.

Yet I actually had an epiphany one night while sitting all alone on a beach in Mexico. I remember cursing at God; I was so angry for what he had let happen to me. When suddenly I heard this voice in my head explaining to me that I really hadn't been forgotten, wasn't being punished, or anything else. It had all been a life lesson given to me and that I had passed with flying colors. And because of those experiences, I was to help other people who had also been harmed. While I'm still not a churchgoer to this day, my belief in a Higher Power has given my life a strength and insight it never had before. (The story is much more involved than that and you can read it in detail in my book, *Get Out of Your Boxx*, if you're interested.)

> *But the bottom line was this:*
> *By living through my pain, I realized that my life's mission*
> *was truly to help others find their healing too.*

So stop for a moment and ask yourself if you believe in a Higher Power, do you think that all things happen for a reason? And if so, what might be the reason that you had to live through such tough stuff?

Could it be so that you could show your kids what a true loving relationship should look like, when no one had taught that concept to anyone in your family for several generations? Could it be that by learning to stand up for yourself at last, you might become an advocate for others in some way? (Lawyer, psychologist, social worker.) Could it be that by learning to be strong and rallying against your narcissist, you are actually teaching him tough lessons of his own?

Who can say? The important thing is that your faith can indeed guide you through the tough times as well as give you perspective on healing.

What I know personally is that the feedback I get from people now is always amazing. What I learned through my personal journey – and the healing that came out of it – is helping others do the same. So I no longer look back at my sexually abusive background as a punishment or God not stepping in to help me. I look at it as my gift. Certainly not one I'd ever wish upon anyone else, but one that brought me to where I am today. And each time someone approaches me to tell me that they too had been abused, and that after hearing my story they were at last willing to tell theirs and start the road to healing, I absolutely know I'm on my life's mission.

> *Can you turn your life's difficulties*
> *into something meaningful?*
> *If so, you'll speed your healing along tenfold!*
> *Let your faith be your guide.*

Giving Back

Once you're healed, you'll be a great role model for others and a great resource to those who have not yet come to understand the confusing world of narcissism. It's amazing just how great it feels to help others who are struggling. For one thing it really helps you see how far you yourself have come. I smile a lot when I see my clients go forth to make a difference in the lives of others. I think back on what they were like when I first met them and am still awed at the incredibly different people they have become.

Without the fear, depression (many who required antidepressants no longer do after they escape their emotional prison), guilt, shame, uncertainty, and all the rest of the unhealthy symptoms consistent with Narcissism Victim Syndrome (a term I coined to explain the confusing phenomenon), they are truly new people. They have energy, happiness, goals, and even new relationships with healthy people. And their kids … well, needless to say, they are different people too.

While helping others is extremely cathartic, I must caution you on one point:

Do not become a mentor until you are fully healed!
(And this is actually a bit hard to see in yourself.)

I discovered this in my own rocky path on this journey. Shortly after my divorce I was introduced to a gal who had been through some tough relationship stuff herself, and like me, had spent some time in Mexico hiding out and healing. Because of that, mutual friends of ours introduced us as they thought we might want to share stories and develop camaraderie of survivors or something. Jan was a bit ahead of me in the healing process, was a bit older and a bit wilder than I, and was a professor at a local university with a doctorate degree in education.

She listened to my story patiently and when I got to the part where I explained how I was going to hold seminars and support groups for other victims, she simply smiled and said, "You've got to quit being so angry first."

I looked at her honestly and replied, "Angry? I'm not angry."

Jan smiled again and said, "Have you been listening to yourself? You've spent the last half hour saying 'He did this and he did that.' Of course you're still angry, and it will overflow on all the others you try to help until you get healthy yourself. And by the way, you never once said what you did in the relationship that contributed to its collapse."

Wow! I felt like she'd pulled the rug out from under me, but was she ever right! And the fact that she was further along in her healing than I was allowed her to see my festering pain and help me recognize it. However, had we both been in the same spot that I was in, odds are we'd have just vented and whined and complained to each other during the entire lunch and neither of us would have truly benefited.

See what I mean? That's why it's so important that you heal fully before you attempt to lead others. They need a strong, positive force to hold their hands while they're still struggling. And once you're ready, they'll be so thankful that you're there for them. And if we all keep the cycle perpetuating, just think of the changes we can make in the world!

Kim's story should clearly demonstrate that there is hope for us all ...

Kim

I can't tell you how wonderful my relationship is now with a great guy. We spend hours together and just can't get enough of each other. I guess I'd have to attribute it to building my own self-esteem more than anything. I had been in some not-so-great relationships and just got tired of them. I also saw a friend who had done some spiritual growth and once she felt more contented with herself I saw how it changed her relationship with men and everyone else.

So, I got myself into therapy, read everything I could get my hands on about building self-esteem, put myself on a diet and exercise program, and basically just decided if anything was to change it was going to have to be me.

I hadn't ever felt great about my body, and by making the diet and exercise commitment I started seeing results that really helped me in every facet of my life and certainly left me feeling more comfortable with men. But it also helped me feel more valuable to myself and because of that, I just didn't accept men in my life anymore who didn't respect themselves or anyone else. I really learned to take my time with guys – find out more about who they were before feeling like I had better grab on to whichever one happened to come along because another one might not.

Many of my friends are still amazed that for the longest time I went out with guys on only one date. I guess I just started getting picky. Maybe it was because I also got more comfortable just being alone and not worrying that I was going to die an old maid. I got busy taking classes and filling my time with "me things" so that I didn't sit around and wait for the phone to ring.

I think the new vibes I was putting out must have been what started letting me connect with more folks who were on my same wavelength and eventually lead me to meeting Ross. He was genuinely nice to begin with but it also lasted. He had a life too and although he was busy with his work and hobbies, we both quickly cherished the time we could give to each other.

I was careful to let the relationship develop very slowly. I just had to feel like I trusted this guy completely before I made any kind of commitment to him. I even tested him a bit – you know – didn't kiss him for the first several dates. Didn't call him, just let him call me. God, it was tough, but it was kind of like an experiment for me while I considered whether he liked me for me, or if he was just looking for something superficial or an easy "quickie"? I'd been through enough of those before.

Well, he proved to be a one in a million! But the other thing I realize is that if I hadn't learned to be true to myself, I never would have found him. So it always comes back to each person finding and loving herself first and understanding that she deserves great things in any relationship she's in. If you want to find gold at the end of the rainbow, look inside yourself to find it! And, if you can't find it there but keep expecting everyone else to provide it for you, you will always come up disappointed.

My kids have a chance to grow up happy and healthy now and I don't worry about them becoming either narcissistic or codependent. They have already been changing before my eyes. My son is more patient and compassionate with others. My daughter has more self-esteem and confidence. Thank God they are getting the chance I never had for a truly healthy relationship.
Graham – survivor

Chapter 34
The Next Relationship?

So how do you begin to pick up the pieces after a not-so-great relationship? And how do you make the transition from one relationship to another – especially if things ended painfully?

Well, one of the biggest gifts you can give yourself is time alone.

Yes – I said time alone. (This is when I hear my clients say, "But I hate being alone! It's like torture. I miss being with someone so much!") Of course, that's been part of their problem to begin with, which is why it's the first huge step towards making change and finding healthy love.

But how much time is enough? Again, my clients hate to hear this but the reality of the situation is this:

You should spend a minimum of six months to one year before you get into a relationship with anyone. It simply takes that long to figure out who you are without anyone else defining your life for you.

You need to figure out (perhaps for the first time in your life) things such as what you like and dislike, what your passions are, and what your boundaries need to be. You need to understand your needs, feelings, and dreams. And you need to assess what you can live with and what you can't before you let someone else's life and issues influence yours.

And above all, you need to feel absolutely comfortable being alone, for if you get involved with someone and something doesn't feel right about it, you'll feel quite comfortable coming home to your own safe place and leaving him behind. (Which you probably weren't doing in your earlier relationships, and is partly what got you into trouble to begin with.)

Yet, it is taking this time and space to regroup before you move on to someone new that will be one of the biggest steps to healing your wounds. By rushing into replacing your last love with a new one, you only take your painful baggage with you and I can guarantee you that it will be a setup to repeating your unhealthy patterns.

On your journey to valuing yourself and seeking out healthy and rewarding relationships, here are a few simple beliefs to embrace. Keep them in front of you constantly and they may keep you out of a bunch of bad relationships...

I believe that people have to...

Earn the right to be in my life.
Earn the right to date me.
Earn the right to sleep with me.
Earn the right to marry me.

And I also must earn a place in their lives as well.

And just think; starting over in a new relationship will give you the chance to try out some new techniques for setting boundaries, communicating your needs better, and taking your time to really decide if this Mr. Right or Ms. Right is really right for you.

Like Attracts Like

It's also important to recognize that if you are lonely, sad, depressed, angry, resentful, fearful, or fighting within yourself about your self-worth, that's exactly what you are going to attract to your life! Either someone similar or a predator in search of a target. What we put out to the universe is what we get back. It's called the Law of Attraction.

So decide what you really want and who you want to be, and then give the universe that message! Catch yourself whenever you fall into negative thoughts and behaviors. They eat your energy and send out to the world the absolute opposite message from what you're hoping for. Ask yourself how you can change your own inner messages about yourself. Remind yourself what's great about you. And spend some serious time thanking the universe for the wonderful things in your life and quit focusing on the things that aren't perfect!

Changing your inner self starts with taking one baby step at a time. It doesn't have to be a huge leap. Even if you have to walk around with a pretend smile on your face for a few days until you get back into a genuine belief that you're happy, that's a start! You'll be amazed how just changing your attitude about yourself and what you want from the universe can change everything!

Mix and Mingle

Now just because I told you that you shouldn't get into another relationship for six months or more doesn't mean I expect you to live in a convent! While you're learning all these new things about yourself, go try out a bunch of new things. Take up dancing, hiking, walking your dog at the park. Attend some singles functions or divorce recovery classes. There are so many organizations out there now that would be a great place to meet a huge variety of folks in a safe, non-threatening, and no pressure atmosphere.

One particular website you might find helpful is Meetup.com. It lists hundreds of groups that meet regularly in your area. From book clubs to cycling groups to dog lovers, there is something for everyone. Now this is the kind of activity I highly recommend that you immerse yourself in. Meet tons of people. See what they're like. Make a bunch of new friends. But don't let yourself get emotionally or romantically involved with any of them for that crucial six months. Remember – this is YOUR time to grow, and if you hook up with someone right away, you only stunt your own growth.

A Word About Desperate Daters

In researching my book, *The Seven Secrets of Love,* I uncovered what I think is the most dangerous phenomenon in the dating world ... the Desperate Dater. Why? Because Desperate Daters end up doing things that their common sense tells them is simply not smart – like not reading the Red Flags early on, staying with a partner who treats them badly, and not knowing when it's time to leave an unhealthy relationship. (Sound familiar?)

You too may have been a Desperate Dater originally, but with conscious work and your new knowledge, you will hopefully make wiser choices this time. Just in case, here's a quiz so you can see for yourself if you used to be one, or perhaps if you or your friends might still be falling prey to some desperation. Keep in mind that while I tend to see this more in females, males can be as desperate as gals, so this quiz applies to both genders.

Desperate Dater Quiz

- ❑ Do others consider you the caretaker type?
- ❑ Does it feel like you're always putting your partner's needs first?
- ❑ Are you willing to invest more than a couple of months in a relationship where you don't feel a special connection to your mate?
- ❑ Do you make excuses for your partner's behaviors? (Not calling when he says he will? Being chronically late? Drunkenness? Harsh words?)
- ❑ Do you do whatever you can to not "rock the boat" in your relationships?
- ❑ Do you compromise more than your mate in decision-making?
- ❑ Do you feel less smart, less able, or less important than your mate?
- ❑ Do you ever wonder if your partner is lying to you about his whereabouts, his job, his responsibilities, or other women?
- ❑ Do you choose your dates based on their financial status?
- ❑ Do you ever distrust your partner?
- ❑ Has it been so long since you've been in a relationship that you'll do almost anything to get one?
- ❑ Do you ever fear that if your partner leaves, you may not find another one?
- ❑ Have you given up things that are important in your life as they simply don't fit with your mate? (i.e., dancing, sports, social events, time with your friends, etc.)
- ❑ Do you ever feel uneasy around your partner? Even if you can't put your finger on why?
- ❑ Have you ever caught your partner in a lie?
- ❑ Has your partner ever called you names?
- ❑ Has your partner ever harmed you in some way (physically, emotionally, verbally, and/or sexually)?
- ❑ Do you expect that love means your partner should be able to read your mind?
- ❑ Does your mate claim his love for you but then does things to the contrary?

- Are you staying in a relationship that you know is unhealthy for you?
- Do you have children involved who may be being affected by an unhealthy partner as well?
- Are you the one always apologizing for all that is wrong in your relationships?
- Does your mate apologize but the apology always comes with a "but?" ("I'm sorry I yelled, but if you hadn't gotten me mad first, I wouldn't have had to say that, do that, treat you like that.")
- Do you keep staying in a relationship where no one claims their love for each other?
- Do you jump into bed with a new potential partner before you really know him well, worrying that if you don't, he may find someone else?

SCORE:

Add up your "yes" answers and find out if you are (or were) a Desperate Dater...

0 – 5. While you're clearly not a Desperate Dater, you may have some slight tendencies not to be loving and caring for yourself as much as you probably should be. Ask yourself why you don't deserve better? Then remind yourself that you have value and that you deserve to be happy!

5 – 10. You're beginning to show a clear behavior path that indicates you don't feel as important as those around you. This is the first step to accepting bad behaviors from others ... and falling victim to any old relationship that might come along.

10 – 15. You've probably had some crummy relationships before and wonder what it is you keep doing that leaves your relationships in ruins. You're becoming desperate for love and not recognizing when others are taking advantage of you. And you generally lose yourself to any relationship you're in.

15 and up. I'm sad to report that you are a Desperate Dater. You don't feel complete if you don't have someone validating you through a relationship – any relationship! Until you learn to value yourself first and foremost, your relationships will be frustrating, emotional roller coasters that leave you in a heap and wondering how you got there!

Dance Without a Partner

Most of us spend way too many years in unfulfilling relationships. Yet there we stay, feeling stuck in a situation we created, and not always convinced that the work to extricate ourselves from it is worth the effort. Well, let me tell you something …

> *"I'd rather spend the rest of my life*
> *wanting what I don't have*
> *than having what I don't want!"*

Thanks to my great cousin Scott Olsen for this fabulous quote, for it certainly sums up the perfect way to put any relationship under the microscope, wouldn't you say? Living a life with things you don't want is unfulfilling, stressful, and a terribly sad way to spend this gift called life! But living it with the ongoing hope of always finding new and exciting adventures is incredibly healthy!

So now that you're on your way to a new life, I highly suggest you keep that mantra handy and repeat it daily. It can be your compass to helping you decide if that next relationship you eventually discover is the right one for you, or if you should keep shopping!

Again, I cannot stress enough … take time to find out who you are and what you like first and foremost, *without a partner* to define you! I know being alone can be tough but being with the wrong person can be an even more difficult.

And remember that there is someone out there for you. You might just find them where you least expect. Maybe in that Spanish class you've always wanted to take, or hiking on that mountain you finally got in shape enough to climb! Think of the new people you will meet as you get out of the house more and start rebuilding your self-esteem in ways you never imagined. What might that spin class do to your figure and your self-image? Of course a simple cooking class or book club could do the trick too. So keep your mind open and just jump into the deep end of the pool! You never know what you'll discover!

> *How you live your life,*
> *choose your mates,*
> *or become smarter in your relationships*
> *is always your choice to make.*
>
> *So choose wisely.*

If you are interested in learning more specifics about how to handle dating again, including how to traverse the intricate minefield of Internet dating, you might want to read *The Seven Secrets of Love – Unlocking the Mysteries Behind Truly Great Relationships*. I wrote this book to help my clients recognize Red Flags before they got themselves into some dating dilemmas, to discover their own personal dating issues, and to learn what to expect if they've been out of the dating world for a while.

Dating can be great fun again, once you know today's rules, games, and behaviors. So take care but have fun as you dip your toes back into the dating pool again! And think of it as you might think of shopping for that special little black dress (or if you're a guy – the perfect wrench.) There are many different kinds out there and shopping for the perfect one is half the fun! Don't just settle for the first one you run across. Who knows who you might miss that way?

Chapter 35
Breaking the Cycle

So now you know more about narcissism than you ever imagined. You also realize that there's no cure or given treatment. And you're probably wondering if there is anything that can be done to stop this cycle of developing this devastating personality.

To the best knowledge of those in psychology, providing a healthy environment for our children seems to be our best bet for healthy emotional development. As we raise our children, there are many things that we can do to help them feel safe and secure at the same time we help them build strong self-esteem and develop feelings of empathy and compassion for others.

There is a poem I run across periodically in pediatrician's offices and schools that says it all so simply, "Children Learn What They Live." If we criticize our children, they learn to criticize. If we hit them as punishment, they learn to hit. If we do not trust them, they learn not to trust. If we show them our anger, they learn to be angry. The list goes on. However, if we show them love, compassion, kindness, and caring, they learn those behaviors as well.

Providing an environment of unconditional love is absolutely vital for our children to learn to feel safe and to develop trust in others. Yet, unconditional love does not mean that we never punish our kids for misbehaviors. For it is through love that we know it is important to teach them boundaries and to be responsible. It is also crucial that our children know that while their behavior may be unacceptable, they themselves will always be loved by us, no matter what.

> *In addition,*
> *it is important to remember that punishments*
> *can be effective without being abusive.*

If you are someone who believes in spanking, the best advice I heard years ago when my daughter was a toddler, was this: The first hit is for the child, any hits after that are for the parent. In other words, one spank on the butt will get your child's attention. More than one is done purely to make the one doing the spanking feel something. That something might be vindication, an outlet for the parent's stress or anger, or simply a demonstration of power. There is a fine line between punishing and abusing. It is crucial we understand the difference.

While spanking may have been the punishment of choice when I was young, there are so many great alternatives today that seem to carry more weight than spanking ever did, yet don't lead to physical punishment. In this age of high technology, cutting your child off from the Internet, video games, or the telephone may have more impact than any trip to the woodshed ever did.

Loving your child unconditionally is the goal. However, idolizing your children is not the same thing. Idolizing involves putting your child on a pedestal. As I mentioned earlier, this can actually become an abusive situation as well. If children believe they are always perfect, or better than any other kids in the eyes of their parents, they will expect the rest of the world to believe this as well. When they grow up and reality hits, revealing the fact that others do not recognize the perfect child for who he believes he is, his ongoing debate with reality will be a huge shock. This constant inner conflict can possibly begin to lead him on the journey down the road towards narcissism … the road of the ever-unsatisfied inner self, always searching for external validation.

In addition, our American culture has done us no favors in creating certain unhealthy beliefs we hold dear. We are a fast-paced, instant gratification, "competition is everything" society. "Me, me, me" seems to abound. If our needs are not met instantly it becomes a crisis. It also seems we can develop feelings of frustration and self-doubt if we do not measure up to everything everyone else has or does.

As parents, it's so easy to fall into this rut. Of course everyone wants the best for their children. It only makes sense that we want them to have a better life than we have. Yet it is still key that our children learn responsibility in some of the same ways we learned it as children. Kids can baby sit, mow lawns, wash cars, or any number of odd jobs to earn money. Just handing them the keys to a brand new car on their sixteenth birthday isn't necessarily the greatest gift we can give them.

I know so many college kids who have never had to earn a dime to attain anything they wanted and I wonder how they will adjust to the real work world upon graduation. Do they expect the world will be handed to them on a silver platter? If so, they may be in for a big surprise.

There is no perfect answer to any of this. In many homes it takes both parents working full-time to provide for the average American family. Parents come home exhausted and barely able to care for themselves at that point, much less able to meet the emotional needs of the children. Yet, this is the time when children need to know they are loved and cared for and are the most important entity in their parents' lives.

Our culture isn't going to slow down and change for us, but we can be attentive to how we raise our children despite our culture.

❏ Make sure your kids feel loved, safe, and protected within the environment you create.
❏ Avoid criticizing them for their mistakes – rather, discuss your unhappiness with their *behavior* at the same time you remind

them how much you love them as people.
- ❏ Offer hugs, kisses, and a caring touch whenever possible, all the way from infancy through adulthood.
- ❏ Do not let your punishments exceed their crimes.
- ❏ Do not idolize them and live vicariously through them or see them as extensions of yourself.
- ❏ Encourage them to compete for the sake of competing, not because winning is everything.
- ❏ Spend quality and quantity time with your kids! It's better than any gift you can ever buy them.

These are only a few ideas to help you establish an environment where children feel safe and unconditionally loved. Building strong self-esteem, respect, and understanding for others and being able to show and feel emotions, are some of the most incredible gifts we can bestow upon our children. As has been evidenced by the many stories throughout this book, a life without these blessings is a life full of pain and suffering – for all involved.

The more we all know about this confusing and frustrating behavior called narcissism, the more we have the ability to break the cycle that has affected so many for so long. Once it's a household word, narcissists won't be able to hide their abusive and controlling natures anymore.

They will be unmasked for who they really are.

The Real Closure

You may think that your journey has included many lost years of suffering, but remember, you didn't waste those years. Instead you earned your PhD in Narcissism. So heal yourself first, then share what you have learned with so many others.

Remember these important keys...

- ❑ Take your life back! Quit letting a narcissist control you.

- ❑ Don't let yourself be treated as less than your partner or others.

- ❑ Don't sacrifice yourself to a lion. You're worth more.

- ❑ Remember, you don't have to be bleeding to be a victim.

- ❑ Do raise your children with unconditional love and appropriate boundaries for safety and love.

- ❑ Don't allow yourself *or your kids* to remain victims any longer.

- ❑ Don't let your years of pain and suffering be meaningless. Teach others about narcissism – you'll never know the impact your voice may have on someone else in pain and confusion.

Never forget that knowledge is power!
Empower yourself and others!

Your To-Do List

By now you've read so much stuff you probably don't even know where to start. So I will leave you with your head swimming with new knowledge and a checklist to help you get started.

❑ Pick up the following movies to watch as soon as possible: *Gaslight, 9 ½ Weeks, Sleeping With the Enemy,* and *Shine*

❑ Read as many of the following books as possible:
Malignant Self-Love: Narcissism Revisited by Sam Vaknin
Get Out of Your Boxx by Mary Jo Fay
Why We Stay Stuck by Tom Joseph
The Seven Secrets of Love by Mary Jo Fay

❑ Let your friends and family know what is going on in your relationship. Find out who might be able to help (financially, with a place to stay, with your kids) should you need to leave.

❑ Interview therapists to help you deal with the situation, but be sure they understand narcissism and NPD in depth. (Ask them to tell you just what they know and if you know more than they do, keep searching.)

❑ Talk with survivors or join a support group to help you realize that you are neither alone nor crazy. Be cautious, however, that you are guided by someone who has healed, and don't place yourself in a group of total victims without a healthy leader.

❑ Gather information about your financial status and make copies. You may need to open your own account in another bank, just in case...

- ❑ Interview several lawyers to determine what your legal options are. Again, be sure they understand narcissism and NPD in depth. (Just as with the therapist, ask them to explain the subject to you. If you're still more knowledgeable than they are about it, keep searching.)

- ❑ Document things that just aren't right or that might be necessary in court to prove that your narcissist is unhealthy for you or your kids. For example, describe any excessive physical punishment of the children, with dates, locations, and witnesses.

- ❑ Visit your family doctor if you are feeling that your health is at stake. While antidepressants may seem like a crutch, you may need to be on them for a while to handle the stress you're dealing with. And remember, most of these medications take several weeks to become fully effective. (Note: there are some holistic options you may want to explore that act more quickly and do not require a prescription. Check with your local health food store for info on such things as Phenylalanine and others.)

- ❑ Above all, take care of YOU, for if you are a mess, you can't take care of your kids either.

There are certainly more steps you can take, but this list should give you a starting place. There will be lots more ideas as you move along the path of leaving your emotional roller-coaster lifestyle behind and attaining one that's healthy and safe for all of you. But it all starts with a single step, and since you've just read this book, you're already on your way.

My best to you on your journey.

We will all welcome you on the other side!

Acknowledgements

My thanks go out to so many who made this book possible. First and most notably, to all who sent me their stories. Without them, this book would not exist. Many took substantial risks, fearing retribution from the narcissists they described. Some actually declined at the last moment for the same fears. I have done what I can to change names, occupations, and other identifying factors to keep these survivors safe while still holding true to their incredible accounts. I have even buried many of my own experiences within these pages to avoid issues with the narcissists in my past as well. It is my hope that this sampling of various people's lives and thoughts will give some insight to their struggle to see the light and leave the darkness behind. Perhaps it will help others find the path as well.

Second, my deep appreciation goes to Sam Vaknin, PhD, for all his help and feedback on this book. His in-depth knowledge on the subject of narcissism, in addition to his first-hand experience living with the disorder himself, has lent credibility and insights to this writing that would have otherwise been impossible.

As always, thanks to the many technical folks who helped make my books what they are: Barb Munson, my fabulous editor and great friend. Graphic artist Janice Green, for the weeks we struggled with this cover to get it right! Talented makeup artist and photographer Margie Le Bow, for a great photo for the book jacket. And to Cameron Fay from Friesen's Printing for steering all the pieces together and getting them to me in a timely manner. Thank you all for your support, creativity, and perseverance.

Lastly, a world of thanks to my close friends and family, who once again put up with me during my intense frenzy and craziness as I wrote. To my daughter, Shaun, for frequently asking how I was progressing and always reminding me how she knows I'm going to help people with my work. To my mother, Betty Olsen, for her understanding about this road I've chosen to take, despite the hurdles. To my greatest cheerleaders: my sister, Barb Walker, and friends, Sara Coley and Janet Kline, for being there and encouraging me during each step of my life journey. Go Ya-Ya's! And to my friend, J. Scott Laudenslager, and the many other nice guys I've met along the way, who have all shown me that there really still are "a few good men" out there.

And of course to Cool Carol – my great friend who has also had her journey of discovery with her fabulous match, Jeff. You two have taught me much about great, fun, unconditional love. You are inspirational!

Of course I always have to thank my canine pal, Asher for being my greatest little buddy, hanging out with me for hours on end (and often into the wee hours of the night) while I was madly writing, when he'd much rather have gone for a walk instead!

Above all, my thanks to God above for experiences, both good and bad, that have taught me incredible lessons and sent me on a mission to help others.

I would never have found this path any other way.

If you enjoyed this book...

Give the gift of a book to your friends, family members, business associates, or loved ones. Simply fill out our convenient form on one of the next pages and we'll mail the books anywhere in the United States. (Contact us for shipping to foreign countries.) Let us know if it's a gift or if you wish to remain an anonymous donor for someone you love. We have several other relationship books to choose from as well. And all will be autographed if you like.

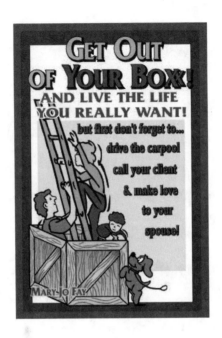

Are you:
Stuck in a rut and don't know how to change it?
Meeting everyone else's needs but not your own?
Wishing for "someday" but someday never comes?
On the never-ending treadmill and can't get off?

Then maybe it's time to **Get Out of Your Boxx!**

Learn about Boxxes such as:
Workaholism, Perfectionism, Denial, Your Past,
The Expectations of Others, The Sex Boxx, and more.

Once you recognize what your boxxes are …
YOU HAVE THE POWER TO CHANGE THEM
AND CHANGE YOUR LIFE
ONCE AND FOR ALL!

Enjoy all the opportunities life has to offer
By getting Out of Your Boxx!

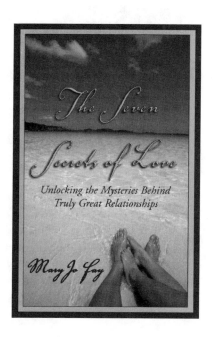

The Seven
Secrets of Love
*Unlocking the Mysteries Behind
Truly Great Relationships*

Mary Jo Fay

**Dating, Mating, and Relating is sometimes HARD!
Have you ever asked yourself...**

Can I really find love on the Net?
Why is my relationship in DIS-harmony?
What am I doing that messes up every first date?
How can I sort out good possible partners from bad?
Why do I keep attracting the wrong sort of mate?
How can I find a truly great relationship?

Let **The Seven Secrets of Love** help you:

Learn how to navigate the many possible dating minefields!
Discover how to read between the lines on dating profiles.
Define your own dating issues to choose the right mate and
NOT be a Desperate Dater!

The reality is that you actually *choose* who you fall in love with —
good, bad, or ugly. So why not choose the right mate from the start?
Believe it or not, it all starts with YOU!

Is bad sex better than no sex?
Do women really have all "those" headaches?
Is making love just another thing on your "to do list?"
Why do some men just want to "get lucky?"
(If they know what to do, there is absolutely no luck involved!)

**This is not your run of the mill sex book or stuffy manual.
It's real people with real things to say about their sex lives.
What works. What doesn't. What they secretly wish for.
And what keeps them connected!**

If you wish your sex life had
a little more zip,
a little more satisfaction,
or even just a little more understanding,
then this book is for you!

With Quickie Crib Notes for men!

WANT TO KNOW MORE?

There's plenty more from Out of the Boxx, Inc!

♥ Would you like to have Mary Jo Fay speak to your group? From the boardroom to the bedroom, Mary Jo speaks on a wide variety of relationship and motivational issues. Please check our website for specific topics or contact us for custom programs.

♥ Would you like your own one-on-one phone consultation to help get you back on track, unstuck, or just give some clarity to your relationship questions? Through the wonders of technology, Mary Jo works with people all over the world!

♥ Want to order any additional copies of this or our other books, audio CD's, or seminar DVD's? We ship almost anywhere in the world! And give bulk discounts for various groups.

Then visit us online for more information at:

www.OutOfTheBoxx.com

or send us an email to:
OutOfTheBoxxInc@aol.com
(Be sure to use 2 x's on boxx, or you won't find us!)

End Notes

1. Vaknin, Sam. *Malignant Self Love, Narcissism Revisited*. Skopje and Prague, Narcissus Publications, 2003.
2. American Psychiatric Association, *Diagnostic and Statistical Manual of Mental Disorders, 4th Edition*. 2000. pp 714-717. Washington, D.C.
3. Ibid.
4. Vaknin, Sam. http://samvak.tripod.com
5. Ibid.
6. McClain, Gina C. "The Human Sexuality Web," The University of Missouri – Kansas City web page.
7. Jacobson, Neal and Gottman, John. "Anatomy of a Violent Relationship." *Psychology Today*, Mar – April 98.
8. Carver, Joseph. www.drjoecarver.com. "Love and the Stockholm Syndrome: The Mystery of Loving an Abuser."
9. Ibid.
10. CIA Human Resource Exploitation Training Manual. 1983. "Psychology of Torture."
11. Carver, Joseph. www.drjoecarver.com. "Identifying Losers in Relationships."
12. Kubler-Ross, Elizabeth, *On Death and Dying*, Scribner Book Company, 1997.

Order Form

Name _____

Address _____

City, State, Zip_____

Phone _____

(If there are questions about your order)

Email address _____

I would like to order the following number of copies of each book:

The Seven Secrets of Love

#_____ copies @ $20 each $20 x _____ = $_____

When Your Perfect Partner Goes Perfectly Wrong – 2nd Edition

#_____copies@ $29 each $29 x _____ = $_____

Get Out of Your Boxx!

#_____copies@$20 each $20 x _____ = $ _____

Please Dear, Not Tonight

#_____copies @ $21each $21 x _____ = $_____

Shipping and handling add $5 for the first book,   = $_____
$2 for each additional book.

                                        Total = $ _____

You may charge your Visa or Master Card

Card Number _____ Expiration Date _____

Please make sure your address above is your billing address, (for Credit Card verification.) If we are to mail your books to a different address, please add a note with the additional address.

Or mail your check or money order to:

    Out of the Boxx, Inc.

    PO Box 803

    Parker, CO 80134

Notes